The AI Educa

The AI Educator traces how artificial intelligence is reshaping the purpose, practice and ethics of education. Rather than treating AI as a threat or cure-all, the book situates it within a long history of technological disruption, from the printing press to the internet, revealing the recurring patterns of fear, adaptation and renewal that accompany each wave of innovation.

Drawing on classroom research, case studies and contemporary scholarship, it examines how generative AI challenges traditional pedagogies, assessment practices and professional identities. Chapters explore the erosion and restoration of academic integrity, the evolving role of teachers, the design of ethical guardrails and the shift from product-oriented to process-based learning. Central to the book is the argument that AI's educational value lies not in automation, but in how thoughtfully it is integrated to deepen reflection, creativity and critical inquiry.

Through accessible examples and practical frameworks, such as AI-permission models, generative assessment design and prompt engineering for learning, the book offers educators concrete strategies to harness AI as a collaborative partner rather than a replacement. It introduces concepts such as meta-AI literacy and generativism to help teachers and students navigate new forms of authorship and knowledge-making.

Ultimately, *The AI Educator* calls for a human-centred pedagogy grounded in empathy, integrity and purposeful innovation. It invites educators to reclaim agency in the design of AI-enhanced classrooms and to reaffirm what remains irreplaceably human in teaching and learning.

Dr Penny de Byl is the Program Director of the Bachelor of Computer Science and Senior Educational Specialist at Adelaide University, dedicated to advancing STEM education through innovative teaching and learning design. Formerly a professor of Games and Interactive Multimedia at Bond University, she is also the founder and CEO of Holistic3D.com, where she develops and delivers online courses in game development, computer graphics, artificial intelligence, mathematics and related fields. Her award-winning work, including a Queensland State Government Award, a Unity/Google Mobile Curriculum Development Award, a Smart Women in ICT Award and a State Government Research Fellowship, reflects her long-standing commitment to educational innovation. Dr. de Byl has authored several influential books and collaborated with industry leaders such as Unity Technologies, continuing to pioneer the integration of games-based learning and AI into contemporary education.

The AI Educator

From Disruption to Design: Practical Pathways for AI-Empowered Teaching

Penny de Byl

CRC Press
Taylor & Francis Group
Boca Raton London New York

CRC Press is an imprint of the
Taylor & Francis Group, an **informa** business

Designed cover image: Penny de Byl

First edition published 2027
by CRC Press
2385 NW Executive Center Drive, Suite 320, Boca Raton FL 33431

and by CRC Press
4 Park Square, Milton Park, Abingdon, Oxon, OX14 4RN

CRC Press is an imprint of Taylor & Francis Group, LLC

ISBN: 978-1-041-03709-5 (hbk)
ISBN: 978-1-041-03707-1 (pbk)
ISBN: 978-1-003-62498-1 (ebk)

DOI: 10.1201/9781003624981

Typeset in Minion
by SPi Technologies India Pvt Ltd (Straive)

Contents

Preface

On finalising Chapter 8 herein, I was forced to reflect on a question I asked there: In what ways has the integration of AI affected my relationships with students, positively or negatively? That question took me back to the end of Semester 1, 2025, at the University of Adelaide, my first semester back in front of a class after seven years teaching online through my own business, Holistic3d.com. Just before returning to face-to-face teaching, I had published a course on how to use generative AI.

When I first introduced generative AI into my university teaching practice, I thought I was being strategic. I had read enough, experimented enough and scaffolded enough. I imagined it as an augmentation, not a disruption. But somewhere between the prompts and the plagiarism detectors, I found myself staring at student submissions that felt like strangers. Polished, plausible, impersonal and often very much identical!

For someone continuously embedded in face-to-face teaching, this shift may have emerged gradually. But for me, coming off a hiatus, it felt like a slap in the face. I noticed not just a disconnection in the submitted work, but in the students themselves. Dialogue thinned. Curiosity faltered. Trust frayed. I realised I wasn't just losing authorship; I was losing relationship. My initial response was to ban the use of generative AI in some assessments. But that didn't work. Assignment after assignment bore the signature of GenAI-crafted answers. It was frustrating, disheartening and deeply soul-destroying.

How dare they replace my teaching with a prompt? How dare they seek easy answers from a chatbot when I had poured myself into designing what I hoped was an engaging curriculum? I became a kind of vigilante, obsessed with catching out the cheaters. At the time, the only solution I could see was to retreat to in-person invigilated exams, hoping fear might compel authentic study.

But that was a knee-jerk reaction, no different from the initial instincts to ban books, calculators, personal computers or Google. It couldn't stand. I've always been a first adopter in the classroom: building online marking systems before there were learning management systems, chasing every teaching innovation grant, trialling iPads before they were mainstream. And I wasn't going to let AI, something I had studied and taught in various ways for over 25 years, be the thing that beat me.

This book is, in many ways, the product of that reckoning. It has been my own learning journey and a mission to empower educators to navigate this brave new world without turning them into AI experts. It resists the growing expectation that teachers must sacrifice disciplinary content to accommodate technology, or worse, become tech facilitators. Teaching is not an IT support role (although sometimes it feels like it). And while AI may dazzle with its scalability, speed and data-processing power, these are not pedagogical ends. They are tools. Powerful, yes, but inert without human intention.

What we need now is not teachers who are fluent in AI, but AI that is legible to teachers, not just in its mechanics, but in its consequences for pedagogy, for assessment and for the fragile web of trust that underpins all learning.

This book does not idealise nor catastrophise. Instead, it documents, with honesty, the ways AI is reshaping how we teach, how we learn and how we relate. And more than anything, I hope it helps you ask your own difficult questions. Not what AI can do, but what we still must do ourselves.

Acknowledgements

I would like to give a big thanks to my students, Anamika Cherukat and Vishesh Purnanada, who assisted in reading over my drafts, formatting text, checking references and basically making me look good.

And I would like to thank Carl without whom I'd have once upon a time stuck my head in the sand with respect to ChatGPT, and this book would never have been a reality.

Blog and Online Resources

This book is accompanied by a live blog containing discussion and extra resources. Drop by and join in the conversation and share your own experiences with GenAI in education at: www.the-ai-educator.com.

CHAPTER 1

Brave New World?

> These concerns reveal that educators aren't just fearful of AI itself but of what it reflects about systemic weaknesses in educational design and purpose.

CHAPTER AIMS

The aim of this chapter is to introduce key themes explored in this book in relation to:

1. *recurring fears surrounding new educational technologies;*
2. *historical patterns shaping today's responses to AI;*
3. *the evolving roles of teachers and learners;*
4. *tensions between innovation and core educational values;*
5. *the importance of using technology with clear pedagogical intent.*

EVERYTHING OLD IS NEW AGAIN

All around the world, educators are trying to find their footing as artificial intelligence (AI) becomes an increasingly present force in our classrooms and learning environments. On the one hand, there's real excitement about the potential AI holds for transforming how we teach and learn. On the other hand, there's no shortage of apprehension. Questions about academic integrity, critical thinking and data privacy are cropping up

DOI: 10.1201/9781003624981-1

everywhere, and rightly so. But before we dive headfirst into these modern concerns, it helps to take a step back and look at where we've come from.

This isn't the first time education has been disrupted by a technological leap. Think back to the invention of the printing press, the rise of radio and television or the sudden ubiquity of the internet. Each shift changed the way knowledge was created, shared and controlled, and each brought its own wave of fears. Educators throughout history have worried about losing control of content, undermining traditional literacy, threatening moral development and widening the gap between the privileged and the disadvantaged.

Sound familiar? It should. The fears we're facing with AI echo many of those same historical anxieties. That's not to downplay them, but rather to put them into context. Recognising these patterns helps us see AI not as an unprecedented threat, but as the latest chapter in a long story of educational transformation. So if you're feeling overwhelmed or unsure about where this is all heading, know that you're not alone and you're certainly not the first. Change has always made us a little uncomfortable. But as history shows us, it's also how education grows.

Before we jump wholly into the disruption generative AI (GenAI) is causing in education, let's take a journey through the concerns that educational technologies have been causing us over the past hundred-odd years, beginning with an area that has always plagued assessment: *academic integrity.*

ACADEMIC INTEGRITY

Academic integrity represents the foundational values of honesty, trust, fairness, respect and responsibility that guide all scholarly activity. It is the ethical compass by which academic communities measure the authenticity of learning, assessment and research. These principles have long shaped the expectations placed upon students and educators alike. Yet, with the emergence of each new technology, these values are inevitably called into question.

A significant disruption occurred in the 1990s with the arrival of widespread internet access. For the first time, students could access vast amounts of digital content with minimal effort. Entire paragraphs of information could be copied and inserted into assignments without attribution, and many did so. Banks (2008) documented that over 60% of students admitted to pasting unreferenced material directly into their work, a trend labelled *cyber-plagiarism*. In response, plagiarism detection services such as Turnitin were introduced, not only to discourage this behaviour but to reinforce the importance of academic honesty in an increasingly digital landscape.

But fears of technological interference in education did not originate with the internet. In the 1970s, the classroom introduction of calculators raised parallel concerns. Would allowing students to rely on machines for basic arithmetic erode their understanding of core mathematical principles? Banks (2008) noted that such concerns reflected a deeper anxiety: that learning might be replaced with automation and comprehension would take a back seat to convenience.

Each of these episodes brought educators back to a recurring set of questions: If technology can complete the task, what then is left for the learner? Will students still engage deeply with the material, or will they opt for efficiency over understanding? Can assessment remain valid when shortcuts are readily available?

In contemporary classrooms, these same questions resurface with the advent of AI tools. From automated summarisation to essay generation and equation solving, AI appears poised to take on the very tasks once reserved for students themselves. And while banning these tools may seem like a straightforward solution, history suggests a more nuanced approach. As with calculators and the internet, the challenge lies not in the existence of the tool, but in how it is integrated into pedagogical practice. With careful guidance and well-articulated expectations, educators can help ensure that AI enhances, rather than undermines, the pursuit of genuine academic inquiry.

These considerations naturally lead us to broader questions about student cognition and learning strategies, particularly when digital tools are capable of doing the intellectual work once considered essential to the educational journey.

CRITICAL THINKING

Critical thinking, the capacity to pause, reflect and reason through information, has long stood as a pillar of effective education. It encourages learners to move beyond rote memorisation, prompting them to question assumptions, weigh evidence and form considered judgements. However, each wave of technological innovation in education has brought with it a renewed concern: is technology enhancing students' ability to think critically, or is it doing the thinking for them?

In the mid-20th century, the introduction of television into classrooms sparked apprehension among educators. Parrish et al. (2025) describe how passive viewing was seen as a threat to intellectual engagement. The worry was that students would absorb information without interrogation, mistaking presentation for truth. In response, innovative educators began to reframe television as a starting point rather than a substitute. Carefully chosen segments were followed by guided discussions and supplementary readings, transforming screen time into a catalyst for deeper cognitive engagement.

Decades later, the rise of internet search engines reignited these concerns. With vast information now just a click away, the act of recalling facts became less important than knowing how to find them. Sparrow et al. (2011) identified this shift as *Google thinking*, a cognitive shortcut that, while efficient, often came at the cost of reflection and long-term retention.

But the tension between technology and critical thinking is not confined to the digital age. As early as the 18th century, moralist and educational writer Sarah Trimmer cautioned against the unchecked consumption of fiction. She argued that fairy tales, rich in imagination and fantasy, might erode children's capacity for rational thought and moral reasoning (Grenby, 2014). Even books, now celebrated as gateways to knowledge, were once viewed by some as distractions from disciplined learning.

These episodes reveal a recurring theme in educational history. Each new medium, whether book, screen or search engine, prompts the same questions: Will it replace reasoning with convenience? Will it dull students' capacity to evaluate, synthesise and interpret? Or can it be used to sharpen those very skills?

Today, AI invites us to revisit these questions with fresh urgency. From AI-generated summaries and explanations to entire essay drafts, students can now bypass the intellectual effort of analysis and composition. As with previous technologies, the issue is not the existence of AI tools, but their uncritical use. The challenge lies in designing learning environments where AI supports the thinking process rather than short-circuits it, where students are prompted to reflect on, critique and build upon AI-generated content rather than simply accept it.

While critical thinking remains central to educational aims, it must be understood in tandem with the systems behind the tools. Increasingly, these technologies do more than assist. They collect, sort and shape the learning experience through the use of data.

DID YOU KNOW?

When the printing press was invented in the 15th century, some educators feared it would lead to intellectual laziness. Scholars worried that easy access to books would discourage memorisation and weaken the discipline of study, echoing modern concerns about internet search engines and AI tools. Even Socrates once warned that writing itself might "create forgetfulness in the learners' souls" (as recorded by Plato in *Phaedrus*).

DATA PRIVACY

Data privacy in education refers to the responsible collection, storage and use of students' personal and learning-related information within digital environments. As educational technologies advanced through the 2000s, the ability to track every keystroke, click and pause opened new possibilities for understanding how students learn. With this growth in insight came a parallel growth in concern.

Initially, data collection was seen as a promising development. Educators gained access to real-time analytics on student performance, allowing for targeted feedback, adaptive learning pathways and early intervention strategies. However, as platforms became more sophisticated, questions about the ethical boundaries of surveillance and data ownership emerged. Who was entitled to access this data? How long would it be stored? Could it be sold, repurposed or exploited?

In response, legislative efforts such as the revision of the Family Educational Rights and Privacy Act (FERPA) in the United States attempted to reassert transparency and control (U.S. Department of Education, 2008). At the institutional level, schools and universities began scrutinising third-party vendors, updating data governance policies and making efforts to clarify privacy terms to educators, students and families.

Yet, legal frameworks alone have not resolved the dilemma. When educators lack clarity or confidence in how student data is handled, they may avoid digital tools that rely on formative assessment or learning analytics tools, which, ironically, hold great potential for improving student outcomes. On the other hand, when data collection is driven by institutional accountability or commercial gain, pedagogical priorities risk being sidelined. In such cases, educational platforms may begin to reflect managerial objectives more than learning needs.

A striking example is the widespread adoption of ClassDojo (classdojo.com), a classroom management application designed to track student behaviour. Although it is framed as a tool for promoting positive reinforcement, research by Manolev et al. (2019) suggests that its use may encourage compliance at the expense of curiosity, fostering a surveillance culture that shapes student behaviour more than student thinking.

Historically, these concerns have raised a series of vital questions: Is the data collected truly supporting learning, or is it feeding institutional metrics? Are students able to take intellectual risks, or does constant monitoring inhibit exploration? And how might such tools alter the relationship between teacher and learner, shifting it from a partnership to one of control?

Today, the introduction of AI adds new dimensions to these concerns. Beyond academic performance, some platforms now interpret facial expressions, tone of voice and patterns of engagement, venturing into emotional analytics and biometric feedback. These advances raise profound questions about the limits of privacy in the digital classroom and challenge us to consider not just what is possible, but what is appropriate.

As data becomes increasingly entangled with algorithms, we must also turn our attention to the ways in which technology determines what students see. This leads us directly into the adjacent concern of *content control* where AI-driven systems play a growing role in shaping educational exposure and limiting what is left unseen.

CONTENT, CENSORSHIP AND ACADEMIC FREEDOM

Content, censorship and academic freedom concern the often-contentious terrain of what material is included or excluded in educational contexts, who holds the authority to make those decisions and to what extent educators are free to explore controversial or challenging ideas. As technologies evolve and become embedded within educational systems, these concerns are revisited often with renewed urgency each time a new tool, platform or policy is introduced.

Historically, debates over appropriate content have mirrored broader cultural anxieties. A century after Sarah Trimmer was warning about the bad influence of fairy tales, fears about the corrupting influence of comic books culminated in US Senate hearings, prompting the formation of the Comics Code Authority, a regulatory body established to restrict content deemed unsuitable for youth.

Even canonical literature has not escaped scrutiny. Works such as *The Merchant of Venice* and *Oliver Twist* were, for a time, removed from school curricula due to perceived antisemitic themes. It was only through legal challenges, such as *Rosenberg v. Board of Education* (1949), that the educational value of engaging with difficult material was reaffirmed. Such decisions underscored the role of education not merely in protecting students, but in preparing them to grapple with complexity.

Each of these moments resurfaced familiar pedagogical questions: Who gets to determine what knowledge is valid or appropriate? Does shielding students from controversy hinder their development as critical thinkers? At what point do moral concerns impinge on the educator's role as facilitator of inquiry?

The digital age has amplified these tensions. Teachers are no longer the sole gatekeepers of classroom content. Instead, content filters, algorithmic age restrictions and digital curation systems, from YouTube's recommendation engine to eBook library platforms, now quietly shape what learners see. These decisions often occur without explanation, driven by opaque algorithms rather than transparent pedagogical reasoning.

With the rise of AI, the stakes have increased. Algorithms trained on skewed datasets can replicate and reinforce dominant ideologies, marginalising alternative or minority perspectives. A stark illustration of this came in 2020, when Ofqual's algorithm for grading UK students disproportionately downgraded those from state-funded schools by relying on historical performance trends (Weale, 2020). Although not a case of traditional content censorship, it exposed how data-driven systems can silently reproduce systemic inequalities and influence educational outcomes.

These developments echo long-standing concerns: Are students being subtly shielded from diverse perspectives by algorithmic design? Is educational content increasingly shaped by corporate or computational priorities rather than pedagogical intent? Is the autonomy of educators being eroded by digital systems that filter learning materials without consultation or accountability?

As AI becomes more embedded in content delivery, whether recommending resources, filtering reading lists or tailoring lesson plans, the question remains: are we creating more responsive learning environments or simply narrowing the educational lens through which students view the world? The challenge, as it has always been, is to balance the need for protection and appropriateness with the imperative to expose students to the breadth and complexity of human thought.

As content and delivery systems evolve, so too must teaching practices. These shifts naturally give rise to broader pedagogical debates, inviting renewed reflection on what meaningful, effective education should look like in a technology-rich classroom.

PEDAGOGICAL DEBATES

Pedagogical debates reflect the ongoing conversations and often tensions among educators about how best to teach and foster meaningful learning. These debates are rarely settled. Instead, they evolve in response to social, cultural and technological change. Whenever a new tool enters the classroom, traditional practices are reassessed, sparking new discussions about the role of the teacher, the nature of instruction and what constitutes effective education.

One of the most prominent examples emerged in the mid-20th century during the so-called *reading wars*. At the heart of this debate was the question of how children should learn to read. Advocates of the phonics approach emphasised decoding letter sounds as the foundation of literacy, while proponents of the whole-language method encouraged learning words through context and exposure. Commercial reading schemes like the *Dick and Jane* basal readers popularised the "look-say" technique, which relied heavily on memorisation. Critics of this approach argued it neglected the systematic building of reading skills, eventually leading to a renewed emphasis on phonics-based instruction (Allington, 2002)

Similar pedagogical tensions surfaced with the classroom arrival of calculators in the 1970s. Concerns were raised that dependence on these devices would hinder students' development of arithmetic fluency. Kerr (1989) noted that while calculators could enhance efficiency, they also risked bypassing conceptual understanding if introduced too early or without sufficient scaffolding.

The pattern repeated with the introduction of personal computers in the 1980s and 1990s. Enthusiasts celebrated their potential for creativity, interactivity and student-centred learning. Yet, others feared that computers might diminish the teacher's role from subject-matter expert to mere facilitator. The classroom dynamic was shifting, and not all educators were convinced it was for the better.

These transformations provoked important questions: Would emerging technologies undermine tried-and-true instructional methods? Would they serve all learners equally, or widen existing disparities? And what would become of the teacher's authority when digital platforms increasingly guided the learning process?

The rise of mobile phones added new complexity. Once strictly prohibited in classrooms due to their perceived disruptive nature, smartphones have since been reimagined as learning tools enabling real-time polls, collaborative research and immediate access to information. Studies such as those by Thomas and O'Bannon (2013) and Kukulska-Hulme (2009) chart this shift, revealing how teacher perceptions adapt as devices become embedded in daily life and pedagogy.

Artificial intelligence now reopens these debates with a new sense of urgency. AI-powered systems can generate lesson plans, deliver instant feedback and even provide personalised tutoring, raising legitimate concerns about the deskilling of educators and a potential loss of autonomy. Yet, others argue that, when used thoughtfully, such tools can relieve teachers of repetitive administrative tasks, allowing them to focus more deeply on complex instructional design, creativity and meaningful student engagement.

As with previous technologies, the core issue is not whether AI should be used in education, but *how* it should be used. The debate centres on the reshaping of teaching, not merely its support. In this way, pedagogical debates offer a useful lens through which to evaluate the educational impact of emerging technologies, highlighting the importance of intention, context and teacher agency.

Naturally, these discussions spill into broader concerns about student motivation and participation. How we teach is intimately connected with how students engage. And engagement, in turn, depends heavily on what students encounter and what they don't. Increasingly, this is determined by algorithmic systems that filter and prioritise content, which raises crucial questions about access and opportunity.

STUDENT ENGAGEMENT

Student engagement describes the degree to which learners are intellectually and emotionally invested in their educational experiences. It encompasses interest, motivation and active participation and is consistently recognised as a vital predictor of both academic performance and long-term success. While each wave of technological advancement has brought promises of heightened engagement, it has also prompted educators to ask a critical question: Does the technology deepen learning, or simply hold attention?

As previously noted, the introduction of personal computers into classrooms was met with both enthusiasm and caution. Advocates hailed them as transformative tools that could level the educational playing field. Yet, others expressed concern that computers might foster shallow engagement where students clicked through software exercises without meaningful cognitive investment. Wenglinsky (1998) underscored this tension, noting that computer use was beneficial when directed towards complex, problem-solving tasks, but had a detrimental effect when used for rote drill-and-practice activities.

The arrival of the internet magnified these concerns. It opened doorways to collaboration, independent inquiry and global research opportunities, but only for those who used it purposefully. Warschauer (2004) found that students who were guided to engage deeply with online content reaped intellectual rewards, while others developed habits of multitasking and skimming that disrupted concentration and weakened long-term understanding.

In recent years, new technologies such as virtual reality, gamified learning platforms and AI tutors have been introduced with similar claims: that they can captivate students and reinvigorate learning. Lindgren et al. (2016) demonstrated that immersive virtual reality experiences could significantly enhance both engagement and knowledge retention. At the same time, Lee and Hammer (2011) warn that such tools often benefit from a novelty effect, one that may fade over time without thoughtful instructional integration.

These developments have kept alive enduring pedagogical questions: Are students more engaged, or simply more entertained? Is technology fostering meaningful connections with content, or encouraging superficial interaction? And can we truly distinguish between active learning and passive compliance when engagement is measured through screen time or clicks?

Today, AI promises to personalise engagement like never before. Intelligent tutoring systems, automated feedback platforms and learning analytics dashboards offer tailored experiences designed to respond to each student's needs. But these systems raise familiar concerns. Will learners become passive recipients of AI-curated tasks? Is time-on-task a genuine indicator of engagement, or just activity? As before, the potential of AI lies not in its novelty but in how it is embedded within pedagogical frameworks that prioritise human connection, critical thought and purposeful learning.

Ultimately, even the most engaging technologies are only as effective as the educators who implement them. The next logical concern, then, is not just how students interact with technology, but how teachers are prepared to use it. This leads us to a longstanding issue in educational innovation: the persistent lack of training and support for educators.

INSUFFICIENT TRAINING AND SUPPORT FOR EDUCATORS

Insufficient training and support for educators refers to the persistent gap between the emergence of new technologies in education and teachers' ability to integrate them meaningfully into their practice. No matter how advanced or promising a digital tool may appear, its effectiveness in the classroom ultimately hinges on the confidence, pedagogical understanding and professional autonomy of the educators who use it.

This gap is not new. It has accompanied nearly every innovation in classroom technology. In the 1950s, overhead projectors were introduced with the promise of enhancing visual learning. By the 1960s and 1970s, they had become standard in many schools. Yet, as Saettler (2004) notes, these tools often reinforced traditional, lecture-based instruction rather than enabling more interactive or student-centred approaches. Their transformative potential was limited not by the technology itself, but by the way it was introduced, often without pedagogical training or conceptual frameworks.

The personal computer boom of the 1980s and 1990s followed a similar trajectory. While computers entered classrooms in increasing numbers, Cuban (2001) observed that many teachers received little to no training in how to incorporate them meaningfully into their teaching. As a result, computers were often used for isolated tasks, relegated to the periphery of the learning experience. Later technologies such as interactive whiteboards, tablets and mobile apps repeated this pattern, highlighting a structural issue: new tools arrive faster than the systems designed to support their integration.

MINI CASE STUDY: INTERACTIVE WHITEBOARDS

CONTEXT

In the early 2000s, a well-resourced urban school district implemented a comprehensive rollout of interactive whiteboards (IWBs) across all classrooms. This initiative aimed to enhance student engagement and modernize teaching practices by integrating emerging educational technologies.

CHALLENGE

Despite high initial enthusiasm and the provision of basic training for teachers, the integration of IWBs failed to produce the anticipated pedagogical transformation. Most educators reverted to using the technology in conventional ways such as displaying static slides or handwriting notes which effectively replicated chalkboard-based instruction.

SOLUTION

The district's approach emphasized hardware deployment over instructional innovation. Teachers were provided with the tools but lacked sustained professional development focused on interactive pedagogy, collaborative practices, and learner-centered design.

IMPLEMENTATION

The rollout strategy prioritized infrastructure and minimal orientation rather than a comprehensive change management process. Training sessions were limited in scope and duration, leaving a gap between technological capability and pedagogical implementation.

RESULTS

As documented by Higgins, Beauchamp, and Miller (2007), the integration of IWBs had little measurable effect on classroom practice or student engagement. The boards became high-tech chalkboards, reinforcing traditional teacher-centered methods rather than fostering active learning or collaboration.

CONCLUSION

This case illustrates a recurring challenge in educational technology initiatives: the mistaken belief that tools alone can drive transformation.

> Without a clear pedagogical vision, ongoing professional development, and systemic support, even advanced technologies are likely to reinforce rather than disrupt established practices.
>
> Source: (Higgins et al., 2007) Reviewing the literature on interactive whiteboards. *Learning, Media and Technology, 32*(3), 213–225. https://doi.org/10.1080/17439880701511040

These moments raised important professional questions: Are educators being supported with the time and resources they need to adapt? Is professional development keeping pace with technological change? And are training efforts rooted in sound pedagogical practice, or are they reactive and tool-focused?

Artificial intelligence has brought these questions to the fore once again. AI-powered platforms now offer real-time feedback, adaptive assessments and even automated lesson planning. While many educators express interest in these capabilities, research by Zawacki-Richter et al. (2019) shows that teachers often feel unprepared to understand the underlying algorithms or evaluate the broader ethical and educational implications of AI in the classroom.

The challenge here is not simply one of access, but of readiness. Without clear guidance and purposeful training, AI risks becoming yet another underutilised or misapplied technology, one that fails to deliver on its educational promise. Equipping teachers with the time, support and professional learning opportunities they need is essential to ensuring that technology serves student learning rather than replacing it.

As history has shown, professional development must go hand in hand with thoughtful implementation. Without it, even the most powerful tools can be reduced to superficial add-ons. The recurring struggles around teacher preparedness also point to a broader systemic issue: the lack of policies to guide technology use in education. This brings us to the next area of concern: the ongoing absence of consistent frameworks and guidelines for digital integration in schools.

LACK OF CLEAR POLICIES AND GUIDELINES

When schools and universities adopt new technologies without clear policies or guidelines, educators are left in a difficult position. The absence of consistent frameworks means that teachers must make decisions on their own about how, when and why to use digital tools. This lack of direction becomes even more pressing as innovations emerge at a pace faster than institutions can regulate. Without established legal, ethical or pedagogical structures to draw upon, many teachers find themselves experimenting in uncharted territory, often with little assurance that their choices are equitable or sustainable.

Historically, technological adoption in schools has frequently outpaced policy development. In the 19th century, the humble chalkboard entered classrooms without formal direction. Teachers devised their own methods of use, resulting in wide variability across classrooms. By the 1980s, the UK's Microelectronics Education Programme (MEP) sought to modernise education by introducing microcomputers into schools. Yet, as Watson (2001) observed, while hardware distribution was systematic, guidance on pedagogical integration was inconsistent. Some teachers used these devices for exploratory, constructivist learning, while others defaulted to rote drills. This was not out of resistance, but due to a lack of structured support.

These inconsistencies sparked foundational questions: Who is responsible for setting the standards for technology use in education? What does ethical, appropriate implementation look like? And how can systems ensure consistency and equity without overarching national or institutional policies?

The early 2000s brought another surge in technological experimentation, as laptops, tablets and online platforms entered classrooms. Reactions were mixed. Some schools adopted new tools enthusiastically; others banned them altogether. In the absence of shared frameworks, decisions were often reactive, based on isolated events or individual leadership preferences. This created not only pedagogical inconsistency but systemic inequity, particularly between well-resourced and under-resourced schools.

The introduction of AI has intensified the urgency of these concerns. With AI tools capable of generating essays, grading work and adapting instruction in real time, educators are left to interpret their role in the absence of concrete guidance. Key issues around data privacy, academic honesty, copyright and algorithmic bias remain unsettled. Holmes et al. (2019) highlight the widespread uncertainty that persists in classrooms as educators attempt to reconcile AI with established educational norms.

Some governments and international bodies have begun responding. Miao and Holmes and Australia's *Framework for Generative AI in Schools* (Australian Government Department of Education 2023) represent early efforts to address these challenges. Yet, a familiar gap remains between the creation of policy and its effective implementation at the classroom level. Educators continue to bear the burden of interpretation, often without the time, resources or professional development needed to operationalise these frameworks.

As with earlier technologies, the current landscape raises pressing concerns: Are teachers being left to navigate high-stakes decisions alone? Is the absence of policy exacerbating divides across the educational system? And are we responding to change with vision, or with crisis management?

The need for thoughtful, inclusive and adaptive policy has never been greater. As AI technologies evolve, so too must the frameworks that govern their use. Without clear guidance, the weight of adaptation falls disproportionately on educators, feeding into deeper anxieties about their evolving role, responsibilities and professional security in an increasingly automated landscape.

THREAT TO THE TEACHING PROFESSION

The threat to the teaching profession refers to long-standing concerns that technological advancements may erode, undervalue or altogether replace the role of educators. While innovations are often framed as tools to enhance teaching, they have consistently prompted fears of deskilling, automation and the gradual loss of professional autonomy. Beneath each new wave of technology lies a deeper question: what happens to the teacher when machines take over tasks once considered uniquely human?

These anxieties are not new. In the early 20th century, film reels and instructional radio broadcasts were heralded as revolutionary teaching aids and ones that might allow expert instruction to reach remote and rural learners. Yet, these same tools raised troubling questions about whether human educators might one day be rendered obsolete. The arrival of internet-based education reignited such concerns. Online courses and open educational resources, including platforms like TED Talks, edX and Udemy, made lectures by leading global scholars available to anyone with a connection. For some, this sparked a utopian vision of borderless learning; for others, it cast doubt on the continued necessity of classroom-based educators.

Learning Management Systems (LMS) such as Blackboard, Moodle and Canvas further amplified the tension. With their capacity for automated content delivery, grading and communication, LMS platforms shifted aspects of teaching into the domain of systems administration. As these platforms grew in sophistication, educators worried that their role was being reduced to that of content curators or data monitors, which was far from the relational and pedagogical core of the profession (Selwyn, 2016).

Each of these developments raised enduring questions: Would teachers be replaced by more scalable, cost-effective digital solutions? Would institutions prioritise automation and efficiency over the value of human connection? And would educators retain agency over curriculum, assessment and classroom dynamics in a data-driven system?

The rise of AI has brought these concerns into sharp relief. AI systems now offer real-time feedback, automated lesson planning and adaptive tutoring tools with undeniable potential for efficiency and personalisation. Yet, as Williamson and Hogan (2020) caution, this integration risks reframing educators as overseers of algorithmic processes rather than facilitators of dynamic, responsive learning. The richness of pedagogy, its improvisation, empathy and nuance cannot easily be translated into code.

However, history also offers a more optimistic view. With each wave of innovation, there have been calls not for the replacement of educators, but for a reimagining of their role. AI, like film, radio and the internet before it, can be harnessed to enhance rather than diminish teaching. By offloading routine administrative tasks, AI may create space for teachers to focus on what matters most: nurturing curiosity, fostering connection and guiding critical inquiry.

The challenge, as always, lies in implementation. It is not the presence of technology, but its purpose and context that determine its impact. To preserve the integrity of the teaching profession, educators must remain central in decision-making processes, helping to shape how tools are used and why.

As teachers adapt to these evolving landscapes, attention must also be paid to those who remain underserved. Technological innovation, while promising, often risks widening existing inequalities. Ensuring that equity remains a guiding principle in educational technology adoption is not just an ethical imperative; it is a professional one.

ACCESS INEQUITY

Access inequity refers to the uneven distribution of digital tools, infrastructure and support that limits students' ability to participate fully in technology-enhanced learning. While educational technologies hold the potential to transform learning environments and expand opportunity, they have historically magnified existing disparities when access is not equitably addressed.

This dynamic has been visible in nearly every phase of educational technological adoption. During the 1980s and 1990s, as personal computers entered schools, wealthier institutions were often first to acquire devices, provide teacher training and maintain technical infrastructure. Under-resourced schools, by contrast, frequently struggled to keep up, lacking not only hardware but also the expertise to integrate it meaningfully into teaching and learning (Selwyn, 1999). The digital divide became a structural issue shaped not by pedagogical intent, but by socioeconomic conditions.

The same pattern recurred with the expansion of broadband internet and mobile technologies. While many students in urban or affluent areas gained access to high-speed connections and individual devices, those in rural or lower-income households often faced unreliable connectivity, shared or outdated devices, and a lack of technical support. These disparities raised urgent equity questions: Who gets to benefit from digital innovation? Are certain students being left behind through no fault of their own? And how should schools and systems respond to ensure fair access to opportunity?

The COVID-19 pandemic sharpened these questions with stark clarity. As learning moved rapidly online, the absence of consistent access to devices, the internet and quiet study spaces caused significant disruption for many students. Dorn et al. (2020) report that these inequities exacerbated learning loss, disproportionately affecting students already facing educational disadvantage.

Today, the emergence of AI in education threatens to replicate or even deepen these divides. AI-powered tools, from personalised tutors to predictive analytics, may only reach learners in well-funded schools or households with reliable digital infrastructure. Students without adequate devices, high-speed internet or adult support risk being excluded from these benefits altogether. Miao and Holmes (2021) warns that such exclusions raise not only questions of access but also broader concerns about fairness, representation and ethical inclusion in the digital age.

As with earlier technologies, the challenge is clear: to ensure that innovation does not come at the cost of equity. This means going beyond hardware provision to address systemic needs such as culturally inclusive design, targeted support for disadvantaged communities and long-term investment in digital infrastructure. Only then can educational technologies, including AI, serve as bridges rather than barriers to meaningful, inclusive learning.

To understand the stakes more clearly, it helps to examine past reactions to educational innovations with the outcomes they produced.

AND IN HINDSIGHT?

Following an in-depth examination of educators' concerns surrounding the adoption of various educational technologies, we turn now to consider whether those fears materialised. From the earliest literary warnings against fairy tales to later apprehensions about calculators, computers and the internet, this section evaluates the outcomes of those anxieties. Drawing on retrospective studies and empirical evidence, we investigate which concerns were validated by experience, which were overstated, and what implications this has for the continued integration of technology in educational contexts.

Books: Early critics, such as Sarah Trimmer, warned that fairy tales and novels could undermine reason and morality, but these fears have since proven largely unfounded. Literary scholars now suggest that early exposure to fiction develops empathy, imagination and critical reasoning skills (Mar et al., 2009). Rather than corrupting judgement, books have proven to be fundamental to literacy and reflective thought. The richness of narrative literature has also been shown to activate complex cognitive processes that support long-term academic development. In fact, books, and indeed textbooks, became the foundation of today's education system.

Calculators: The major concern around calculators was that they would erode arithmetic skills. Subsequent studies have shown that when used in conjunction with strong instructional design, calculators do not impair numerical competency (Suydam, 1987). Instead, students using calculators frequently showed advanced concept development and enhanced problem-solving skills compared to those who did not. In fact, a meta-analysis by

Ellington (2003) found that students who used calculators during instruction performed as well or better on conceptual mathematics tasks than those who did not. Far from eroding foundational skills, calculators allowed students to engage more deeply with complex problem-solving.

Computers: The spread of personal computers ignited fears of academic dishonesty, shallow engagement and potential deskilling. Research has shown, however, that the impact of computers depends heavily on how they are implemented. Collaborative platforms, simulations and interactive tools have been shown to increase student engagement and enhance learning outcomes (Stahl, Koschmann, & Suthers, 2006). However, when used passively, such as for browsing or unsupervised assessments, computers have facilitated academic dishonesty (Lancaster & Clarke, 2008). The COVID-19 pandemic magnified these risks, with remote learning environments seeing a measurable rise in cheating incidents (Holden, Norris, & Kuhlmeier, 2021). We will discuss more about cheating below.

The Internet: The advent of the internet brought unparalleled access to information. It came with fears that this immediacy would erode deep thinking, promote superficial learning and exacerbate privacy violations. Indeed, researchers (Sparrow et al., 2011) found that internet users were more likely to remember where information was located than the information itself. Nevertheless, when used intentionally, internet-based tools can support inquiry-based learning and foster critical thinking. Structured digital inquiry, supported by teacher scaffolding, has been shown to deepen engagement and analytical skill development (Warschauer, 2004).

Nevertheless, concerns about student privacy and the lack of academic integrity have proved to be valid. The Electronic Frontier Foundation (2017) documented numerous cases where educational technology platforms collected more data than necessary, often without parental consent or clear data governance policies. These findings spurred international calls for greater transparency and regulation in the educational technology sector.

HAS CHEATING BECOME AN EPIDEMIC?

The discourse around academic cheating in the era of GenAI often appears polarised. On one hand, media headlines and institutional responses suggest a crisis of academic integrity, with students allegedly turning to tools like ChatGPT in droves to complete assignments dishonestly. On the other hand, empirical research presents a more tempered view, indicating that the prevalence of cheating has remained relatively stable for decades.

Argument 1: Cheating Is Rampant and Increasing

Advocates of this view often cite spikes in AI-related misconduct as evidence of a growing epidemic. For instance, a recent report in *The Guardian* highlighted that UK universities documented nearly 7,000 confirmed cases of AI-enabled cheating in the 2023–2024 academic year, more than triple the number recorded the previous year (Adams, 2025). These figures fuel fears of a declining ethical standard and a breakdown of traditional assessment models. Anecdotal accounts, such as the UCLA graduate who publicly credited ChatGPT for completing his degree (Lee and Hammer, 2011), reinforce the perception that cheating is becoming normalised and increasingly difficult to detect.

Argument 2: Cheating Rates Have Remained Stable

In contrast, longitudinal studies paint a different picture. Bowers' landmark 1964 study found self-reported cheating rates among college students ranged from 11% to 49%, depending on the behaviour in question. Decades later, McCabe and Bowers (1994) reported similar rates, suggesting little change over time. Vandehey et al. (2007) tracked cheating at one institution and found a modest increase from 54.1% in 1984 to 57.4% in 2004. More recently, a high school survey study found that while the methods of cheating have evolved, from handwritten crib notes to Google, and now GenAI, the overall rate of student dishonest behaviour has remained broadly consistent (Lee et al., 2024). This suggests that cheating is a persistent feature of educational systems rather than a growing anomaly.

The ChatGPT Spike: A Question of Timing and Access

It's also important to contextualise the current wave of concern about GenAI. Tools like ChatGPT only became widely accessible to the public in late 2022, with usage dramatically increasing through 2023. As such, the surge in studies examining AI-facilitated cheating may reflect not only a behavioural shift but also the novelty and unprecedented availability of these tools. Birks and Clare (2023) argue that AI-based academic misconduct represents a new form of an existing issue, inviting comparisons with past prevention frameworks.

Moreover, extensive publicity surrounding the rapid uptake of GenAI platforms, particularly ChatGPT, has intensified scrutiny of academic integrity, even before we see definitive changes in cheating rates (Birks and Clare, 2023; The Guardian, 2025). The attention may say as much about the tech adoption curve as it does about actual moral decline.

Reconciling the Two Perspectives

These two arguments need not be mutually exclusive. It may be that *visibility* of cheating has increased due to the traceability of digital misconduct, or that *institutional responses* are more reactive to new technologies than to older, analogue forms of dishonesty. The moral panic surrounding AI may be less about actual changes in behaviour and more about shifts in *how* students cheat and how well-equipped educators feel to address it. Ultimately, these debates should prompt deeper reflection on the pedagogical and structural conditions that allow cheating to persist, rather than simply focusing on the tools students use.

WHAT WE KNOW NOW

Having examined the concerns that have accompanied each wave of educational technology and weighed them against historical outcomes and research evidence, it becomes clear that many fears, while valid at the time, have either evolved or been tempered by experience. Some anxieties have proven well-founded, others overstated, and many have offered critical insight into how technology should (or shouldn't) be used in learning environments. Table 1.1 gathers the key questions raised throughout the chapter and pairs them with the answers we've uncovered. Together, they serve as a map of persistent tensions and emerging resolutions that continue to shape the intersection of education and innovation.

The questions outlined in Table 1.1 reflect the enduring concerns educators have faced with each new wave of technology. While the specifics have changed, the underlying themes remain remarkably consistent: fears of diminished understanding, loss of autonomy and inequity in access. Yet, as the answers reveal, many of these concerns have been met with adaptation, innovation and evidence-informed practice. Understanding this lineage not only helps in understanding current debates but also equips us to respond with greater confidence and clarity. With this perspective in place, we now turn to what all of this means for the future.

TABLE 1.1 Concerns Surrounding the Introduction of New Technologies in Education and Some Answers

Category	Question	Answer
Academic Integrity	Would allowing students to rely on machines for basic arithmetic erode their understanding of core mathematical principles?	No. Studies show machines, when used with strong instructional design, enhance concept development and problem-solving.
	If technology can complete the task, what then is left for the learner?	Learners are expected to engage with higher-order thinking tasks; educators are to integrate tech to enhance inquiry.
	Will students still engage deeply with the material, or will they opt for efficiency over understanding?	Depends on implementation; history shows both outcomes possible, requiring careful pedagogical design.
	Can assessment remain valid when shortcuts are readily available?	Yes, but requires adaptation and reinforcement of academic honesty frameworks.
Critical Thinking	Is technology enhancing students' ability to think critically, or is it doing the thinking for them?	Depends on use; guided use fosters deeper thinking, unguided may hinder it.
	Will it replace reasoning with convenience?	Risk exists (e.g., Google thinking), but can be mitigated with instructional design.
	Will it dull students' capacity to evaluate, synthesise and interpret?	Uncritical use may do so, but reflective engagement can sharpen these skills.
	Or can it be used to sharpen those very skills?	Yes, when students critique, reflect on and build upon generated content.
Data Privacy	Who was entitled to access this data?	Policies like FERPA and institutional reviews aim to clarify access rights.
	How long would it be stored?	Not always clear; regulatory frameworks are evolving to address this.
	Could it be sold, repurposed or exploited?	Yes, examples such as ClassDojo raise these concerns.
	Is the data collected truly supporting learning, or is it feeding institutional metrics?	Both occur; tension between pedagogical use and institutional control noted.

	Are students able to take intellectual risks, or does constant monitoring inhibit exploration?	Monitoring can inhibit curiosity; promotes compliance over creativity.
	How might such tools alter the relationship between teacher and learner shifting it from a partnership to one of control?	Surveillance risks changing dynamic to managerial oversight.
Content, Censorship and Academic Freedom	Who gets to determine what knowledge is valid or appropriate?	Historically contested; digital algorithms now shape decisions without transparency.
	Does shielding students from controversy hinder their development as critical thinkers?	Yes; legal cases affirm educational value of engaging with complexity.
	At what point do moral concerns impinge on the educator's role as facilitator of inquiry?	Moral panic historically curtailed educator autonomy (e.g., fairy tales, comics).
	Are students being subtly shielded from diverse perspectives by algorithmic design?	Yes; filters can replicate biases and exclude minority views.
	Is educational content increasingly shaped by corporate or computational priorities rather than pedagogical intent?	Yes; algorithms and vendors influence what students encounter.
	Is the autonomy of educators being eroded by digital systems that filter learning materials without consultation or accountability?	Yes; platforms often override teacher decisions through opaque systems.
	Are we creating more responsive learning environments or simply narrowing the educational lens through which students view the world?	Depends on implementation; risk of narrowing lens if algorithmic bias isn't addressed.
Pedagogical Debates	Would emerging technologies undermine tried-and-true instructional methods?	Yes, if not integrated thoughtfully; pattern repeated with calculators, PCs.
	Would they serve all learners equally, or widen existing disparities?	Disparities have often widened without inclusive frameworks.
	What would become of the teacher's authority when digital platforms increasingly guided the learning process?	Teachers risk deskilling and loss of agency; need to stay central in decisions.

(*Continued*)

TABLE 1.1 (Continued)

Category	Question	Answer
Student Engagement	Does the technology deepen learning, or simply hold attention?	Depends; novelty fades if not paired with deep instructional use.
	Are students more engaged, or simply more entertained?	Both possible; critical distinction between active learning and passive use needed.
	Is technology fostering meaningful connection with content, or encouraging superficial interaction?	Effective use can support depth; passive use risks surface-level interaction.
	Can we truly distinguish between active learning and passive compliance when engagement is measured through screen time or clicks?	No; current metrics often conflate activity with engagement.
	Will learners become passive recipients of AI-curated tasks?	Risk exists; requires pedagogical oversight.
	Is time-on-task a genuine indicator of engagement, or just activity?	Time alone is insufficient; deeper indicators needed.
Insufficient Training and Support for Educators	Are educators being supported with the time and resources they need to adapt?	Often, no; support lags behind tech rollout.
	Is professional development keeping pace with technological change?	No; historically reactive, not proactive.
	Are training efforts rooted in sound pedagogical practice, or are they reactive and tool-focused?	Too often reactive and focused on tools, not pedagogy.

Lack of Clear Policies and Guidelines	Who is responsible for setting the standards for technology use in education?	Unclear; governments and bodies like UNESCO attempt guidance.
	What does ethical, appropriate implementation look like?	Still under debate; few operationalised models exist.
	How can systems ensure consistency and equity without overarching national or institutional policies?	They can't easily; equity gaps widen without consistent frameworks.
	Are teachers being left to navigate high-stakes decisions alone?	Yes; lack of support and clear policies noted.
	Is the absence of policy exacerbating divides across the educational system?	Yes; creates inconsistency and inequity.
	Are we responding to change with vision, or with crisis management?	Too often, crisis management dominates over proactive planning.
Threat to the Teaching Profession	What happens to the teacher when machines take over tasks once considered uniquely human?	Risk of dehumanisation and deskilling; empathy and judgement hard to replicate.
	Would teachers be replaced by more scalable, cost-effective digital solutions?	Some fear this; others call for reimagining teacher roles.
	Would institutions prioritise automation and efficiency over the value of human connection?	Concern noted; balance needed between efficiency and pedagogy.
	Would educators retain agency over curriculum, assessment and classroom dynamics in a data-driven system?	Not guaranteed; teacher voice must be central in tech decisions.
Access Inequity	Who gets to benefit from digital innovation?	Often, the privileged; underserved communities lag behind.
	Are certain students being left behind through no fault of their own?	Yes; inequity linked to resources and infrastructure.
	How should schools and systems respond to ensure fair access to opportunity?	With systemic investment, inclusive design and targeted support.

LOOKING BACK TO MOVE FORWARD

If history has taught us anything, it's that every new educational technology arrives accompanied by a wave of uncertainty. From fairy tales and novels to computers and the internet, each innovation has prompted fears about moral decline, eroding attention spans, compromised privacy and even the disappearance of the teacher. And yet, over time, many of these concerns have been reassessed, some justified, others exaggerated and all of them instructive. As we've seen throughout this chapter, hindsight offers valuable insight into how we might move forward with intention.

Too often, educational technologies are adopted not for their pedagogical value, but simply because they are new. The case of interactive whiteboards serves as a cautionary tale: heralded as transformative, they frequently reinforced existing teacher-centred practices rather than fostering deeper engagement or collaboration. The lesson here is clear: effective integration depends not on what the technology *can* do, but on how and *why* it is used.

Today, AI is reigniting many of these long-standing debates. With its promises of personalised learning, instant feedback and streamlined assessment, AI has captured the imagination of educators and institutions alike. Yet, as Holmes et al. (2019) remind us, such tools can reinforce inequities and displace the subtle, human dimensions of teaching. Personalisation may benefit some learners, but it also risks scripting their learning journeys in ways that limit autonomy and critical agency. These are not merely technical issues. They strike at the core of what it means to educate. These concerns reveal that educators aren't just fearful of AI itself but of what it reflects about systemic weaknesses in educational design and purpose.

At the same time, technologies like mobile devices continue to reshape how we think about student engagement. No longer is it enough to simply hold attention. Engagement now demands participation, critical thought and meaningful collaboration. When used with care and purpose, tools such as smartphones can support these goals, enriching student experiences and connecting learning to their lived realities. But the success of this approach hinges not on the tools themselves, but on the pedagogical frameworks that guide their use.

Ultimately, the challenge we face is not just one of implementation, but of imagination. Educators must be supported not only with training, but with time and space to rethink how curriculum, classroom practice and assessment evolve in tandem with technological change. Professional learning must move beyond operational know-how to encompass ethical reflection, disciplinary fluency and an adaptive mindset. Only then can we ensure that the technologies we bring into the classroom serve learning, rather than the other way around.

As the dust of past disruptions begins to settle, one thing becomes clear. It is no longer enough to react to technology; we must learn to understand it. If AI is to play a meaningful role in the future of education, we need more than surface-level familiarity. We need to unpack how these systems work, what they're capable of and where their limitations lie. In the next chapter, we'll turn our focus to exactly that: demystifying AI in the classroom, so that educators are empowered not just to use it, but to shape its role with confidence and care.

REFLECT AND REFRAME

1. Which historical concerns about educational technology do you see echoed in current debates about AI?
2. Have any of your own assumptions about technology in education been challenged by the historical patterns explored in this chapter?
3. In your context, are new tools being adopted for their pedagogical value or simply because they're available?
4. How might awareness of past overreactions or underestimations shape your response to AI in the classroom?
5. What role should educators play in guiding how technology is used, and who currently holds that decision-making power?
6. What does meaningful engagement look like in a technology-rich learning environment?

REFERENCES

Adams, 2025. Revealed: Thousands of UK university students caught cheating using AI.

Allington, R. L., 2002. What I've learned about effective reading instruction. *Phi Delta Kappan*, 83, 740–747. https://doi.org/10.1177/003172170208301007

Australian Government Department of Education, 2023. *Australian framework for generative artificial intelligence in schools*. Commonwealth of Australia. https://www.education.gov.au/schooling/resources/australian-framework-generative-artificial-intelligence-ai-schools (Accessed: 3 September 2025).

Banks, S., 2008. A historical analysis of attitudes toward the use of calculators in junior high and high school math classrooms in the United States since 1975.

Birks, D., and Clare, J., 2023. Linking artificial intelligence facilitated academic misconduct to existing prevention frameworks. *International Journal for Educational Integrity*, 19(1), 20.

Cuban, L., 2001. *Oversold and underused: Computers in the classroom*. Harvard University Press.

Dorn, E., Hancock, B., Sarakatsannis, J., and Viruleg, E., 2020. COVID-19 and student learning in the United States: The hurt could last a lifetime.

Electronic Frontier Foundation, 2017. *Spying on students: School issued devices and student privacy*. Electronic Frontier Foundation. https://www.eff.org/wp/school-issued-devices-and-student-privacy (Accessed: 3 September 2025).

Ellington, A. J., 2003. A meta-analysis of the effects of calculators on students' achievement and attitude levels in precollege mathematics classes. *Journal for Research in Mathematics Education*, 34(5), 433–463.

Grenby, M. O., 2014. *The child reader, 1700–1840*. Cambridge University Press.

Higgins, S., Beauchamp, G., and Miller, D., 2007. Reviewing the literature on interactive whiteboards. *Learning, Media and Technology*, 32, 213–225. https://doi.org/10.1080/17439880701511040

Holden, O. L., Norris, M. E., and Kuhlmeier, V. A., 2021. Academic integrity in online assessment: A research review. *Frontiers in Education*, 6, 639814.

Holmes, W., Bialik, M., and Fadel, C., 2019. *Artificial intelligence in education: Promises and implications for teaching and learning*. Center for Curriculum Redesign.

Kerr, S. T., 1989. Technology and the future of schooling. *Ninety-fifth Yearbook of the National Society for the Study of Education*, Part II.

Kukulska-Hulme, A., 2009. Will mobile learning change language learning? *ReCALL*, 21, 157–165. https://doi.org/10.1017/S0958344009000202

Lancaster, T., and Clarke, R., 2008. The phenomena of contract cheating. In T. Roberts (ed.), *Student plagiarism in an online world: Problems and solutions*. Idea Group.

Lee, J., and Hammer, J., 2011. (PDF) Gamification in education: What, how, why bother?. ResearchGate. https://www.researchgate.net/publication/258697764_Gamification_in_Education_What_How_Why_Bother

Lee, V. R., et al., 2024. Cheating in the age of generative AI: A high school survey study of cheating behaviours before and after the release of ChatGPT. *Computers and Education: Artificial Intelligence*, 7, 100253.

Lindgren, R., Tscholl, M., Wang, S., and Johnson, E., 2016. Enhancing learning and engagement through embodied interaction within a mixed reality simulation. *Computers & Education*, 95, 174–187. https://doi.org/10.1016/j.compedu.2016.01.001

Manolev, J., Sullivan, A., and Slee, R., 2019. The datafication of discipline: ClassDojo, surveillance and a performative classroom culture. *Learning, Media and Technology*, 44, 36–51. https://doi.org/10.1080/17439884.2018.1558237

Mar, R. A., Oatley, K., and Peterson, J. B., 2009. Exploring the link between reading fiction and empathy: Ruling out individual differences and examining outcomes. *Communications*, 34(4), 407–428.

McCabe, D. L., and Bowers, W. J., 1994. Academic dishonesty among males in college: A thirty year perspective. *Journal of College Student Development*, 35(1), 5–10.

Miao, F. and Holmes, W., 2021. *AI and education: A guidance for policymakers*. UNESCO Publishing.

Parrish, B., and Others, 2025. Television in the classroom: Critical viewing/thinking skill development. Ed.gov. https://eric.ed.gov/?id=ED216337 (Accessed: 1 January 2025).

Rosenberg v. Board of Education of the City of New York, 92 N.Y.S.2d 344 (N.Y. Sup. Ct. 1949).

Saettler, P., 2004. *The evolution of American educational technology*. Emerald Publishing Limited.

Selwyn, N., 1999. Schooling the information society? The place of the information superhighway in education. *Information, Communication & Society*, 2(2), 156–173.

Selwyn, N., 2016. Education and technology. Bloomsbury. https://www.bloomsbury.com/au/education-and-technology-9781350145566

Sparrow, B., Liu, J., and Wegner, D. M., 2011. Google effects on memory: Cognitive consequences of having information at our fingertips. *Science*, 333, 776–778. https://doi.org/10.1126/science.1207745

Stahl, G., Koschmann, T., and Suthers, D., 2006. Computer supported collaborative learning: An historical perspective. In R. K. Sawyer (ed.), *Cambridge handbook of the learning sciences*. Cambridge University Press, pp. 409–426.

Suydam, M. N., 1987. What are calculators good for? *The Arithmetic Teacher*, 34(6), 22–28.

The Guardian, 2025. Revealed: Thousands of UK university students caught cheating using AI. *The Guardian*, 15 June 2025. https://www.theguardian.com/education/2025/jun/15/thousands-of-uk-university-students-caught-cheating-using-ai-artificial-intelligence-survey (Accessed: 3 September 2025).

Thomas, K., and O'Bannon, B., 2013. Cell phones in the classroom: Preservice teachers' perceptions. *Journal of Digital Learning in Teacher Education*, 30, 11–20.

U.S. Department of Education, 2008. *Family Educational Rights and Privacy Act (FERPA)*. U.S. Department of Education.

Vandehey, M. (Michael A.), Diekhoff, G., and LaBeff, E., 2007. College cheating: A twenty-year follow-up and the addition of an honor code. *Journal of College Student Development*, 48, 468–480. https://doi.org/10.1353/csd.2007.0043

Warschauer, M., 2004. *Technology and social inclusion: Rethinking the digital divide*. The MIT Press.

Watson, D. M., 2001. Pedagogy before technology: Re-thinking the relationship between ICT and teaching. *Education and Information Technologies*, 6(3), 251–266.

Weale, S., 2020. Have you been protesting against A-level downgrading?

Wenglinsky, H., 1998. *Does it compute? The relationship between educational technology and student achievement in mathematics*. Policy Information Center.

Williamson, B., and Hogan, A., 2020. Commercialisation and privatisation in/of education in the context of Covid-19.

Zawacki-Richter, O., Marín, V.I., Bond, M. and Gouverneur, F., 2019. Systematic review of research on artificial intelligence applications in higher education–where are the educators?. *International journal of educational technology in higher education*, *16*(1), 39.

CHAPTER 2

Understanding AI's Place in the Classroom

AI is transforming the landscape of education, reshaping how students engage with learning activities, how educators develop and present teaching materials, and how institutions operate.

CHAPTER AIMS

The aim of this chapter is to introduce key themes explored in this book in relation to:

1. *The evolving role of educators in AI-enhanced learning environments.*
2. *The foundational concepts and structure of artificial intelligence.*
3. *The practical applications and benefits of AI in contemporary classrooms.*

THE DEATH OF A KNOWLEDGE WORKER

Among the top ten knowledge worker roles most susceptible to AI-driven transformation are financial analysts, radiologists, lawyers, journalists, paralegals, pharmacists, insurance underwriters, software testers, market

DOI: 10.1201/9781003624981-2

researchers and notably, teachers and professors. Once seen as the stewards of intellectual labour, educators are increasingly exposed to automation pressures from AI-powered grading systems and adaptive learning platforms to virtual tutors and content generators. As algorithms begin to deliver personalised instruction and assess student progress with remarkable precision, the role of human educators is being reshaped. The threat is not complete displacement, but disintermediation, where once the teacher was the sole source of knowledge, now intelligent systems compete for that central role.

Faced with this disruption, educators and other knowledge professionals stand at a crossroads: be augmented by intelligent systems or risk being replaced by them. The choice is not about resisting technology, but about reimagining one's role in a world where machines can think, adapt and even teach. In their influential work *Only Humans Need Apply*, Davenport and Kirby (2016) propose five strategies for thriving in the age of smart machines. These strategies include Step In, Step Up, Step Aside, Step Narrowly and Step Forward. They offer a roadmap for how professionals can reposition themselves not in competition with AI, but in collaboration with it. Each strategy highlights a distinct way to maintain relevance and contribute value where human insight, empathy or creativity remains indispensable.

In the context of education, these strategies can be directly applied to how educators design learning experiences, support students and shape institutional innovation. From deeply integrating AI into pedagogy to focusing on human-only capabilities like empathy and mentorship, each path, described in Table 2.1, offers a way to remain relevant and impactful in an AI-enhanced educational ecosystem.

Rather than retreating from intelligent technologies, you should embrace the augmentation path to work *with* AI, not against it. The goal is to empower teachers, lecturers and education leaders to identify where they can thrive alongside AI by cultivating the skills, mindsets and strategies needed to remain central to the learning experience. Before we explore these practical approaches, however, we will take a step back to define artificial intelligence, trace its evolution across everyday life and lay the conceptual foundation for how AI has come to influence the classroom.

TABLE 2.1 Professional Thriving Strategies for Educators in the Face of AI

Strategy	Description	Education Example
Step In	Collaborate closely with AI systems by understanding their strengths and limits.	A teacher uses an AI-driven tutoring system and tailors instruction based on its feedback.
Step Up	Manage and guide the strategic use of AI tools in the institution.	A department head sets guidelines for ethical AI use in curriculum and assessment.
Step Aside	Focus on uniquely human skills like empathy, motivation and mentoring.	A professor holds in-person reflective discussions and offers emotional support to students.
Step Narrowly	Specialise in a niche area less impacted by AI.	An educator teaches hands-on arts or ethics seminars that require nuanced human interaction.
Step Forward	Contribute to the development of new AI tools for learning.	An instructional designer collaborates with developers to build adaptive learning platforms.

WHAT IS AI?

Today, when people think of artificial intelligence (AI), they often picture ChatGPT or similar chatbots. These advanced language models have become the face of AI, dominating headlines and public perception.

However, AI is far more than just conversational agents. It is an expansive field that has been shaping our world for decades, often in ways we don't even recognise. From the recommendation algorithms curating our entertainment choices to the smart assistants managing our schedules, AI has been subtly woven into our daily lives for much longer than you might realise.

The idea of intelligent machines has been a topic of philosophical and scientific inquiry for centuries, with early myths and legends often depicting artificial beings endowed with intelligence, such as the automata of ancient Greece and the Golem of Jewish folklore. Philosophers like René Descartes and Gottfried Wilhelm Leibniz speculated about mechanical reasoning, proposing ideas that anticipated the logic-based structures used in AI today (Russel & Norvig, 2020). *Father of the Computer*, Charles Babbage, designed the Analytical Engine (Swade & Babbage, 2001), which laid the groundwork for modern computing. Ada Lovelace, working alongside Babbage, conceptualised the first machine-computed algorithm specifically for calculating Bernoulli numbers using the Analytical Engine. This algorithm, which involved a series of operations designed to be carried out sequentially by the machine, is widely regarded as the first example of a computer program (Britannica, n.d.). However, modern AI research truly began in the mid-20th century.

In 1956, the Dartmouth Conference, often considered the birth of AI as a formal discipline, brought together pioneering thinkers such as John McCarthy, Marvin Minsky, Claude Shannon and Nathaniel Rochester to explore how machines could simulate human intelligence (McCarthy, et al., 2006). Since then, AI has evolved through various phases, from symbolic AI in the 1960s and expert systems in the 1980s to the popularity of machine learning in the 21st century.

AI draws from the fields of computer science, mathematics, cognitive science, linguistics and related disciplines, and its subfields have evolved over decades to address specialised challenges and domains. It can be examined as the hierarchical structure as presented in Figure 2.1, which

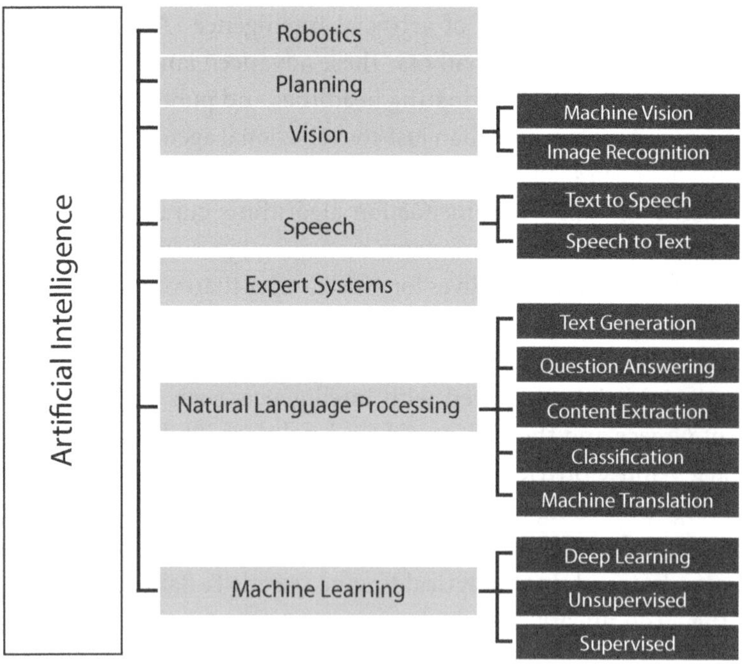

FIGURE 2.1 A hierarchy of artificial intelligence.

provides a conceptual framework through which to examine the major branches of AI, each contributing distinct capabilities and applications.

At the broadest level, Artificial Intelligence refers to the design and implementation of computational systems that exhibit intelligent behaviour. This includes capabilities such as learning from data, making decisions, understanding natural language, interpreting visual inputs and acting autonomously in the physical world. AI finds application across countless domains, from simple systems that filter spam emails to more sophisticated agents capable of navigating real-world environments.

One of the most visible applications of AI is in robotics, where intelligence is embedded in physical machines. Robotic systems combine hardware and software to perform autonomous actions in physical environments. For example, Boston Dynamics' Spot robot can traverse rough terrain, avoid obstacles and perform routine inspections of industrial sites. These systems often rely on additional subfields of AI, such as planning and vision, to operate effectively.

Planning, as a subdomain of AI, involves determining sequences of actions needed to achieve specific goals under constraints. It is central to logistics and scheduling problems. Companies such as Amazon and FedEx employ AI planning algorithms to optimise delivery routes, balancing efficiency with time constraints and resource availability. These systems reason about possible future states and select optimal paths of action accordingly.

Computer vision, often referred to simply as vision in AI contexts, enables machines to interpret and analyse visual information. Within this domain, machine vision is typically employed in manufacturing settings, where systems automatically inspect products for defects. A more general and widely known application is image recognition, used in platforms such as Facebook, where AI systems can identify and tag individuals in photographs.

Speech-based AI technologies support the conversion between spoken and written language. Text-to-speech (TTS) systems are commonly used in virtual assistants, navigation devices and accessibility tools, enabling machines to "speak" in a human-like voice. Conversely, speech-to-text (STT) systems, such as those used in Zoom's real-time transcription feature, allow spoken language to be captured and converted into written text, supporting note-taking and accessibility.

Expert systems were among the earliest forms of AI to be adopted in professional settings. These systems mimic the decision-making processes of human experts by applying rules to a structured knowledge base. A well-known example is the bacterial infection diagnosis system called MYCIN, developed in the 1970s. While expert systems have declined in prominence due to their limited adaptability, they remain historically significant in the development of AI.

Natural Language Processing (NLP) is the branch of AI aimed at enabling computers to understand and generate human language. NLP underpins applications such as machine translation, sentiment analysis and chatbots. Within this field, text generation refers to the creation of coherent text based on a prompt, as exemplified by models like ChatGPT. Question answering systems, such as those embedded in modern search engines, retrieve relevant information or generate answers to user queries. Context extraction, classification and language translation are also integral parts of NLP, enabling machines to summarise content, assign categories (such as spam detection) and convert text across languages with increasing fluency.

The foundation for many of these capabilities lies in machine learning, a subfield of AI that focuses on algorithms that improve performance through experience. Supervised learning algorithms are trained on labelled data and are used in applications such as email classification or fraud detection. Unsupervised learning algorithms identify patterns in unlabelled data and are used in market segmentation or anomaly detection. A major advancement in this domain, which uses neural networks with multiple layers to model complex relationships in data, is deep learning. Deep learning powers many of today's most advanced AI systems, including those used for speech recognition, image classification and natural language generation.

Some well-known examples of working neural networks include:

- **Google's DeepMind AlphaFold**: This model predicts 3D structures of proteins based on their amino acid sequences, revolutionising biological research.
- **Meta's Segment Anything Model (SAM)**: A computer vision model that can identify and segment any object in an image without needing training for specific object types.
- **Tesla Autopilot**: Uses deep neural networks to interpret real-time video from vehicle cameras for self-driving capabilities.

- **DeepFace (by Meta)**: A facial recognition system that identifies individuals with high accuracy by learning facial features.
- **Google Translate**: Uses neural machine translation (NMT), a deep learning model that improves the fluency and accuracy of translated text.

In education, neural networks power systems such as:

- Automated essay scoring platforms: These use NLP and pattern recognition to assess student writing, offering quick feedback on grammar, structure and even argument strength (Educational Testing Service, n.d.).
- Intelligent tutoring systems: AI tutors like Carnegie Learning analyse student responses in real time, adapting lesson delivery based on where students struggle or excel (MDPI, 2024).
- Student engagement monitoring tools: Vision-based systems use neural networks to track attention, engagement or even emotional states through webcam analysis, helping identify students who may need support (Pabba & Kumar, 2023).

In popular discourse, particularly on social media platforms, the term "my algorithm" has become shorthand for the personalised outputs of such systems. This occurs when users perceive recommendation engines (such as those on TikTok, YouTube or Spotify) to be uniquely tuned to their preferences. While there is no distinct algorithm assigned to each individual, machine learning systems adjust their predictions based on user interactions, creating the illusion of a bespoke experience. This phenomenon reflects both the power and opacity of machine learning: the model is general, but the feedback loops make its outputs feel personal.

DID YOU KNOW?

"**My algorithm**" is a colloquial way of referring to the personalised content curation a person experiences on a digital platform. It's not a unique algorithm, but rather a personalised output of a shared system based on user data and engagement history.

COMMON MISUNDERSTANDINGS

Myth	Reality
"Everyone has a separate algorithm."	There's **one algorithm**, but it creates **personalised outcomes** based on individual data.
"My algorithm is broken."	What people perceive as a glitch is usually just a change in their behaviour or platform tweaks.
"I can trick my algorithm."	Sort of true. If you actively change your behaviour (e.g., search for different content), the system may adjust over time.

Large language models like ChatGPT live at the crossroads of two major areas in artificial intelligence: deep learning and natural language processing. Instead of following hard-coded rules written by humans, these models learn by example. They study vast amounts of text and notice patterns of how words and phrases tend to appear together, how sentences are structured and how meaning flows through language. Their architecture, known as a transformer, helps them focus on the most relevant parts of the input so they can respond in a way that makes sense. The result is a system that doesn't just spit out memorised facts but can generate responses that sound natural, stay on topic and often make good sense.

Although ChatGPT does not perform physical actions like a robot, perceive images like a vision system or plan in the classical AI sense, it can be integrated with these systems to form multimodal agents. For instance, when combined with speech recognition and synthesis, ChatGPT can function as the conversational core of a virtual assistant. In educational contexts, it can serve as an automated tutor, generating explanations, answering student questions or even producing customised learning materials. Its strength lies in language: in understanding, generating, translating and transforming text.

The term *generative AI* (GenAI) refers to software capable of producing original content, including text, images, sounds, code or data, through training on very large datasets. We categorise GenAI along two intersecting dimensions: *output modality* and *reasoning type*, and enhance this taxonomy by incorporating *Explainable AI (XAI)* principles, which are increasingly essential in scholarly and educational deployments.

1. Modality-Based GenAI

   - **Text-based GenAI**: Transformers like GPT-4 (OpenAI, 2023), Claude (Anthropic, n.d.) and Gemini (Google, n.d.) generate coherent natural language for tasks such as summarisation, translation, question answering and essay composition.
   - **Image-generating AI**: Models like DALL·E (OpenAI, 2021), Midjourney (Midjourney, n.d.) and Stable Diffusion (Diffusion, n.d.) create visual content by mapping textual prompts to image representations.
   - **Code-generating AI**: Tools such as Codex (OpenAI, 2025) or CodeWhisperer (AWS, n.d.) produce code snippets, assist with debugging or generate full scripts based on natural language input.
   - **Multimodal GenAI**: Systems like GPT-4 (OpenAI, 2023) with vision or Gemini 1.5 (Google, n.d.) process diverse inputs such as text, image, audio and synthesise responses across modalities.

2. Reasoning-Based GenAI

   - **Retrieval-Augmented Generation (RAG)**: Models that supplement generative output by querying external sources and thus grounding responses and improving factual reliability.
   - **Tool-using Models**: These invoke external tools (e.g., computation engines or knowledge bases) to enhance correctness, such as solving math problems via external calculation.
   - **Agentic Models**: Examples include AutoGPT (AutoGPT, n.d.) and BabyAGI (BabyAGI, n.d.), which conduct autonomous planning, memory-based decision-making and feedback-driven workflows.
   - **Reasoning-Augmented Models**: These use structured reasoning techniques like chain-of-thought, scratchpads or tree-of-thought to simulate intermediate inference steps, improving performance on logic-based tasks.

3. Explainability in GenAI (XAI for GenAI)

   As GenAI systems gain complexity and application in sensitive domains, users and stakeholders increasingly require transparency. The evolving field of GenXAI addresses the distinct need to explain generative artefacts rather than classifications (Schneider, 2024). The key explainability dimensions for XAI include:

- **Verifiability**: Ability to trace generated outputs to external sources or evidence.
- **Interactivity**: Explanations that can be queried or refined by users.
- **Security and Cost**: Trade-offs involving data access, computational overhead and explanation reliability (Schneider, 2024)

In summary, the AI hierarchy provides a conceptual map for navigating the diversity of methods and applications in the field. While the boundaries between subfields increasingly blur in contemporary systems, understanding their historical and functional distinctions helps clarify how tools like ChatGPT fit within the broader AI ecosystem. By situating ChatGPT (and other GenAI systems) within deep learning and NLP, we recognise it not as a general AI, but as a specialised system, powerful in its domain, yet dependent on integration with other technologies to achieve more comprehensive intelligence. This contextual understanding becomes especially significant when we examine how such specialised systems are being adapted for real-world domains and none more transformative, or contested, than education.

AI MEETS EDUCATION

AI is transforming the landscape of education, reshaping how students engage with learning activities, how educators develop and present teaching materials, and how institutions operate. From personalised learning experiences to automated grading and intelligent tutoring systems, AI is becoming an integral part of modern education.

AI is revolutionising education in multiple ways. Machine learning algorithms can personalise learning experiences by analysing vast amounts of student data to adapt content to each student's strengths and weaknesses (Abbas et al., 2023; Sajja et al., 2025). AI-driven tutoring systems, such as Carnegie Learning's MATHia, help students practice skills in an adaptive and interactive manner (Fancsali, Sandbothe & Ritter, 2023). Additionally, AI-powered assessment tools can automate grading, providing instant feedback and freeing educators to focus on student engagement (Darad, 2023).

In the previous chapter, we examined the concerns that educators are raising around the introduction and use of AI in the classroom. Now let's take a look at some of the benefits.

Benefits of AI in Education

AI is increasingly offering innovative solutions to augment learning, streamline educational processes and improve student outcomes. Its applications in education extend beyond personalised learning, accessibility, automation and data-driven insights. Additional key benefits include:

Personalised Learning

AI-driven platforms adapt learning materials to individual student performance, identifying strengths and weaknesses to deliver customised content. This personalisation is achieved through machine learning algorithms that continuously analyse learner behaviour, quiz results and interaction patterns to tailor educational experiences in real time (Wang et al., 2023). Such adaptive systems not only promote mastery learning by allowing students to progress at their own pace but also reduce cognitive overload by focusing on relevant content. Moreover, these systems have shown measurable benefits in improving student engagement and retention, especially in large-scale online courses (Zawacki-Richter, et al., 2019). Educators also benefit, gaining insight into student performance trends and intervening more effectively when learners struggle (Luckin, 2016). This dynamic, feedback-rich approach ensures that students receive targeted support precisely where they need it most (Akintola et al. 2025)

MINI CASE STUDY: BOOSTING ACADEMIC PERFORMANCE WITH A PERSONAL AI TUTOR

CONTEXT

UniDistance Suisse sought to boost student learning outcomes in a neuroscience psychology course by integrating evidence-based learning strategies with artificial intelligence (AI). The course was part of the university's online psychology degree program and included traditional online lectures and quizzes.

CHALLENGE

Although learning sciences highlight the effectiveness of spaced repetition, retrieval practice, and personalization, these techniques are often difficult to implement at scale. The institution aimed to bridge this gap using AI to simulate the benefits of one-on-one tutoring.

SOLUTION

A semester-long intervention introduced a personal AI tutor app developed by MAGMA Learning. The AI tutor used GPT-3 to generate 800 microlearning questions from course materials and employed a neural network to model each student's evolving grasp of concepts. The app personalized the delivery of questions based on individual progress and knowledge decay patterns.

IMPLEMENTATION

Students could voluntarily use the app at any time during the course. They were reminded regularly to engage with it as a complement to regular study. The app tracked learning over time, visualized knowledge mastery via a "learnet," and delivered appropriately challenging questions.

RESULTS

- **Higher Grades**: Students who actively used the AI tutor achieved final exam grades significantly higher than their inactive peers with on average, 0.71 grade points higher (on a 1–6 scale).
- **Improved Rankings**: Compared to a parallel course without the AI tutor, active users improved their class rankings by up to 15 percentile points.
- **Better than Quizzes**: Usage of Moodle quizzes did not show the same performance gains, indicating the AI tutor's unique benefit.
- **Model Accuracy**: The AI's predictions of student grasp showed a strong correlation ($r = 0.81$) with actual exam results, validating the AI's learning model.

CONCLUSION

This study demonstrates that AI tutors grounded in the learning sciences can meaningfully enhance student achievement. Unlike generic AI tools, the app's integration of personalized spaced repetition and retrieval practice created an effective, scalable, and student-centered learning experience.

The intervention suggests that tailored AI solutions, when well-designed, can replicate the benefits of one-on-one tutoring in higher education.

Source: (Baillifard, et al., 2024) Effective learning with a personal AI tutor: A case study. *Education and Information Technologies*. https://doi.org/10.1007/s10639-024-12888-5

Increased Accessibility

AI tools such as STT applications, real-time transcription and language translation software significantly enhance inclusivity in education (Zaki & Ahmed, 2024). These technologies are particularly beneficial for students with disabilities, such as those with hearing or motor impairments, as well as non-native speakers who face linguistic barriers in traditional classrooms (Navas-Bonilla et al., 2025; Al-Azawei, Serenelli and Lundqvist, 2016). By converting spoken language into text, real-time transcription supports deaf and hard-of-hearing students in accessing lecture content synchronously. Similarly, automated translation services allow multilingual learners to engage with course materials and participate in discussions more fully.

The Universal Design for Learning (UDL) framework (www.cast.org) further emphasises the significance of providing multiple means of engagement, illustration and expression, principles that AI-powered tools directly support (Meyer, Rose, & Gordon, 2014). Some such tools are presented in Figure 2.2 as they would fit in the UDL framework. These innovations not only accommodate diverse learner needs but also contribute to more equitable and culturally responsive learning environments (Popenici & Kerr, 2017).

Efficiency and Automation

AI simplifies administrative tasks such as grading, attendance tracking and scheduling, thus significantly reducing educators' workloads and releasing valuable time for more meaningful teaching activities. Automated grading systems can evaluate multiple-choice tests, short answers and even essays using natural language processing, providing timely feedback to students and reducing turnaround time (Zawacki-Richter, et al., 2019). Attendance can be monitored using facial recognition or AI-integrated learning management systems that track login and participation patterns.

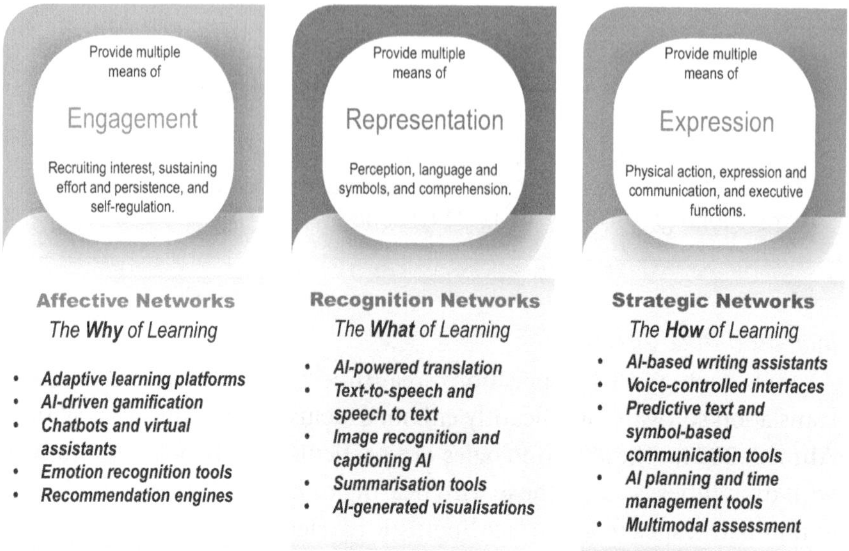

FIGURE 2.2 The universal design for learning framework adapted to include AI capabilities.

MINI CASE STUDY: AUDEMY – AI FOR ACCESSIBLE LEARNING IN BLIND AND VISUALLY IMPAIRED EDUCATION

CONTEXT

Blind and visually impaired (BVI) students often struggle with conventional educational tools that lack adaptability, emotional sensitivity, and interactive feedback.

CHALLENGE

Standard screen readers and braille materials provide only limited accessibility. Tools rarely personalize instruction or adapt to varying engagement, pacing, and comprehension needs of BVI learners.

SOLUTION

Audemy, an AI-powered audio-based learning platform, was developed through collaboration with 20+ educators from specialized BVI schools. It integrates adaptive learning, conversational AI, and privacy-conscious design to personalize instruction based on real-time student performance.

IMPLEMENTATION

Over 2,000 BVI students now use Audemy. The platform adjusts content difficulty, playback speed, and question types dynamically. It also supports screen readers and other assistive technologies while ensuring data privacy via on-device processing with Intel-powered systems.

RESULTS

- **Student engagement increased** significantly, as the platform's personalized and interactive features helped sustain attention and interest.
- **Learning outcomes improved** through adaptive question difficulty and the inclusion of varied formats such as real-world contextual problems.
- **Teachers gained valuable AI-generated insights** into student performance, which enabled them to deliver more targeted and effective instruction.

CONCLUSION

Audemy demonstrates how AI can advance inclusive education by creating accessible, adaptive, and emotionally supportive learning environments for students with disabilities.

Source: (Yang & Taele, 2025) AI for accessible education: Personalized audio-based learning for blind students. *CHI 2025 Workshop on Augmented Educators and AI.* https://arxiv.org/abs/2504.17117

AI tools also support complex scheduling by analysing educator availability, room assignments and student timetables to optimise class timetables, a task that is often highly time-consuming for school administrators (Holstein, et al., 2019). These efficiencies allow educators to redirect their attention from routine administrative duties to curriculum design, differentiated instruction and one-on-one student support. As a result, AI not only improves institutional operations but also contributes to improved teaching quality and student experience.

MINI CASE STUDY: AI STREAMLINING ADMINISTRATIVE WORK FOR EDUCATORS IN HIGHER EDUCATION

CONTEXT

Faculty in higher education often manage heavy workloads, juggling grading, content development, feedback, and administrative reporting. These tasks can reduce time available for student engagement and innovation in teaching.

CHALLENGE

Time-consuming administrative responsibilities like grading, lesson planning, and managing student queries diminish instructional quality and increase stress, contributing to educator burnout.

SOLUTION

A quantitative study conducted by Gupta, Kumar, and Rao (2024) analyzed the impact of AI tools, such as ChatGPT, Turnitin, automated grading systems, and learning management platforms, on teacher productivity across higher education institutions in India.

IMPLEMENTATION

The study surveyed 90 faculty members using a stratified random sampling method, collecting data through time logs, surveys, and platform analytics. Faculty using AI tools were compared to those using traditional methods.

RESULTS

- **Time savings** averaged 22.2 hours per week per teacher. Grading time was reduced by 7.1 hours, and lecture preparation by 6 hours.
- **AI tool adoption** showed a strong correlation ($r = 0.85$) with time saved.
- **Teacher satisfaction** increased, with 95% agreeing that AI saved them time, and 90% reporting higher job satisfaction.
- **Research efficiency** also improved significantly (mean rating: 4.4 vs. 3.6 for non-users, $p < 0.001$).

CONCLUSION

The study confirms that AI tools can substantially reduce teacher workload and improve productivity. By automating repetitive tasks, educators can focus more on high-impact areas such as student mentoring, research, and instructional design, ultimately enhancing the quality of education delivery.

Source: (Sharad et al., 2024) *AI and Teacher Productivity: A Quantitative Analysis of Time-Saving and Workload Reduction in Education*. Dr. Ambedkar Institute of Management Studies and Research. https://www.researchgate.net/publication/387980511

Data-Driven Insights

AI analytics can deliver educators with real-time statistics on student progress, enabling early intervention for struggling students and data-informed decision-making to improve learning outcomes (SchoolAI, 2025). By collecting and analysing data from online activities, assessments and engagement metrics, AI systems can detect patterns that indicate a learner is struggling or losing interest (Long & Siemens, 2011). Dashboards powered by learning analytics tools, such as *Microsoft Insights for Education* or *Canvas Analytics*, present these trends visually, allowing educators to pinpoint which students may need additional support. More advanced systems can even suggest specific interventions, such as targeted revision materials, personalised feedback or peer mentoring opportunities (Ifenthaler & Yau, 2020). These tools also assist in curriculum refinement by highlighting which concepts are consistently misunderstood across cohorts. In large-scale or online learning environments, where individual monitoring is challenging, AI analytics serve as a critical mechanism for maintaining responsiveness, equity and academic achievement.

MINI CASE STUDY: AI-POWERED LEARNING ANALYTICS IN EARLY CHILDHOOD EDUCATION

CONTEXT

In early childhood education, understanding each child's unique learning trajectory is crucial. Traditional assessment methods often lack the immediacy and specificity needed to address individual learning needs promptly.

CHALLENGE

Educators face difficulties in identifying early signs of learning challenges due to delayed feedback and limited data on student engagement and comprehension. This delay can hinder timely interventions, potentially impacting a child's developmental progress.

SOLUTION

The integration of AI-powered learning analytics tools has transformed the educational landscape by providing real-time data on student interactions and performance. These tools analyse various metrics, such as response times, accuracy, and engagement levels, offering educators immediate insights into each student's learning process.

IMPLEMENTATION

Educators employ AI-driven systems that continuously collect and analyse data as students engage with learning activities. For instance, in a case study involving a 3-year-old student named Ravi, teachers utilized AI analytics to monitor his responses during interactive tasks, identifying patterns that indicated specific areas where he required additional support.

RESULTS

- **Identification of learning challenges** was made possible through AI's ability to detect subtle performance patterns, enabling early intervention.
- **Personalized instruction** was achieved as teachers used real-time analytics to adapt learning activities to each student's needs.
- **Improvement in academic performance** was observed in students who received targeted support based on AI-generated insights.
- **Confidence in instructional decisions** increased among educators, supported by continuous, data-informed insights into student progress.
- **Ongoing monitoring and adaptation** of teaching strategies became more effective, allowing timely reinforcement or remediation.

CONCLUSION

The use of AI-powered learning analytics in early childhood education empowers educators with actionable insights, facilitating early interventions and personalized instruction. This proactive approach not only addresses individual learning needs effectively but also fosters improved educational outcomes from the outset of a child's academic journey.

Source: (Lakshmi et al., 2024). *How AI-powered learning analytics are shaping early childhood education and instruction*. https://ceinternational1892.org/article/how-ai-powered-learning-analytics-are-shaping-early-childhood-education-and-instruction/

Enhanced Engagement and Motivation

Gamification strategies powered by AI, such as adaptive quizzes, personalised challenges and interactive learning environments, make education more engaging and enjoyable. By integrating game design elements, like points, levels, badges and rewards, into educational platforms, AI enhances these experiences through real-time personalisation based on learner performance and preferences. Adaptive quiz engines, for instance, can adjust question difficulty and content dynamically to match a student's current mastery level, maintaining an optimal challenge-to-skill ratio that sustains motivation (Wang & Tahir, 2020). AI also personalises challenge sequences or narrative-driven tasks that align with individual learning goals, as seen in systems like *Duolingo*, *Classcraft* and *Squirrel AI*. Moreover, AI-driven feedback loops provide immediate, meaningful responses that reinforce progress and maintain learner autonomy (Chen et al., 2020). These interactive, responsive environments not only increase participation and persistence but also cultivate a growth mindset by framing errors as learning opportunities. As a result, AI-driven gamification supports deeper engagement and improved academic performance across diverse learning contexts.

MINI CASE STUDY: ENHANCING PEER REVIEW THROUGH AI-DRIVEN GAMIFICATION WITH SOCRATIQUE

CONTEXT

In software engineering education, developing students' abilities to provide constructive peer feedback is essential. However, traditional peer review processes often suffer from low engagement and variable feedback quality.

CHALLENGE

Students frequently exhibit limited motivation to participate actively in peer assessments, leading to superficial feedback that lacks depth and specificity.

SOLUTION

The Socratique platform integrates GenAI with gamification elements to enhance the peer review process. By providing real-time AI assistance in crafting feedback and incorporating game-like features such as points and leaderboards, the platform aims to motivate students to engage more deeply with peer assessments.

IMPLEMENTATION

In a controlled study within a master's-level functional programming course, students were divided into two groups: one using the Socratique platform with AI-driven gamification and another using a standard peer review process. The platform offered AI-generated suggestions to improve feedback quality and employed gamified incentives to encourage participation.

RESULTS

- **Increased participation** was observed among students using the Socratique platform, who provided significantly more peer feedback than those in the control group.
- **Enhanced feedback quality** was achieved, with peer reviews from the Socratique group rated higher for clarity, relevance, and specificity.
- **Positive student perception** emerged, as participants reported that the gamified features made the peer review process more engaging, enjoyable, and motivating.

CONCLUSION

The integration of AI-driven assistance with gamification strategies in the Socratique platform effectively enhanced student engagement and the quality of peer feedback in a software engineering education context. This approach demonstrates the potential of combining AI and gamification to improve educational outcomes in peer assessment activities.

Source: (Wlodarski, et al., 2025). *Level Up Peer Review in Education: Investigating genAI-driven Gamification system and its influence on Peer Feedback Effectiveness*. arXiv preprint arXiv:2504.02962. https://arxiv.org/abs/2504.02962arxiv.org

Real-Time Adaptive Feedback

AI provides timely, tailored feedback on assessment and learning exercises, allowing students to identify and correct mistakes and then refine their understanding in real time, rather than waiting for instructor evaluation (eLearning Industry, 2025; Educational Innovation at Sydney, 2024; Matelsky et al., 2023). Unlike traditional feedback methods that can be delayed and generalised, AI-powered systems analyse student inputs instantly and deliver tailored responses based on performance, learning history and common misconceptions. Tools such as *Gradescope, Khan Academy* and AI-driven writing assistants like *Grammarly* or *Write & Improve* offer contextual suggestions, highlight errors and explain underlying concepts. This feedback not only promotes self-regulated learning but also reduces anxiety by providing supportive guidance during the learning process (Balfour, 2013). In STEM subjects, intelligent tutoring systems like *Carnegie Learning* and *ALEKS* use knowledge tracing algorithms to pinpoint exactly where a student is struggling and suggest the next best step to take. Furthermore, educators benefit by receiving aggregated performance data, allowing them to intervene strategically and support students more effectively. By enabling continuous learning and real-time course correction, AI-enhanced feedback systems are transforming how learners engage with educational content.

MINI CASE STUDY: ENHANCING STUDENT LEARNING THROUGH IMMEDIATE, PERSONALIZED AI FEEDBACK

CONTEXT

Education Perfect (https://www.educationperfect.com/ai/), an educational technology company, developed an AI-powered feedback tool designed to provide instant, personalised criticism to students across a multitude of subjects, including English, Science, History, Geography, and Language learning.

CHALLENGE

Traditional feedback methods often take days, weeks or even months, preventing students from promptly addressing misunderstandings. Teachers also face challenges in providing individualized feedback at scale, limiting opportunities for students to refine their understanding in real time.

SOLUTION

The AI-powered feedback tool provides instant, tailored comments and suggestions that support students in building and expanding their understanding. It fits smoothly into current teaching and learning routines, making sure feedback arrives when it's most useful and directly connected to the task at hand.

IMPLEMENTATION

Education Perfect introduced the AI feedback tool across its platform, aligning it with the Australian Framework for Generative Artificial Intelligence (AI) in Schools and educational best practices. The tool was tested with a diverse user base, incorporating feedback from teachers and students globally to refine its functionality.

RESULTS

- **92% of students found the AI feedback helpful**, indicating high acceptance and perceived value.
- **85% of students reported enhanced learning**, demonstrating the tool's effectiveness in deepening understanding.
- **83% of students felt motivated to improve their answers**, highlighting increased engagement and proactive learning behaviours.

CONCLUSION

The implementation of Education Perfect's AI-powered feedback tool has significantly enhanced the learning experience by providing immediate, personalized feedback. This approach empowers students to correct mistakes and refine their understanding in real time, fostering a more effective and engaging educational environment.

Source: (The Educator, 2024). *New AI tool gives students instant, tailored feedback*. Retrieved from https://www.theeducatoronline.com/k12/news/new-ai-tool-gives-students-instant-tailored-feedback/284739theeducatoronline.com

Scalability in Education

AI enables institutions to offer quality education at scale, particularly through AI-powered MOOCs (Massive Open Online Courses), expanding access to learning opportunities for students in remote or underserved areas. By leveraging AI technologies, MOOCs can now deliver bespoke learning experiences to thousands of learners simultaneously. AI-driven systems create adaptive pathways by analysing learner interactions, recommending content and generating tailored feedback that supports mastery learning at scale (Patil, 2025). Recent developments in GenAI further enhance these environments by enabling real-time assessment, automated grading and adaptive quizzes that align with individual skill levels, improving retention and reducing dropout (IJTPE, 2025; Springer, 2025). Moreover, AI-powered translation tools are breaking down linguistic barriers, enabling global participation in MOOCs and fostering inclusive, multilingual learning communities (Tariq 2024; MyLearnOmics, 2023).

AI chatbots and virtual tutors can enhance learner support by providing continuous assistance, answering questions and guiding students through course content, particularly in contexts where access to instructors is limited (Holmes et al., 2022; Zhai et al., 2021).

These capabilities allow institutions to extend their reach far beyond traditional classrooms, helping bridge educational gaps and democratising access to high-quality learning regardless of geographic or socioeconomic barriers.

MINI CASE STUDY: KWAME FOR SCIENCE: SCALING QUALITY SCIENCE EDUCATION WITH AI IN WEST AFRICA

CONTEXT

Sub-Saharan Africa faces high student-to-teacher ratios (average 35:1), leading to limited access to qualified science educators. The COVID-19 pandemic further widened this educational gap. The project aimed to address the lack of scalable, quality teaching resources in science for secondary school students preparing for the WASSCE (West African Senior School Certificate Examination).

CHALLENGE

One of the primary challenges faced in deploying Kwame for Science was the limited access to locally relevant educational content. Copyright restrictions prevented the use of officially approved science textbooks from Ghana, making it difficult to align AI-generated responses with the national curriculum. Compounding this issue was the difficulty in scaling individualized support to students, especially given the high student-to-teacher ratio typical in Sub-Saharan Africa. Additionally, efforts to digitize past exam papers were hampered by the limitations of OCR (Optical Character Recognition) technology, particularly with regard to scientific and mathematical symbols. Finally, while user engagement with the system was strong in terms of usage, gathering feedback through answer ratings proved to be difficult, with only a small percentage of students voting on whether the AI-provided answers were helpful.

SOLUTION

Kwame for Science was developed as a bilingual (English and French) AI teaching assistant. It leverages Sentence-BERT (SBERT) models to retrieve relevant scientific content and WASSCE past questions based on user queries. The tool also categorizes content into curriculum topics using a custom machine learning model.

IMPLEMENTATION

To overcome these barriers, the developers of Kwame for Science built a web-based AI teaching assistant powered by a Sentence-BERT (SBERT) model for semantic question answering. The system was populated with content drawn from open educational resources such as the CK-12 curriculum and Simple Wikipedia, supplemented by a unique dataset of over 3,500 past WASSCE exam questions and expert-written answers. These past papers were manually curated and annotated by local subject-matter experts to ensure contextual relevance and scientific accuracy. The entire knowledge base was indexed using ElasticSearch to support fast and scalable retrieval of responses. In addition to answering queries, the platform allowed students to browse past exam questions, filter them by year, topic, and type, and view detailed explanations. The system was deployed across 32 countries over an eight-month period, reaching 750 users and demonstrating its capacity to deliver curriculum-aligned science education at scale.

RESULTS

- **High scalability demonstrated with 750 users across 32 countries** in an 8-month pilot.
- **High accuracy of responses with an 87.2% Top-3 success rate**, meaning at least one of the top three AI-generated answers was helpful.
- **Increased educational resource access with 3.5K past exam question-answer pairs** covering nearly three decades of WASSCE science content.

- **Frequent student engagement with 2,173 detailed answer views and 931 past question expansions**, indicating consistent use of feedback and review tools.
- **Efficient topic classification model achieved 91 % unweighted average recall**, helping organize questions into 48 curriculum topics.

CONCLUSION

Kwame for Science illustrates how AI can offer scalable, high-quality education in underserved regions. Despite challenges in data sourcing and evaluation, its real-world deployment showed that AI-powered MOOCs and virtual teaching assistants can bridge teacher shortages and expand learning access, especially for critical subjects like science.

Source: (Boateng, et al., 2023). *Real-world deployment and evaluation of Kwame for Science, an AI teaching assistant for science education in West Africa*. arXiv. https://doi.org/10.48550/arXiv.2302.10786

Collaboration and Global Learning

AI-powered translation tools and virtual learning assistants facilitate seamless collaboration among students from diverse linguistic backgrounds, promoting global learning experiences and cultural exchange. Real-time translation technologies, for example, those embedded in platforms like *Google Translate*, *Microsoft Teams* and *Zoom*, enable multilingual communication in live discussions, chat and written assignments, allowing students to express ideas in their native languages while still participating fully in group activities. Virtual learning assistants, powered by NLP, provide multilingual support, clarify instructions and offer personalised explanations in multiple languages, reducing reliance on human translators or bilingual educators (Chen et al., 2022). These tools are especially beneficial in international online courses and virtual exchange programs, where cultural and linguistic diversity is both a strength and a potential barrier. By removing language as a limiting factor, AI fosters more inclusive, equitable and culturally enriched learning environments that prepare students to engage in a globally connected world (Huang et al., 2019). Moreover, this enhanced accessibility promotes mutual understanding and respect across cultures, contributing to the development of global citizenship competencies in education.

MINI CASE STUDY: PROMOTING GLOBAL LEARNING THROUGH AI-POWERED TRANSLATION AND VIRTUAL ASSISTANTS

CONTEXT

In multicultural and multilingual classrooms, ensuring equitable learning opportunities for all students presents a growing challenge. With increasing numbers of international students and linguistic diversity, educators are turning to AI to promote inclusion and collaboration. AI tools, particularly real-time translation and virtual learning assistants, are being used to ensure that language differences no longer limit participation, comprehension, or academic success.

CHALLENGE

The complexity of delivering personalized education in linguistically diverse settings is significant. Language barriers often prevent students from engaging meaningfully with peers and instructors. These barriers can lead to social isolation, reduced academic performance, and difficulty in accessing educational resources. Furthermore, traditional translation methods and human interpretation services are not scalable or always available, leaving many students without adequate support.

SOLUTION

To address these challenges, schools and institutions are integrating AI-powered translation tools and virtual learning assistants. These technologies include speech-to-text systems, real-time subtitling, automatic translation of course materials, and intelligent agents that support multilingual interaction. Fitas (2025) explores how these tools improve communication, enhance access to information, and support peer collaboration across language divides.

IMPLEMENTATION

In educational settings studied by Fitas, AI solutions were deployed to support inclusive learning environments through multiple strategies. Tools like Microsoft Translator and Google Translate were used in real-time to enable communication in live classroom sessions. Virtual assistants with multilingual capabilities were integrated into learning management systems to provide students with contextualized support and translation of materials. These implementations also emphasized accessibility for students with cognitive or physical challenges, showcasing the intersectionality of AI's potential for equity. Educators reported smoother collaboration in group work and increased student confidence in participating in global learning communities.

RESULTS

- **Inclusivity in classroom communication was improved** as real-time translation tools enabled students to follow lessons and participate regardless of their native language.
- **Collaboration across cultural and linguistic groups was enhanced** because students could work together effectively on group projects with reduced misunderstandings.
- **Social isolation among non-native speakers was reduced** by making classroom interactions more accessible and engaging.
- **Accessibility for students with additional learning needs was strengthened** as AI tools supported those with cognitive and physical challenges.
- **Teacher workload related to multilingual support was lowered** through automated translation and feedback, reducing the need for manual intervention.

CONCLUSION

This case demonstrates that AI-powered translation tools and virtual assistants are critical enablers of inclusive, global education. By lowering language barriers, these technologies support collaboration, enhance participation, and foster intercultural understanding empowering students from diverse backgrounds to thrive in shared learning environments.

Source: (Fitas, 2025). *Inclusive education with AI: Supporting special needs and tackling language barriers*. arXiv. https://arxiv.org/abs/2504.14120

Teacher Professional Development

AI not only supports students but also aids educators by providing data-driven insights, personalised professional development plans and automated tools for lesson planning and classroom management (Mounkoro et al., 2024). By analysing classroom data, such as student performance trends, engagement levels and learning gaps, AI platforms like *Edthena* and *TeachFX* help teachers reflect on their practice and tailor instruction accordingly. These systems offer real-time dashboards and predictive analytics that assist educators in identifying which teaching strategies are most effective and where adjustments are needed (Ifenthaler & Yau, 2020). Additionally, AI can generate personalised professional development recommendations based on teacher experience, subject area and student needs, supporting continuous improvement without a one-size-fits-all model (Holstein, et al., 2019). Tools like *ScribeSense* and *LessonPlans.ai* automate routine tasks such as lesson planning, resource curation and classroom scheduling, making time for more personal interactions with students. In classroom management, AI-enabled platforms can monitor class participation, flag disengaged learners and suggest interventions, helping educators maintain productive learning environments. Collectively, these applications of AI enhance instructional quality, streamline workload and empower teachers to focus on what matters most: student learning and development.

MINI CASE STUDY: AI FOR TEACHER PROFESSIONAL DEVELOPMENT IN THE DIGITAL AGE

CONTEXT

With rapid technological advancement, education systems worldwide are embracing AI not only for student-centered learning but also for supporting teacher professional growth. This study analyzes how AI enhances teacher development through smart learning systems, digital training pathways, and real-time data feedback loops.

CHALLENGE

Traditional professional development for teachers often suffers from limitations such as one-size-fits-all training, lack of personalization, inadequate planning, and disconnection from modern teaching needs. Teachers in many regions remain under-equipped to meet the demands of 21st-century classrooms.

SOLUTION

The study proposes leveraging artificial intelligence to deliver adaptive, personalized, and accessible professional development programs. It emphasizes AI's potential to provide intelligent tutoring, simulate classroom scenarios, offer real-time feedback, and guide long-term career pathways for educators.

IMPLEMENTATION

To implement AI in teacher professional development, the study suggests embedding intelligent learning systems into educational institutions. These systems include knowledge bases that define both subject content and pedagogical strategies, allowing AI to respond dynamically to teachers' needs. Teachers engage in immersive virtual simulations using augmented reality (AR) and virtual reality (VR), gaining experience in classroom management and lesson delivery. Digital platforms supported by AI track progress, analyze learning behaviors, and provide personalized feedback. Additionally, databases containing information about teacher career progression and development needs are integrated into global networks, allowing educators to map their learning journeys and access targeted resources.

RESULTS

- **Training was personalized** through AI-generated development plans tailored to individual job histories and career aspirations.
- **Teachers were better prepared** by rehearsing classroom situations in AR/VR environments before real-world application.
- **Efficiency of training increased** as AI-driven content delivery reduced costs and time traditionally spent on in-person training.
- **Feedback became immediate**, with AI offering real-time performance diagnostics and suggestions for improvement.
- **Lifelong learning was supported** by AI systems that adjusted to an educator's changing needs over time.
- **Access to training expanded**, as intelligent platforms made professional development available across geographic and time constraints.
- **Knowledge transfer improved**, allowing retiring educators to preserve and pass on expertise through AI-mediated systems.

CONCLUSION

Artificial intelligence represents a transformative force in teacher professional development. By shifting from passive, generic training to interactive, data-informed, and personalized learning, AI empowers educators to adapt to a digital-first educational landscape. Future teacher training initiatives should prioritize AI integration, develop relevant infrastructure, and invest in digital literacy for both trainers and trainees.

Source: (al-Zyoud, 2020). The Role of Artificial Intelligence in Teacher Professional Development. *Universal Journal of Educational Research*, 8(11B), 6263–6272. https://doi.org/10.13189/ujer.2020.082265

As AI continues to evolve, its role in education will increase and morph, providing new opportunities for enhancing learning and teaching processes. By leveraging AI responsibly and addressing challenges such as bias, privacy and equitable access, educators and institutions can create an inclusive and efficient educational system for the future.

Foundations and Frontiers

AI is no longer a vision of the future. It is a driving force already transforming the landscape of education. This chapter examined the evolving role of educators in the age of AI, arguing not for resistance but for strategic adaptation and collaboration. The *death of the knowledge worker* is not literal, but symbolic of a shift in roles, where educators move from being sole knowledge providers to becoming facilitators, mentors and designers of AI-augmented learning experiences.

We traced the conceptual roots and historical development of AI, from early automata and Babbage's Analytical Engine to today's large language models like ChatGPT. By exploring a hierarchical view of AI and its subfields, including machine learning, vision, planning, NLP and robotics, we positioned ChatGPT within the broader AI ecosystem as a powerful, yet specialised, language-based tool.

The chapter also highlighted AI's tangible benefits in education: personalised learning, improved accessibility, administrative efficiency, data-driven insights, enhanced engagement, real-time feedback, scalability and global collaboration. Through a series of real-world mini case studies, we demonstrated how AI is improving learning outcomes, supporting teachers, increasing inclusivity and extending educational opportunities worldwide.

Finally, we emphasised that AI not only supports students but also empowers teachers, offering personalised professional development, classroom management tools and actionable data. With the right strategies, educators can step into new roles where human empathy, creativity and ethical judgement complement machine intelligence, ensuring they remain central to the evolving educational landscape.

As we've seen, AI holds immense promise for transforming education, offering new tools to personalise learning, support educators and expand access. However, this transformation is not without tension. The integration of AI into classrooms challenges long-standing pedagogical norms, institutional structures and educator identities. In the next chapter,

AI Challenges in Traditional Pedagogy, we explore the friction between emerging AI-powered approaches and established teaching practices. We'll examine the limits of legacy systems and the complexities of aligning AI with curriculum standards, assessment models and pedagogical values.

REFLECT AND REFRAME

1. Where in your current teaching practice are students most likely to bypass learning processes by using AI tools? Consider which tasks rely heavily on final products rather than visible steps.
2. Have you ever questioned an AI-generated outcome in your role as an educator? What made the result feel opaque or untrustworthy, and how did you respond?
3. How can professional development in your context better prepare educators to critically evaluate and implement AI? What would meaningful support look like for you or your colleagues?
4. In what ways might current assessment strategies unintentionally reward surface-level learning? How could these be adapted to focus more on process and student thinking?
5. What strategies can you use to maintain educator authority and human judgement in an AI-assisted classroom? Think about moments where your professional instinct should guide, not the algorithm.
6. How can you help students develop a critical relationship with AI tools rather than a dependent one? Reflect on how to foster digital agency and metacognitive awareness in learners.

REFERENCES

Abbas, N., Ali, I., Manzoor, R., Hussain, T., and Al Hussaini, M. H. (2023) Role of artificial intelligence tools in enhancing students' educational performance at higher levels. *Journal of Artificial Intelligence, Machine Learning and Neural Network*, 3(5), 36–49. https://doi.org/10.55529/jaimlnn.35.36.49.

Akintola, A. S., Akintayo, M., Kadri, T., Oforgu, C. M., Mgbame, M., and Nwanna, M. (2025) Adaptive AI systems in education: Real time personalised learning pathways for skill development. *International Journal of Advance Computational Engineering and Networking (IJACEN)*, 13(1), 56–62. https://iraj.in/journal/IJACEN/paper_detail.php?paper_id=21586 (Accessed: 3 September 2025).

Al-Azawei, A., Serenelli, F., and Lundqvist, K. (2016) Universal Design for Learning (UDL): A content analysis of peer reviewed journal papers from 2012 to 2015. *Journal of the Scholarship of Teaching and Learning*, 16(3), 39–56.

al-Zyoud, H. M. M., 2020. The role of artificial intelligence in teacher professional development. *Universal Journal of Educational Research*, 6263–6272.

Anthropic, n.d. Claude. [Online]. https://claude.ai/login?returnTo=%2F%3F [Accessed 2025].

AutoGPT, n.d. AutoGPT. [Online]. https://agpt.co/ [Accessed 2025].

AWS, n.d. Amazon web services. [Online]. https://docs.aws.amazon.com/codewhisperer/latest/userguide/whisper-legacy.html [Accessed 2025].

BabyAGI, n.d. BabyAGI. [Online]. https://babyagi.org/ [Accessed 2025].

Baillifard, A., Gabella, M., and Martarelli, C. S., 2024. Effective learning with a personal AI tutor: A case study. *Education and Information Technologies*, 30(1), 297–312.

Balfour, S. P., 2013. Assessing writing in MOOCs: Automated essay scoring and calibrated peer review™. *Research & Practice in Assessment*, 40–48.

Boateng, G. et al., 2023. Real-World Deployment and Evaluation of Kwame for Science, An AI Teaching Assistant for Science Education in West Africa. *arXiv.org*.

Britannica n.d. Ada Lovelace: The first computer programmer. *Britannica.com*. https://www.britannica.com/story/ada-lovelace-the-first-computer-programmer (Accessed: 3 September 2025).

Chen, B., Wang, Y., and Wang, L., 2022. The effects of virtual reality-assisted language learning: A meta-analysis. *Sustainability*, 14(6), 3147.

Chen, L., Chen, P., and Lin, Z., 2020. *Artificial intelligence in education: A review*. IEEE.

Darad, K., 2023. Revolutionizing Education with AI-Driven Assessments. [Online]. https://elearningindustry.com/revolutionizing-education-with-ai-driven-assessments

Davenport, T. H., and Kirby, J., 2016. *Only humans need apply: Winners and losers in the age of smart machines*. Harper Business.

Diffusion, S., n.d. Stable Diffusion Online. [Online]. https://stablediffusionweb.com/ [Accessed 2025].

Educational Innovation at Sydney 2024. How generative AI can make personalised feedback at scale more consistent and efficient. *Teaching@Sydney*, 11 June. https://educational-innovation.sydney.edu.au/teaching%40sydney/how-generative-ai-can-make-personalised-feedback-at-scale-more-consistent-and-efficient/ (Accessed: 3 September 2025).

Educational Testing Service, n.d. About the e rater Scoring Engine. [Online]. https://www.ets.org//erater.html [Accessed 2025].

eLearning Industry, 2025. Revolutionizing education with AI driven assessments. *eLearning Industry*, 21 March. https://elearningindustry.com/revolutionizing-education-with-ai-driven-assessments (Accessed: 3 September 2025).

Fancsali, S. E., Sandbothe, M., and Ritter, S. (2023) Orchestrating classrooms and tutoring with Carnegie Learning's MATHia and LiveLab. In Thomas, D. R., Lin, J., and Koedinger, K. R. (eds), *Proceedings of the workshop "Towards the Future of AI augmented Human Tutoring in Math Learning"*, AIED 2023, July, Tokyo.

Fitas, R., 2025. Inclusive education with AI: Supporting special needs and tackling language barriers. *arXiv.org*.

Google, n.d. Gemini – Google AI. [Online]. https://gemini.google.com/app [Accessed 2025].

Gupta, M.S., Kumar, N. and Rao, V., 2024, November. AI and teacher productivity: A quantitative analysis of time-saving and workload reduction in education. In *Proceedings of the Conference on Advancing Synergies in Science, Engineering, and Management (ASEM 2024)*, Virginia Beach, VA (pp. 6–9).

Holmes, W., Persson, J., Chounta, I.A., Wasson, B. and Dimitrova, V., 2022. Artificial intelligence and education: A critical view through the lens of human rights, democracy and the rule of law. *European Journal of Education*, 57(3), 384–401.

Holstein, K., Mclaren, B., and Aleven, V., 2019. Designing for Complementarity: Teacher and Student Needs for Orchestration Support in AI-enhanced Classrooms Designing for Complementarity: Teacher and Student Needs for Orchestration Support in AI-enhanced Classrooms.

Huang, R., Spector, J. M., and Yang, J., 2019. *Educational technology: A primer for the 21st century*. Springer Singapore.

Ifenthaler, D., and Yau, J. Y.-K., 2020. Utilising learning analytics to support study success in higher education: a systematic review. *Educational Technology Research and Development*, 68(4), 1691–1990.

IJTPE (2025) Personalizing MOOC assessments with AI: Fine-tuning ChatGPT for personalized quizzes and adaptive learning paths. *International Journal of Advances in Engineering & Technology (IJTPE)*, 17(1), 192–203.

Lakshmi, K., Khan, S., Kumar, P.A., Wagh, V. and Vasanti, G., 2024. AI-Powered learning analytics: transforming educational outcomes through ICT integration. *Library of Progress-Library Science, Information Technology & Computer*, 44(3), 17910–17919.

Long, P., and Siemens, G., 2011. Penetrating the fog: analytics in learning and education. *Journal of Educational Technology*, 22(3), 132–137.

Luckin, R., 2016. Intelligence Unleashed: An argument for AI in Education.

Matelsky, J.K., Parodi, F., Liu, T., Lange, R.D. and Kording, K.P., 2023. *A large language model-assisted education tool to provide feedback on open-ended responses*. arXiv preprint arXiv:2308.02439.

McCarthy, J., Minsky, M., Rochester, N., and Shannon, C., 2006. A proposal for the dartmouth summer research project on artificial intelligence, August 31, 1955. *AI Magazine*, 27(4), 12.

MDPI (2024) Leveraging AI in e learning: Personalized learning and adaptive. *Electronics*, 13(18), Article 3762. https://www.mdpi.com/2079-9292/13/18/3762 (Accessed: 3 September 2025).

Meyer, A., Rose, D. H., and Gordon, D., 2014. *Universal design for learning: Theory and practice*. Cast Professional Publication.

Midjourney, n.d. Midjourney. [Online]. https://www.midjourney.com/home [Accessed 2025].

Mounkoro, I., Uberas, A. D., Cadelina, F. A., Saleem, M. U., Maryam, S., Almagharbeh, W. T., Majeed, A. A., and Hidayatallah, Z., 2024. Integrating AI in Classroom Management: Improving Educational Efficiency and Teacher Workflows.

MyLearnOmics (2023) AI translation tools in overcoming language barriers. *MyLearnOmics*, 12 October. https://mylearnomics.com/ai-translation-tools-in-overcoming-language-barriers/ (Accessed: 3 September 2025).

Navas-Bonilla, C.R., Guerra-Arango, J.A., Oviedo-Guado, D.A. and Murillo-Noriega, D.E. (2025) Inclusive education through technology: a systematic review of types, tools and characteristics. *Frontiers in Education*, 10, 1527851. https://doi.org/10.3389/feduc.2025.1527851

OpenAI, 2021. OpenAI. [Online]. https://openai.com/index/dall-e/ [Accessed 2025].

OpenAI, 2023. OpenAI. [Online]. https://openai.com/index/gpt-4-research/ [Accessed 2025].

OpenAI, 2025. OpenAI. [Online]. https://openai.com/codex/ [Accessed 2025].

Pabba, C., and Kumar, P., 2023. A vision-based multi-cues approach for individual students' and overall class engagement monitoring in smart classroom environments. *Multimedia Tools and Applications*, 83(17), 52621–52652.

Patil, S., 2025. AI-driven personalized learning paths in MOOCS: Optimizing engagement and outcomes in digital education. In Oruganti, Sai Kiran, Karras, Dimitrios, Thakur, Srinesh, Chaithanya, Janapati Krishna, Metta, Sukanya, and Lathigara, Amit 1s), *Digital transformation and sustainability of business* (pp. 387–395). CRC Press.

Popenici, S. A., and Kerr, S., 2017. Exploring the impact of artificial intelligence on teaching and learning in higher education. *Research and Practice in Technology Enhanced Learning*, 12(1), 22.

Russel, S., and Norvig, P., 2020. *Artificial intelligence: A modern approach*, 4th US ed. 4th ed. Pearson.

Sajja, R., Sermet, Y., Cwiertny, D., and Demir, I., 2025. Integrating AI and learning analytics for data-driven pedagogical decisions and personalized interventions in education. *Technology, Knowledge and Learning*, 1–31.

Schneider, J., 2024. *Explainable generative AI (GenXAI): A Survey, conceptualization, and research agenda*. s.l.: s.n.

SchoolAI (2025) How AI helps educators track student progress and outcomes. *SchoolAI*, 9 May. https://schoolai.com/blog/ai-helps-educators-track-student-progress-outcomes [Accessed: 3 September 2025].

Sharad Mitali, Gupta, M. S., Kumar, N., and Rao, V., 2024. AI and teacher productivity: A quantitative analysis of time-saving and workload reduction in education. *ResearchGate*.

Springer (2025) Advancing MOOCs personalization: The role of generative AI in adaptive assessment. In *Proceedings of the International Conference on AI in Education* (pp. 211–223). Springer. https://link.springer.com/chapter/10.1007/978-3-031-99261-2_22 (Accessed: 3 September 2025).

Swade, D. and Babbage, C., 2001. *Difference engine: Charles Babbage and the quest to build the First Computer*. Viking Penguin.

Tariq, M.U., 2024. AI-powered language translation for multilingual classrooms. In *Integrating generative AI in education to achieve sustainable development goals* (pp. 29–46). IGI Global Scientific Publishing.

The Educator, 2024. New AI tool gives students instant, tailored feedback. www.theeducatoronline.com.

Wang, A. I., and Tahir, R., 2020. *The effect of using Kahoot! for learning – A literature review*. Elsevier.

Wang, S., Christensen, C., Cui, W., Tong, R., Yarnall, L., Shear, L., and Feng, M., 2023. When adaptive learning is effective learning: comparison of an adaptive learning system to teacher-led instruction. *Interactive Learning Environments*, 31(2), 793–803.

Wlodarski, R., Sousa, L., and Pensky, A. C., 2025. Level up peer review in education: Investigating genAI-driven gamification system and its influence on peer feedback effectiveness. *arXiv.org*.

Yang, C., and Taele, P., 2025. AI for accessible education: Personalized audio-based learning for blind students.

Zaki, M. Z., and Ahmed, U., 2024. Bridging linguistic divides: The impact of AI-powered translation systems on communication equity and inclusion. *Journal of Translation and Language Studies*, 5(2), 20–30.

Zawacki-Richter, O., Marín, V. I., Bond, M., and Gouverneur, F., 2019. Systematic review of research on artificial intelligence applications in higher education – where are the educators? *International Journal of Educational Technology in Higher Education*, 16(1), 39.

Zhai, X., Chu, X., Chai, C.S., Jong, M.S.Y., Istenic, A., Spector, J.M., Liu, J.B., Yuan, J. and Li, Y., 2021. A review of artificial intelligence (AI) in education from 2010 to 2020. *Complexity*, 2021, Article ID 8812542

CHAPTER 3

AI Challenges in Traditional Pedagogy

Overreliance on automation often stems from good intentions, but when human judgement is replaced, we risk eroding what matters most in education.

CHAPTER AIMS

The aim of this chapter is to introduce key themes explored in this book in relation to:

1. *The systemic and pedagogical tensions emerging from the integration of AI into traditional instructional models, including disruptions to teaching, assessment and curriculum alignment.*
2. *The professional, ethical and institutional sources of resistance that challenge meaningful adoption of AI technologies in educational contexts.*
3. *The risks of overreliance on automation and algorithmic systems, and the imperative to preserve human judgement, agency and pedagogical purpose in AI-assisted classrooms.*

DOI: 10.1201/9781003624981-3

BEYOND THE CHEATING PANIC

In recent years, headlines have been dominated by stories of students leveraging AI tools like ChatGPT to complete assignments, sparking widespread concern among educators and the public. This surge in AI-assisted cheating has led to a media frenzy, with institutions scrambling to implement detection tools and enforce stricter policies (Adams, 2025). A notable incident highlighting the complexities of AI detection in education occurred in May 2023 at Texas A&M University-Commerce. A professor, aiming to identify AI-generated content, used ChatGPT itself to assess whether students' assignments were produced by the AI. ChatGPT responded affirmatively to all submissions, leading the professor to assign failing grades to the entire class (Heinz, 2023).

However, this reactionary approach often overlooks a critical question: *What aspects of our current pedagogical methods are enabling such widespread misuse of AI?* Traditional assessment models, heavily reliant on take-home essays and standardised tests, may inadvertently encourage shortcuts when students perceive assignments as mere hurdles rather than meaningful learning experiences (Chang, 2025). The commodification of education, where degrees are viewed as transactional credentials, further exacerbates this issue, diminishing intrinsic motivation and ethical engagement (Molesworth, Nixon & Scullion, 2009).

To counteract this transactional mindset, education must increasingly be framed as a meaningful process rather than a one-time performance. Learning, like mastery in well-designed computer games, should encourage repeated engagement, strategic experimentation and resilience. In games, players often fail multiple times, yet they return motivated, not solely by the endpoint but by the journey itself. Similarly, educational design should inspire students to value iteration, curiosity and growth over mere completion. When students see learning as an evolving quest rather than a hoop to jump through, the incentive to misuse tools like AI diminishes considerably.

MINI CASE STUDY: REPLAYABILITY IN GAMES

CONTEXT

Released in 2011, *Skyrim* is an open-world role-playing game renowned for its expansive world and player freedom. Its design emphasizes exploration, character customization, and a multitude of quests, contributing to its enduring popularity.

CHALLENGE

Despite its vast content, questions arise regarding the game's true replayability. While players can experience different character builds and choices, the main storyline remains largely unchanged across playthroughs. This raises concerns about the depth of variation and sustained engagement over multiple sessions.

SOLUTION

Skyrim employs procedural content generation to offer a sense of endless gameplay. Randomized quests and encounters aim to provide fresh experiences, encouraging players to explore new paths and character developments in subsequent playthroughs.

IMPLEMENTATION

The game's mechanics allow for diverse character progression, enabling players to experiment with various skills and playstyles. This flexibility, combined with a rich modding community, extends the game's lifespan by introducing new content and mechanics beyond the original design.

RESULTS

Academic analysis suggests that while procedural generation adds variety, it may also lead to a lack of cohesive narrative depth in repeated playthroughs. The main quest's static nature means that, despite different approaches, the core experience remains similar, potentially limiting the game's replay value over time. Nevertheless, *Skyrim* is frequently cited as one of the most replayable games by players themselves. Community rankings and gaming forums consistently highlight its expansive content, diverse playstyles, and modding support as reasons players return to it repeatedly (Joyce, 2023).

CONCLUSION

Skyrim offers a complex interplay between vast content and structured narrative. Its design encourages initial exploration and experimentation, but the static main storyline may hinder long-term replayability. Understanding these dynamics is critical for educators and designers wanting to create engaging, repeatable experiences in both gaming and learning environments.

Furthermore, educational experiences can foster similar engagement when students are invited to see learning not as a linear task but as a progressing quest. In this context, GenAI holds significant potential to support such a shift by offering adaptive feedback, personalised challenges, and dynamic content that responds to individual learning paths. Rather than completing an assignment once and moving on, students, like players, could be encouraged to revisit, reflect, and refine their work, deepening their understanding over time. When thoughtfully integrated, AI can help recreate the conditions that make gameplay compelling: autonomy, discovery, and a sense of meaningful progress.

Sources: (Joyce, 2023). Assessing Mass Effect 2 and Elder Scrolls V: Skyrim: Using Player Choice to Explore Agency and Replayability. *Journal of Games Criticism, 3*(1). Retrieved from https://gamescriticism.org/wp-content/uploads/2023/07/joyce-3-a.pdf, Z League. (2025). *The most replayable games, according to gamers*. Retrieved from https://www.zleague.gg/theportal/gaming-news-the-most-replayable-games-according-to-gamers/

Moreover, the rapid integration of AI into education has outpaced the progress in comprehensive guidelines and training for educators, leaving many ill-equipped to adapt their teaching strategies effectively (Johnson, 2025).

This chapter aims to delve deeper into these underlying tensions between AI-driven innovation and traditional pedagogical approaches. By examining the root causes of AI misuse in education, we seek to explore how educators can uphold pedagogical integrity while embracing technological advancements.

IMPACT ON INSTRUCTIONAL STRATEGIES

While AI has undoubtedly enabled new possibilities for personalised and scalable education, its rise has also exposed the fragility of several long-established instructional strategies. As shown in Table 3.1, GenAI tools

TABLE 3.1 Instructional Strategies Negatively Impacted by AI

Instructional Strategy	Negative Impact of AI
Take-home Essays and Reports	GenAI can write entire assignments, undermining authenticity and making it harder to assess student ability.
Open-ended Homework Assignments	Students can outsource thinking and reflection to AI tools, reducing engagement with the learning process.
Essay-based Exams	AI-generated answers blur authorship, creating challenges in verifying independent student work.
Project-Based Learning (PBL)	When students use AI to complete large portions of a project, the process (where most learning occurs) is bypassed.
Peer Review and Collaborative Writing	AI can be used to mask individual contributions or replace peer feedback, undermining collaborative learning.
Inquiry-Based or Reflective Writing	Prompts designed to foster introspection or personal synthesis can be easily answered by AI with plausible text.
Scaffolded Writing Process	Students may skip brainstorming, outlining and drafting phases by generating a polished product instantly.
Flipped Classroom Models	Pre-class preparation via AI summaries may lead to surface-level understanding without engaging with core material.
Take-home Problem Sets (STEM)	AI tools like WolframAlpha, ChatGPT or Copilot can instantly solve problems, bypassing the development of problem-solving skills.

like ChatGPT have disrupted a range of practices, particularly those reliant on take-home writing, open-ended assignments and unsupervised reflection. These strategies, which once served as robust indicators of student understanding, are increasingly vulnerable to automation. When a student can generate a plausible essay, reflection or even a research paper in seconds, educators are left questioning not only *authorship* but also the *authenticity* of learning outcomes (Cotton, Cotton and Shipway, 2023).

The implications also extend beyond plagiarism. AI challenges the integrity of scaffolded learning processes, such as drafting, revising and peer review, by enabling students to skip directly to polished outputs. Moreover, collaborative and project-based work suffers when AI can quietly complete tasks intended to develop communication, teamwork and sustained engagement. As instructional design and assessment models continue to grapple with the presence of AI, Table 3.1 underscores a need to rethink pedagogical approaches not just for detection and prevention, but for resilience and adaptability in an AI-assisted learning environment.

These instructional strategies share several core characteristics that make them particularly vulnerable to automation and misuse. These commonalities help explain *why* AI so easily disrupts them:

1. Out-of-Class Execution
   Most of these strategies rely on students completing work outside of supervised environments. Take-home essays, projects, problem sets and pre-class flipped learning tasks are typically done at home, where there's minimal oversight. This creates ideal conditions for students to use AI tools undetected.

2. Product-Focused Over Process-Focused
   These strategies emphasise the *final output* (e.g., an essay, a report, a solved problem) more than the *learning journey*. Since AI can produce polished work quickly, students can bypass the messy, formative phases of learning, like drafting, problem-solving or revision, and present an AI-generated product as their own.

3. Text-Heavy or Predictable Formats
   AI models are particularly effective at generating content for tasks with predictable structures, for example, argumentative essays, reflective journal entries or lab reports. The more formulaic or conventional the output, the more likely it is that AI can mimic it convincingly.

4. Lack of Real-Time Interaction or Dialogue
   Strategies like peer review, collaborative writing and reflective journaling often happen asynchronously, without continuous instructor feedback. This lack of interaction makes it easier to substitute AI input without breaking the flow of the activity or raising red flags.

5. Assumption of Internal Motivation and Integrity
   These strategies often rely on the assumption that students are intrinsically motivated and committed to the learning process. They depend on trust rather than verification, making them susceptible when that trust is broken or when external pressures (e.g., deadlines, burnout) outweigh learning goals.

The pedagogical consequences of these vulnerabilities are both systemic and far-reaching. One of the most immediate impacts is the *loss of process visibility*. When students rely on AI to generate polished outputs, instructors are left without insight into the steps that led to those results. These steps are often where the deepest learning occurs. This obscures opportunities for formative feedback, making it difficult to support students (Tertiary Education Quality and Standards Agency [TEQSA], 2023).

Closely tied to this is the *erosion of assessment authenticity*. Traditional assignments such as essays, reports and problem sets have historically functioned as reliable indicators of student understanding and effort. With the increasing use of GenAI, the credibility of these assessments is compromised. Educators can no longer assume that submitted work reflects a student's independent thinking or skill development (*University of Pittsburgh*, 2023).

In parallel, there is a growing concern around *student overreliance on automation*. While AI can support learning when used responsibly, habitual dependence on these tools may reduce students' resilience, critical reasoning and intellectual autonomy. The convenience of instant answers can disincentivise perseverance and reflective problem-solving. These are skills not only in academia but in lifelong learning.

Finally, a more structural issue emerges: *pedagogical misalignment*. Many instructional strategies in current use were designed under the assumption that students engage without AI assistance. This assumption is increasingly untenable. As AI becomes integrated into students' daily academic routines, educators must reconsider how their pedagogical approaches align with the realities of student toolsets and behaviours. Without such recalibration, well-intentioned strategies risk becoming ineffective or even counterproductive (Mazo, 2025).

SOURCES OF RESISTANCE

Despite growing recognition of the need to recalibrate pedagogical strategies in response to GenAI AI, resistance within educational institutions remains widespread. This reluctance is not merely a matter of unfamiliarity with new tools, but stems from deeper epistemological, professional, structural and ethical tensions.

At its core, resistance often reflects long-standing epistemological commitments that prioritise originality, authorship and human cognitive labour. Many educators have been trained to value intellectual production as a deeply personal and effortful process. The introduction of GenAI, which can replicate student outputs with ease, destabilises these assumptions and raises fundamental questions about what constitutes genuine learning (Chen, 2025).

In addition, professional identity plays a significant role. For many educators, teaching is not just a task but an embodiment of disciplinary expertise and pedagogical authority. The incursion of AI into spaces traditionally reserved for human educators, such as generating feedback, scaffolding arguments or summarising readings, can be perceived as a threat to that identity. Resistance in this context is less about technological aversion and more about safeguarding professional autonomy (Yuhne, 2025).

Institutional factors also contribute to inertia. Curriculum frameworks, assessment policies and learning management systems often operate on rigid timelines and protocols. Even educators who are open to pedagogical innovation may find themselves constrained by structural norms and accreditation demands that inhibit experimentation. Such conditions create an environment where meaningful adaptation to AI is perceived as logistically or politically unfeasible (Hutson, 2024).

Tied to this is economies of scale. Long before the emergence of GenAI, computers were introduced into education not primarily to enhance pedagogy, but to solve a more pragmatic problem: the cost and inefficiency of individualised assessment. In large-scale education systems, testing students one-on-one or evaluating open-ended responses face-to-face proved prohibitively expensive and logistically unmanageable. The appeal of machine-scored multiple-choice tests, which could be administered and processed at scale, catalysed the integration of early educational technologies (Brown, 2022).

As enrolments grew and accountability pressures increased, particularly in standardised testing regimes, institutions sought tools that could offer consistency, speed and cost reduction. Automated marking systems emerged as a solution, not to deepen learning, but to facilitate measurement. In this way, the earliest educational uses of computers were less about transforming instruction and more about managing volume (Selwyn, 2022).

This legacy is crucial to understanding present challenges with GenAI. While current tools offer more sophisticated forms of automation, the underlying logic remains familiar: technological efficiency is often privileged over pedagogical nuance. Calls to return to oral exams or in-person demonstrations of learning, though well-intentioned, must grapple with the economic realities that initially led institutions to abandon such labour-intensive practices. Face-to-face assessment is time-consuming, resource-heavy and difficult to scale. Particularly in massified higher education systems.

Thus, the resistance to abandoning automated or product-based assessment is not simply ideological but structural. If we are to reimagine assessment in the age of AI, we must confront not only technological possibilities but also the fiscal constraints and institutional logics that shape how assessment is designed and delivered (Luckin and Holmes, 2016).

Next, ethical and equity-related concerns further compound resistance. The use of AI in education raises important concerns about data privacy, algorithmic bias and digital access. Educators working in under-resourced contexts may be particularly hesitant to integrate AI, fearing it may exacerbate existing inequalities or compromise student welfare (Edutopia, 2024).

Finally, a significant source of resistance lies in uncertainty and cognitive overload. For faculty already navigating the demands of hybrid teaching, assessment reform and student wellbeing, the prospect of mastering yet another technological system can feel daunting. Without sustained institutional support and clear pedagogical guidance, AI integration is seen not as a promising innovation but as an added burden with ambiguous outcomes (Hill, 2025).

CURRICULUM MISALIGNMENT

The rapid proliferation of AI tools in education has exposed a critical fault line that most current curricula were neither designed for, nor responsive to, the capabilities and implications of GenAI. While these technologies now shape how students research, write, solve problems and seek feedback, curriculum frameworks remain largely predicated on assumptions that predate their existence. This structural lag creates profound dissonance between how students learn and how that learning is evaluated.

Curricula are typically designed around standardisation, emphasising uniform content delivery, fixed learning outcomes and summative assessments that can be applied consistently across cohorts. In contrast, AI tools offer dynamic, individualised support by adjusting explanations, feedback and even learning trajectories in real time. These divergent logics create the pedagogical tension where AI invites personalisation, but curricula enforce uniformity. As a result, when students engage with AI to advance their understanding or enhance their work, they often do so in ways that are invisible, or even unintelligible, to formal assessment schemes (Luckin and Holmes, 2016).

This misalignment is particularly evident in feedback and grading systems. For instance, AI writing tools may provide nuanced suggestions to improve argument structure, clarity or rhetorical tone, which are qualities aligned with authentic communication and disciplinary literacy. However, these enhancements do not always map onto standardised grading rubrics. A study by LaJuan Perronoski Fuller and Bixby (2024) found that AI-generated feedback often diverged from the formal assessment criteria used in higher education writing tasks, raising concerns about reliability and alignment. Similarly, a controlled experiment reported by The Wall Street Journal (Randazzo, 2024) demonstrated striking variations in AI grading. The same student essay received scores ranging from 62% to 97%, depending on the platform. Such discrepancies reveal that AI's interpretive logics do not always conform to institutional metrics, potentially confusing students about what constitutes quality or success.

MINI CASE STUDY: ADAPTING EARLY CHILDHOOD CURRICULA FOR AI LITERACY

CONTEXT

As AI permeates everyday life and professional sectors, there is a growing imperative to introduce AI education at earlier stages. While most AI education initiatives target secondary and postsecondary levels, recent developments highlight the need to build AI competencies even in kindergarten, where foundational cognitive, social, and ethical skills begin to form.

CHALLENGE

Despite increasing recognition of AI's significance, early childhood education lacks a standardized, developmentally appropriate AI curriculum. Most existing frameworks and tools are designed for older learners, leaving a critical gap in pedagogical strategies, content integration, and educator support for younger children.

SOLUTION

(Su and Zhong, 2022) propose a structured AI curriculum for children aged 5–7, grounded in a four-part framework encompassing aims, content, methods, and assessment. They identify three crucial competencies for AI literacy: AI Knowledge, AI Skills, and AI Attitudes. These are translated into modules that include hands-on activities like machine learning through drawing games, facial recognition exercises with tools like PictoBlox, and ethical reflection through concept mapping.

IMPLEMENTATION

The curriculum is divided into four modules: Introduction to AI, Machine Learning, AI Techniques, and AI Ethics. Each module consists of lessons supported by structured learning objectives, classroom materials, and evaluation strategies. Problem-based learning is emphasized as the primary pedagogical approach, encouraging inquiry, teamwork, and practical engagement. Teachers are supported with comprehensive guides and suggested assessments, including pre- and post-tests, classroom observation profiles, and self-assessment tools for children.

RESULTS

Pilot implementations showed that children developed basic understanding of AI concepts, improved problem-solving skills, and exhibited increased engagement and curiosity. Group projects like smart plant watering systems helped consolidate technical knowledge with ethical reasoning, fostering 21st-century competencies such as collaboration, creativity, and critical thinking.

CONCLUSION

This case underscores the necessity of evolving early childhood curricula to integrate AI literacy meaningfully. By adopting developmentally appropriate frameworks and active learning strategies, educators can prepare young learners not only to understand AI but to participate ethically and creatively in an AI-driven environment.

Source: (Su and Zhong, 2022). **Artificial Intelligence (AI) in early childhood education: Curriculum design and future directions.** ***Computers and Education: Artificial Intelligence*, 3, 100072**. https://doi.org/10.1016/j.caeai.2022.100072

Compounding this problem is the fact that most curricula offer no explicit guidance on AI use. In the absence of clear policy or pedagogical scaffolding, students and instructors must navigate an ambiguous space where AI is present in practice but absent from curricular logic. AI thus functions as an invisible pedagogical actor, shaping learning while being excluded from the frameworks that govern it.

To bridge this divide, curriculum developers must recognise AI not as an external threat or novelty, but as a fundamental shift in how learners engage with knowledge. Without curricular realignment, AI will continue to operate as a parallel track disconnected from the systems that define, measure and credential student learning.

OVERRELIANCE ON AUTOMATION

As artificial intelligence tools become increasingly embedded in educational environments, a pressing concern arises regarding the potential overreliance on automation. This dependence is not merely a matter of convenience but signals a broader shift in how decisions are made, knowledge is assessed and learning is facilitated.

In 2023, a professor at Texas A&M University-Commerce employed ChatGPT as a tool to detect the presence of GenAI in student essays. While this approach was ultimately unreliable as a method for evaluating academic work, it highlights a growing temptation among educators. Faced with the dual pressures of heavy marking loads and the persistent challenge of upholding academic integrity, automated tools such as ChatGPT offer an appealing, if flawed, shortcut.

A key concern that previously shaped the debate around automation in education was the delegation of pedagogical judgement to algorithms. Automated essay-scoring systems, in particular, had been criticised for emphasising superficial features, such as length, syntactic regularity or keyword frequency, over more meaningful qualities like argument complexity, originality or cultural nuance (Yang *et al.*, 2002; Jeon and Strube, 2021). Researchers documented instances where nonsensical but formulaic essays received high scores because they aligned with algorithmic expectations (Perelman, 2012). This prompted formal protests from educators, including public petitions, which warned that students' motivation would suffer if they believed no human would read their writing (Humanreaders.org, 2013).

RISKS OF OUTSOURCING DECISION-MAKING TO ALGORITHMS

In some domains, such as solving mathematical equations or verifying objective facts, algorithmic tools perform reliably and without controversy. These tasks are governed by formal rules and clear correctness criteria, making automation an effective complement to human judgement. However, once algorithms are deployed for multifaceted educational decisions such as those requiring nuance, contextual awareness or ethical consideration, the stakes become considerably higher.

The expansion of GenAI tools has reframed and intensified earlier concerns about algorithmic decision-making. Generative models, in particular, layer probabilistic *creativity* on evaluations, further obscuring accountability and traceability. When such systems are used by educators or institutions to grade essays, flag misconduct or suggest interventions, they effectively transfer pedagogical authority from human educators to opaque statistical engines.

This shift introduces several risks:

1. **Opacity and accountability**
   One of the biggest challenges with using AI in education is that the decisions these systems make are often difficult to explain, even for the people who designed them. This is what's commonly known as the *black box* problem (Burrell, 2016; Pasquale, 2015). These systems are incredibly complex, and the way they arrive at a decision, like assigning a grade or flagging plagiarism, can be almost impossible to trace. For example, an automated essay scorer might give a student a low grade simply because the essay was shorter than average or didn't use certain vocabulary, without really engaging with the quality of the ideas. In the same way, plagiarism detectors sometimes flag work that's properly cited, while missing more subtle cases. When students can't see why a decision was made, or how to appeal it, it raises real concerns about fairness and trust (Binns, 2018; Diakopoulos 2016; Selbst and Barocas, 2018).

2. **Perpetuation of bias**
   AI systems don't just make decisions in a vacuum; they learn from past data. And if that data reflects existing inequalities in

education, the system will learn those too. This means that tools used in things like admissions or performance prediction can end up reinforcing biases related to race, gender or social background. For instance, if students from wealthier schools were more likely to succeed in the past, the algorithm might unfairly favour applicants with similar profiles going forward. So even though these tools appear neutral, they can quietly carry forward the same unfair patterns we've been trying to fix (Baker and Hawn, 2021; Holstein, McLaren and Aleven, 2018).

3. **Erosion of educator engagement**
   When we hand over parts of teaching, like grading or giving feedback to machines, we risk losing something important in the student-teacher relationship. Good teaching isn't just about efficiency; it's about understanding where a student is coming from and responding with empathy, insight and flexibility. But when algorithms take over these decisions, that space for dialogue can shrink. Teachers may end up feeling disconnected from their students' learning journeys, and students may feel like they're being judged by a system that doesn't truly *see* them (Popenici and Kerr, 2017).

4. **Reduction of learning to surface-level metrics**
   Another issue is that algorithms tend to focus on things they can easily measure, such as word count, grammar or keyword usage. While those features can be useful, they don't capture deeper qualities like originality, creativity or cultural insight. This can nudge students to write in a way that pleases the algorithm, rather than expressing themselves authentically. Over time, the learning experience can start to feel hollow. Focused more on checking boxes than on meaningful thinking and communication (Wilson and MacArthur, 2024).

These risks are not merely technical concerns as they shape how students learn, how teachers teach and how educational values are expressed or suppressed. Table 3.2 maps these four core risks of algorithmic systems to the types of learning they most profoundly affect, illustrating how seemingly neutral technologies can reshape the educational experience in subtle but significant ways.

TABLE 3.2 Impact of AI-Driven Risks on Learning Types

Risk	Description	Types of Learning Most Affected
Opacity and Accountability	AI decisions are difficult to interpret or challenge, limiting feedback and student agency.	- Metacognitive learning (learning how to learn) - Formative learning (learning from feedback) - Self-regulated learning
Perpetuation of Bias	Algorithms replicate historical inequalities, disadvantaging certain groups.	- Culturally responsive learning - Equity-based access to learning - Socially inclusive learning
Erosion of Educator Engagement	Automation reduces teacher involvement in feedback and judgement, weakening pedagogical relationships.	- Relational learning (dialogue and trust) - Constructivist learning - Reflective teaching practices
Reduction to Surface Metrics	AI prioritises measurable features (e.g., word count), overlooking depth, originality and context.	- Critical thinking - Creative and divergent thinking - Cultural and contextual understanding

MINI CASE STUDY: SCORING WITHOUT UNDERSTANDING: A CASE STUDY ON ETS'S E-RATER® AND THE BLACK BOX PROBLEM IN EDUCATION

- https://ejournals.bc.edu/index.php/jtla/article/view/1653
- (Burrell, 2016). How the machine 'thinks': Understanding opacity in machine learning algorithms. *Big Data & Society, 3*(1). https://doi.org/10.1177/2053951715622512
- (Perelman, 2014). When "the state" is not enough: An analysis of SAT essay scoring. In M. D. Williamson, R. J. Mislevy, & I. I. Bejar (Eds.), *Automated Scoring of Complex Tasks in Computer-Based Testing* (pp. 117–135). Erlbaum.

BACKGROUND

As educational institutions increasingly adopt AI-driven tools to streamline assessment, automated essay scoring systems have gained traction for their efficiency and scalability. One of the most widely used systems is e-rater®, developed by Educational Testing Service (ETS). This machine learning-based engine evaluates written responses in high-stakes exams like the GRE and TOEFL, assessing features such as grammar, syntax, word usage, and essay structure.

CONTEXT

In 2012, MIT researcher Les Perelman developed a system called BABEL (Basic Automatic BS Essay Language Generator) to test the robustness of e-rater®. BABEL produced grammatically correct but semantically meaningless essays. Surprisingly, these essays received high scores from the e-rater engine.

The BABEL experiment exploited a critical limitation of e-rater: it evaluates *form over meaning*. The algorithm rewarded essays with longer word counts, advanced vocabulary, and varied sentence structures, regardless of coherence or truthfulness.

THE PROBLEM

Despite being used in high-stakes testing, e-rater lacks semantic understanding. Its decisions are based on surface-level statistical features rather than human-like comprehension. Because of this:

- Well-reasoned but concisely written essays may score poorly
- Verbose or incoherent essays may score highly
- Students and educators are unable to access the system's rationale, making contesting scores nearly impossible

This highlights a classic *black box* problem (Burrell, 2016), where the logic behind decisions is opaque, even to developers. In educational assessment, where fairness, interpretability, and accountability are essential, such opacity undermines trust.

IMPLICATIONS

1. **Ethical Risks**: Using opaque AI systems in grading can exacerbate inequities, especially for students with non-standard writing styles or cultural expressions not favoured by the model's training data.

2. **Pedagogical Concerns**: Students may learn to game the algorithm, focusing on length and vocabulary instead of clarity, argumentation, or creativity.
3. **Accountability Void**: Without clear explanations or appeal processes, students have limited recourse to challenge automated decisions, violating principles of procedural justice.
4. **Need for Human Oversight**: ETS often uses e-rater alongside human raters in critical exams, acknowledging its limitations, but this hybrid approach is not always applied in classroom or lower-stakes settings.

CONCLUSION

The case of e-rater and the BABEL experiment underscores the importance of transparency and accountability in educational AI. While automated scoring tools can provide efficiency, they must be carefully scrutinized, paired with human oversight, and kept aligned with educational values that prioritize fairness, understanding, and student agency.

Sources: (Attali and Burstein, 2006). Automated essay scoring with e-rater® V.2. *Journal of Technology, Learning, and Assessment, 4*(3).

In framing algorithmic evaluation as technical enhancements, institutions risked reducing education to pattern-recognition exercises, where results were optimised for machine readability rather than pedagogical depth. As GenAI becomes embedded in educational platforms, it is no longer sufficient to ask what these tools *can* do, but rather, what they *should* be empowered to decide. Robust human oversight, strong transparency mechanisms and policy frameworks are essential to safeguard against delegating educational judgements to unexamined algorithms.

DID YOU KNOW: PROBABILISTIC CREATIVITY

Generative models operate using probabilities. They don't choose a single *correct* output but generate novel combinations of data based on likelihood. This probabilistic mechanism gives an illusion of creativity: the outputs are original (in form), but not grounded in conscious intention or fixed reasoning. This *layer of creativity* makes the output feel humanlike, but it's fundamentally driven by statistical prediction.

EROSION OF HUMAN JUDGEMENT IN TEACHING AND ASSESSMENT

As AI systems take on a growing role in evaluating student work, generating feedback and even advising on curriculum pathways, the space for human judgement in teaching is steadily narrowing. While automation promises objectivity and speed, it often does so by sidelining the nuanced, context-rich decisions that educators routinely make. Human judgement is shaped by experience, empathy, cultural awareness and pedagogical intent. These qualities are difficult to codify. When these are replaced by data-driven outputs, the result is a flattening of the evaluative process.

In assessment contexts, this erosion becomes especially visible. For instance, automated feedback tools like Turnitin's Revision Assistant or ETS's Criterion offer real-time writing suggestions based on algorithmic analysis. While useful in catching basic errors, these systems often miss subtle rhetorical strategies, creative deviations or culturally informed expressions that a human teacher might value (Perelman, 2014). Similarly, AI-powered plagiarism detectors may flag common phrases or properly cited content as misconduct, requiring students to justify their integrity in front of opaque systems.

Predictive analytics platforms like Civitas Learning and Jisc's Learning Analytics Service have also been implemented in universities to identify students *at risk* of failing or dropping out. These systems use past academic performance, attendance and engagement metrics to generate alerts for intervention. While intended to support struggling students, such systems can easily become deterministic and reinforce assumptions about who will succeed and who won't. Educators, presented with algorithmically generated predictions, may unconsciously internalise these signals and lower expectations or adjust teaching efforts accordingly.

What's concerning is not just the presence of these tools, but the gradual shift in authority they bring. Over time, the algorithm's recommendation may come to outweigh the educator's professional intuition. What begins as support can quietly become substitution. The danger lies in conflating pattern recognition with pedagogical insight.

This isn't an argument against technological assistance in education; rather, it is a call to remain critically aware of what is being displaced when human judgement is automated. At its best, teaching is a human craft grounded in interpretation, dialogue and ethical care. These are elements that no model, no matter how advanced, can fully replicate.

MINI CASE STUDY: THE EROSION OF TEACHING AUTHORITY IN THE AGE OF AI

CONTEXT

The rapid integration of AI tools in education, including intelligent tutoring systems, predictive analytics, and conversational bots, is fundamentally altering the teacher-student dynamic. Globally, these technologies are embedded in smart classrooms and digital learning platforms, often marketed as solutions to improve efficiency and access. However, beneath this promise lies a growing concern about how such systems are redefining the role, and diminishing the authority, of teachers.

CHALLENGE

Drawing on her research, (Gao, 2025) argues that the introduction of AI into educational settings is contributing to the disintegration of both external and internal forms of teacher authority. External authority (traditional and legal) has weakened as AI systems and student-centred reforms shift control away from the teacher. Internal authority (knowledge and charisma), once rooted in the teacher's personal presence and expertise, is also being undermined by the growing role of GenAI as a knowledge producer.

A critical example is the way AI systems now act as dialogic agents, capable of mimicking human responses and delivering feedback. This has led to students viewing AI as more reliable or objective than their teachers, reducing the teacher's role to that of a facilitator or technical overseer rather than an authoritative guide.

KEY ISSUES IDENTIFIED

- **Loss of Subjectivity**: Teachers become passive users of AI content and recommendations, diminishing their capacity for critical judgment, reflection, and personalized pedagogy.
- **Compression of Emotional Space**: Smart classrooms disrupt the intimacy of teacher-student relationships. Emotional cues such as eye contact, tone, and gesture are filtered through screens or replaced with machine interactions.
- **Dependence on AI Output**: Teachers may uncritically rely on AI-generated data and feedback, resulting in generalized and formulaic teaching that ignores individual student needs.

- **Undermining of Charismatic Authority**: The emotional warmth and moral influence traditionally embodied by the teacher is devalued, as students increasingly engage with emotionless, efficiency-driven AI interfaces.

IMPLICATIONS

This erosion of authority is not only a philosophical issue but a practical one with serious implications for *student engagement, emotional development, and moral education*. Gao emphasizes the need to reassert teacher subjectivity through strategies rooted in Nel Noddings' care theory (1984), such as narrative pedagogy, emotional attentiveness, and the co-construction of meaning through trust-based relationships.

CONCLUSION

This case highlights a core dilemma in AI integration: while technology can support instruction, its overuse risks shifting pedagogical authority from teachers to algorithms. If left unexamined, this shift may reduce teaching to a transactional process, stripping it of the emotional, ethical, and human qualities essential to deep learning.

Source: (Gao, 2025). *The Erosion and Reconstruction of Teachers' Authority in the Context of Artificial Intelligence*. Journal of Theory and Practice in Education and Innovation, 2(2), 26–33. https://woodyinternational.com/index.php/jtpei/article/view/182

STUDENT DEPENDENCY ON AI-GENERATED ANSWERS

As AI tools become more embedded in students' daily study routines, a quiet shift is occurring. One that trades curiosity for convenience. With just a prompt, students can now receive detailed summaries, solved equations, rephrased paragraphs and even full-length essays. While these tools offer undeniable support, especially for struggling learners or those with language barriers, there's a growing risk that students may begin to default to AI before engaging their own thinking.

This isn't simply a case of cheating or corner-cutting. In many cases, students use AI in good faith to clarify confusing topics, generate ideas or check grammar. But over time, repeated reliance on AI-generated responses can atrophy essential learning habits. Why wrestle with a difficult question when a polished answer is seconds away? Why explore multiple viewpoints or build an argument when a chatbot can deliver one instantly?

The problem is subtle, but significant. When students bypass the mental struggle that often leads to insight, they also sidestep opportunities to build resilience, creativity and critical thinking. Learning becomes more about retrieving answers than constructing understanding. And unlike a teacher or peer, AI doesn't notice when a student misunderstands, doesn't ask questions in return and doesn't tailor its responses to the student's personal growth. As a result, students may get correct information but miss the deeper process of making meaning from it.

A 2023 report from UNESCO echoes this concern, warning that GenAI tools could lead to over-dependence and reduce learners' capacity for self-regulated inquiry and original thought (UNESCO, 2021). Similarly, Gao (2025) notes that students' overreliance on AI risks diminishing their autonomy and self-efficacy, as they come to see AI systems as more authoritative than their own judgement or reasoning. Furthermore, these findings are echoed by Zhai, Wibowo and Li (2024), whose review of student interactions with AI dialogue systems found a measurable decline in independent reasoning and intellectual perseverance among those who routinely accepted AI responses without question.

What's at stake here isn't just academic integrity; it's the development of intellectual independence. If education is meant to help students learn how to think, not just what to think, then AI must be positioned as a support, not a shortcut. Students need to be encouraged to question, to try, to get stuck and to work things out. Not because it's harder, but because it's in the struggle where students will achieve deep learning.

STRATEGIES FOR MAINTAINING PEDAGOGICAL INTEGRITY

It's tempting to view AI as a neutral tool; something that simply speeds up what we already do. But education isn't a neutral process. It's a deeply human, value-laden practice that depends on judgement, empathy and dialogue. That means any automation in this space isn't just a technical choice, but it's a pedagogical one.

Critically examining the use of AI in education requires us to ask not only what these tools *can* do, but what they *should* do. For example, when we hand over assessment, feedback or even curriculum design to AI systems, we're not just saving time; we're shifting the foundations of how learning is defined and how knowledge is valued. If a student's essay is assessed by an algorithm prioritising structure and keyword density over originality or cultural expression, we need to ask: *Whose values are embedded in this system? Whose voices are being silenced?*

Overreliance on automation often stems from good intentions for reducing workload, improving consistency or closing achievement gaps. But when human judgement is replaced rather than supported, we risk eroding the very aspects of education that matter most: the personal, the unpredictable and the transformative. Worse still, we may train students to become passive recipients of machine feedback, losing confidence in their own thinking and undervaluing the role of uncertainty and exploration in learning.

As Holmes and Tuomi (2022) argue, the core risk of automating educational decision-making is not technical error, but *moral displacement* by means of the gradual handover of educational responsibility to systems that cannot be held accountable. Algorithms do not understand the needs of a struggling student, the nuance of a culturally specific reference or the emotional subtext of a classroom dynamic. That's why critical engagement must guide our use of AI in schools and universities.

This means educators need to stay in the loop both technically and ethically. They must ask: *What does this system assume about learners? What kinds of thinking does it reward? And what gets left out of the picture?* True innovation in education won't come from outsourcing judgement but from more deliberate, thoughtful decisions about *when* and *how* to use automation, and when to lean more heavily on the uniquely human capacities of teaching.

While a more thorough discussion on the strategic integration of AI with pedagogical practices and practical examples will be presented in later chapters, it's important at this stage to begin considering how AI can be positioned not as a replacement for educators, but as a tool that complements and enhances human teaching. The key lies in approaching AI with intention, aligning its use with learning goals, ethical considerations and the relational aspects of education that machines cannot replicate. What follows here is not an exhaustive guide, but a brief overview of some of the ways we can begin thinking about blending AI into classroom practices in meaningful, reflective and student-centred ways.

ENCOURAGING THOUGHTFUL USE OF AI IN THE CLASSROOM

Rather than banning AI altogether or turning a blind eye to its use, educators are better served by modelling and teaching students how to use AI wisely. The goal isn't to avoid technology but to embed it into learning in a way that promotes agency, reflection and curiosity.

One approach is to shift the role of AI from answer-provider to thinking partner. For instance, students might be asked to use an AI tool to generate a response to a question and then critically evaluate it. Where does the answer fall short? What perspectives are missing? How could it be improved? This encourages not just consumption but critique.

Teachers can also design assignments that reward process over product. When students must show how they arrived at their conclusions, whether it be through drafts, reflections or peer feedback, they're less likely to outsource the entire task to a chatbot. Incorporating AI literacy as part of the syllabus can help students appreciate the limitations of these tools, including their tendency to hallucinate facts, flatten nuance or reinforce biases.

Importantly, this kind of engagement reframes AI as a resource to think alongside, not a substitute for thinking. It affirms students' capacity to lead their own learning while acknowledging the realities of the digital age. The message becomes, *AI can support your work, but it can't replace your voice.*

BLENDING AI WITH ESTABLISHED TEACHING PHILOSOPHIES

One of the most effective ways to begin using AI in education is to connect it with teaching approaches we already trust and understand. Rather than treating AI as a radical shift, it makes more sense to see it as something that can work alongside well-established pedagogies, like constructivism, inquiry-based learning or even differentiated instruction.

Take constructivism, for instance, the idea that students learn best when they actively build knowledge through hands-on experience, reflection and collaboration. AI can support that kind of learning environment if it's used with care. For example, an AI tool might help students explore different solutions to a problem, generate alternative explanations or offer feedback that nudges them towards deeper thinking without handing them the answer. In this way, AI becomes a sort of *guide on the side*, helping to stretch a student's thinking while keeping them in the driver's seat.

There's also real potential in how AI can support formative assessment. It can help teachers spot patterns in where students are getting stuck, allowing for quicker adjustments and more responsive teaching. Importantly, in a constructivist setting, this kind of insight isn't used to judge students; it's used to adapt learning in real time, creating space for students to explore at their own pace and in their own way.

This isn't about AI replacing pedagogy. It's about using it in ways that align with what we already value: learner agency, dialogue and deep understanding. A more thorough examination of how AI can complement a range of teaching philosophies will come in Chapter 5: Rethinking AI-Assisted Pedagogy. But for now, this section is about planting the seed and encouraging you to think about AI not as a standalone solution, but as something that can genuinely enhance the teaching practices we already know work.

MINI CASE STUDY: INTEGRATING AI FOR FORMATIVE FEEDBACK IN NORWEGIAN SECONDARY SCHOOLS

CONTEXT

Five secondary schools in Norway participated in a qualitative study to explore how AI technologies can be used to enhance formative feedback practices. The initiative was part of a larger developmental project involving 50 schools, emphasizing digital transformation in classroom assessment.

CHALLENGE

Teachers often face high workloads that limit their ability to provide timely, individualized formative feedback. Students, especially those working independently, may struggle with receiving continuous, subject-relevant guidance. Variability in digital literacy and limited planning also hindered effective AI integration.

SOLUTION

An AI-powered educational platform was implemented across the five schools, drawing on four knowledge bases: a general GPT model, teacher-defined curriculum goals, student work history, and expert fine-tuning. This system allowed for dynamic, personalized feedback throughout students' learning processes. Teachers were able to embed AI feedback tools aligned with their specific learning objectives.

IMPLEMENTATION

Data were collected from 26 students and 13 teachers through interviews and unstructured classroom observations. The AI provided immediate feedback on writing and content development, enabling students to iterate on their work more efficiently. Teachers could focus more on high-level content and individual support while AI handled grammar, structure, and concept suggestions.

RESULTS

- **Students** appreciated the immediacy and usefulness of AI feedback, particularly in improving their writing and managing time effectively. High-performing students used the system to deepen content, while others felt the feedback was occasionally too complex or generic.
- **Teachers** reported that AI improved student output and motivation, supported inclusive practices (e.g., aiding dyslexic students with audio feedback), and enabled more strategic time use. However, the necessity of periodic planning and the teacher's interpretive role remained essential.

CONCLUSION

AI technologies can significantly support formative assessment by delivering personalized, subject-specific feedback that complements teacher input. However, successful implementation depends on thoughtful integration into pedagogical planning, digital literacy development, and maintaining the teacher's role as the final arbiter of assessment.

Source: (Burner, Lindvig and Wærness, 2025). "We should not be like a dinosaur"—Using AI technologies to provide formative feedback to students. *Education Sciences, 15*(1), 58. https://doi.org/10.3390/educsci15010058

BUILDING EDUCATOR CAPACITY THROUGH PROFESSIONAL DEVELOPMENT

Introducing AI into the classroom isn't just a matter of updating tools. It also requires updating teacher confidence, knowledge and professional identity. For many educators, the idea of using AI in teaching feels abstract, overwhelming or even threatening. Without the right support, it's easy for AI to remain on the margins of practice, either underused or misused. That's where professional development becomes essential. It's a recurring theme in this book already!

Teachers need more than technical training. It's not enough to know *how* a tool works; they need time and space to explore *when*, *why* and *whether* to use it. Effective professional development goes beyond software tutorials. It invites educators into open conversations about pedagogy, ethics and student agency. It encourages experimentation, peer exchange and reflection on what it means to teach in an AI-rich world.

This kind of learning should be iterative, embedded in practice and tailored to different levels of readiness. Some teachers might start by using AI for feedback or lesson planning, while others may explore AI co-creation tools with students. What matters is creating a culture where curiosity is encouraged and critical questions are welcomed. How do we maintain trust in human judgement? What happens to teacher-student relationships when feedback comes from a machine? How do we prevent bias from creeping into the data?

In short, building educator capacity is not just about skill acquisition; it's about professional empowerment. If we want AI in education to be meaningful and human-centred, then teachers need to be positioned not as passive adopters, but as informed designers, facilitators and gatekeepers. That starts with giving them the tools, the appropriate guidance and the trust to shape how AI is used in their own classrooms.

We've seen this pattern before. Teachers are often handed new technologies or thrust into teaching subjects like coding, robotics or data science, without adequate training or support. The result? The tech is underused, misunderstood or reduced to surface-level engagement. The same will happen with AI if we're not careful. Rather than delivering a new generation of *AI natives*, we risk perpetuating the cycle of struggle, where both teachers and students are left unsure of how to use these tools thoughtfully or effectively. Preparing future educators isn't a nice-to-have, it's the foundation for everything else that follows.

HOLDING THE HUMAN THREAD

This chapter began with a stark observation: while AI has opened new doors for personalised and scalable education, it has simultaneously exposed the fragility of many long-established instructional practices. As shown in Table 3.1, some of our most trusted strategies, such as take-home essays, open-ended reflection and project-based work, have proven especially vulnerable. These tasks, once seen as rich indicators of student engagement and understanding, are now easily replicated by AI, raising deep questions not only about authorship but also about the authenticity of the learning itself.

More than just a plagiarism problem, this disruption impacts the very processes of learning, including drafting, revising, peer collaboration and problem-solving, that we've long relied on to develop critical thinking, creativity and student agency. When AI is used to skip these formative steps, what we lose isn't just academic integrity; it's also the invisible work of learning. As instructional design struggles to keep pace, this chapter has argued that we need to move beyond detection and prevention alone and start designing for resilience and adaptability in an AI-assisted world.

We've also examined the broader risks of overreliance on automation: the opacity of algorithmic decisions, the potential erosion of professional judgement, the weakening of student autonomy and the devaluing of deep, process-driven learning. Across each of these, a pattern emerges: when technology displaces rather than complements the human elements of education, something essential is lost. The solution isn't to reject AI, but to reassert human purpose in how it is used.

That reassertion begins with educators through professional development, ethical guidance and structural support. Teachers must be trusted as designers and facilitators of AI use, not passive implementers. Students, too, must be encouraged to work with AI critically, not lean on it blindly. The future of AI in education depends on restoring balance between innovation and intention.

And that balance brings us directly to Chapter 4: Guardrails, Ethical Considerations, Security and Privacy. If we are to integrate AI responsibly, we must address the ethical and technical guardrails that keep learners safe, data protected and decision-making accountable. Because the question isn't just what AI can do in education, it's what kind of education we are willing to create with it.

REFLECT AND REFRAME

1. What values or principles guide your decisions when introducing new technologies, like AI, into your teaching? Reflect on how these values align (or clash) with the capabilities of generative tools.
2. Think about a recent assignment or task. Could students have used AI to complete it without truly learning? What changes might make that task more resistant to automation and more focused on authentic engagement?
3. How do you currently model critical thinking about AI for your students? What opportunities exist to openly discuss the risks and benefits of using AI in learning?
4. In what ways might institutional policies or cultures unintentionally encourage overreliance on automation? Are there structural factors pushing educators or students towards efficiency at the expense of reflection?
5. What would it look like to design a unit or project that explicitly incorporates both human and AI contributions? Consider what scaffolding and assessment would be necessary to make the learning transparent and intentional.
6. How can you create space, for yourself and your students, to experiment, make mistakes and question the role of AI in education? Think about how to build a classroom climate that values inquiry over perfection.

REFERENCES

Adams, R., 2025. Revealed: Thousands of UK university students caught cheating using AI. *The Guardian.*

Attali, Y., and Burstein, J., 2006. Automated essay scoring with e-rater® V.2. *The Journal of Technology, Learning and Assessment*, 4(3). https://ejournals.bc.edu/index.php/jtla/article/view/1650

Baker, R.S., and Hawn, A., 2021. Algorithmic bias in education. *International Journal of Artificial Intelligence in Education*, 32(4), 1052–1092.

Binns, R., 2018. Fairness in machine learning: Lessons from political philosophy. *Proceedings of Machine Learning Research.*

Burner, T., Lindvig, Y., and Wærness, J.I., 2025. 'We should not be like a dinosaur'—Using AI technologies to provide formative feedback to students. *Education Sciences*, 15(1), 58.

Burrell, J., 2016. How the machine 'thinks': Understanding opacity in machine learning algorithms. *Big Data & Society*, 3(1), 1–12.

Chang, J., 2025. My students think it's fine to cheat with AI. Maybe they're onto something. *Vox*.

Chen, B., 2025. Beyond tools: Generative AI as epistemic infrastructure in education. *arXiv.org*.

Cotton, D., Cotton, P., and Shipway, J.R., 2023. Chatting and cheating. Ensuring academic integrity in the era of ChatGPT. *OSF Preprints*.

Diakopoulos, N., 2016. Accountability in algorithmic decision making. *Communications of the ACM*, 59(2), 56–62.

Edutopia, 2024. Thinking about equity and bias in AI. *Edutopia*.

Gao, L., 2025. The erosion and reconstruction of teachers' authority in the context of artificial intelligence. *Journal of Theory and Practice in Education and Innovation*, 2(2), 26–33.

Heinz, F., 2023. TAMU-Commerce instructor accuses class of using ChatGPT on final assignments. *NBC 5 Dallas-Fort Worth*.

Hill, P., 2025. Faculty uncertainty about AI in teaching and learning. *On EdTech Newsletter*.

Holmes, W., and Tuomi, I., 2022. State of the art and practice in AI in education. *European Journal of Education*, 57(4), 542–570.

Holstein, K., McLaren, B.M., and Aleven, V., 2018. Student learning benefits of a mixed-reality teacher awareness tool in AI-enhanced classrooms. *Lecture Notes in Computer Science*, 10947, 154–168.

Humanreaders.org, 2013. Professionals against machine scoring of student essays in high-stakes assessment. *Schoolinfosystem.org*.

Hutson, M., 2024. AI is forcing universities to rethink assessment and teaching. *Nature*, 625, 437–439.

Jeon, S., and Strube, M., 2021. Countering the influence of essay length in neural essay scoring.

Johnson, M., 2025. ChatGPT and other AI tools are changing the teaching profession. *AP News*.

Joyce, L., 2023. Assessing Mass Effect 2 and Elder Scrolls V: Skyrim: Using collaborative criteria for player agency in interactive narratives. *Journal of Games Criticism*, 3(1).

LaJuan Perronoski Fuller and Bixby, C., 2024. The theoretical and practical implications of OpenAI system rubric assessment and feedback on higher education written assignments. *American Journal of Educational Research*, 12(4), 147–158.

Luckin, R., and Holmes, W., 2016. Intelligence unleashed: An argument for AI in education.

Mazo, J., 2025. Avoiding pedagogical misalignment, maximizing AI's potential. *LinkedIn*.

Molesworth, M., Nixon, E. and Scullion, R., 2009. Having, being and higher education: The marketisation of the university and the transformation of the student into consumer. *Teaching in Higher Education*, 14(3), 277–287.

Brown, G., 2022. The past, present and future of educational assessment: A transdisciplinary perspective. *Frontiers in Education*, 7(1), 1060633.

Pasquale, F., 2015. *The Black Box Society: The Secret Algorithms That Control Money and Information*. Cambridge, MA: Harvard University Press.

Perelman, L., 2012. Les Perelman. *Wikipedia*.

Perelman, L., 2014. When 'the state of the art' is counting words. *Assessing Writing*, 21, 104–111.

Popenici, S.A.D., and Kerr, S., 2017. Exploring the impact of artificial intelligence on teaching and learning in higher education. *Research and Practice in Technology Enhanced Learning*, 12(1), 1–13.

Randazzo, S., 2024. Teachers use AI to grade papers. Is it any good? *The Wall Street Journal*.

Selbst, A.D., and Barocas, S., 2018. Welcome to Zscaler directory authentication. *Scirp.org*.

Selwyn, N., 2022. Education and technology: Key issues and debates.

Su, J., and Zhong, Y., 2022. Artificial intelligence (AI) in early childhood education: Curriculum design and future directions. *Computers and Education: Artificial Intelligence*, 3(100072), 100072.

Tertiary Education Quality and Standards Agency [TEQSA], 2023. Assessment reform for the age of artificial intelligence.

UNESCO, 2021. AI and education: Guidance for policy-makers.

University of Pittsburgh, 2023. AI, academic integrity, and authentic assessment: An ethical path forward for education.

Wilson, J., and MacArthur, C., 2024. Exploring the role of automated writing evaluation as a formative assessment tool supporting self-regulated learning in writing. In Mark D. Shermis, and Joshua Wilson (eds.) *The Routledge international handbook of automated essay evaluation* (pp. 197–220). Routledge.

Yang, Y., et al., 2002. A review of strategies for validating computer-automated scoring. *Applied Measurement in Education*, 15(4), 391–412.

Yuhne, A.H., 2025. AI resistance in education: The hidden emotional load on teachers. *LinkedIn*.

Zhai, C., Wibowo, S., and Li, L.D., 2024. The effects of over-reliance on AI dialogue systems on students' cognitive abilities: A systematic review. *Smart Learning Environments*, 11(28), 1–37.

CHAPTER 4

Guardrails, Ethical Considerations, Privacy and Security

Across systemic, relational and pedagogical domains, one principle stands out: guardrails are not constraints on innovation but conditions for meaningful innovation.

CHAPTER AIMS

The aim of this chapter is to introduce key themes explored in this book in relation to:

1. *Ethical, pedagogical, technical and institutional guardrails that ensure AI in education supports fairness, transparency and professional responsibility.*
2. *Systemic, relational and epistemic challenges, including bias, surveillance, data ownership and shifts in definitions of knowledge, that shape how AI impacts teaching and learning.*
3. *Practical strategies, case studies and reflection tools that help educators critically evaluate AI use and align it with meaningful learning outcomes.*

DOI: 10.1201/9781003624981-4

REFRAMING FAMILIAR CONCERNS THROUGH AN ETHICAL LENS

In earlier chapters, we examined how AI challenges traditional pedagogical practices, reshapes definitions of learning and alters the roles of both educators and students. We also explored the tensions surrounding automation, authorship, assessment and the use of student data. These are critical operational and instructional considerations. However, in this chapter, we shift our focus not to introduce entirely new concerns, but to reinterpret those already raised through the ethical frameworks that underpin responsible educational practice.

What emerges is not simply a list of best practices, but a series of normative questions: What obligations do educators have when AI intervenes in formative feedback? When does efficiency compromise epistemic integrity? How should consent and transparency be handled in environments shaped by opaque algorithms? And who is accountable when AI decisions influence outcomes that matter?

Here, we are less concerned with the technical workings of the tools (already addressed) and more with what those tools *mean* for autonomy, for justice and for professional responsibility. Bias, data governance and surveillance, previously discussed in terms of risk, are now reconsidered in terms of rights. Similarly, earlier considerations around feedback and assessment are recast through the lens of epistemic ethics: how we come to know, who gets to know and under what conditions that knowledge is considered valid or fair.

This ethical reframing asks us not only to manage AI, but to ask whether its application upholds the values we believe education should serve. It requires moving beyond functionality to intentionality, ensuring that the systems we adopt do not merely fit into our workflows, but also align with our moral commitments to equity, care and intellectual honesty.

Several of the tensions already explored, including feedback automation, AI-authored content and the evolving role of the educator, take on added complexity when viewed through an ethical lens. While these issues were previously examined for their instructional and operational impact, their ethical implications warrant separate attention, especially in light of educational values such as fairness, trust and integrity.

OPACITY AND THE RIGHT TO UNDERSTAND

Earlier in the book, we examined the black-box nature of many AI systems, especially those designed to evaluate student work or generate feedback. These tools often operate without making their internal decision processes transparent, and that presents a serious ethical problem. In education, opacity violates the central tenet of justice that students have the right to understand how decisions affecting their learning are made.

When a student receives AI-generated feedback that lacks explanation, say, a vague suggestion to "improve clarity" without indicating what triggered it, they are left guessing. Was it a weak thesis? A disjointed paragraph? Or did the AI simply misunderstand the tone? The lack of clarity diminishes trust, not only in the system itself but also in the learning process. Students disengage when they can't make sense of their feedback or when they suspect the system isn't accurate. And as research shows, trust is harder to rebuild once it's broken (Dietvorst, Simmons and Massey, 2015). It is worth noting that this problem is not unique to AI. Human tutors are equally capable of offering overly general or unclear feedback. In such cases, AI has the potential to enhance the feedback process rather than replace it. This possibility is explored in more detail later in the book.

The AI issue becomes more troubling when we look at real-world examples. In Germany, a popular AI tool called Fobizz was used to score student writing. However, reviewers found that nonsensical and AI-generated texts often received higher grades than serious student submissions. In the study, one test involved submitting a text with intentionally fabricated facts and nonsense phrasing. Surprisingly, the tool still issued a positive evaluation. The feedback praised the text's structure and clarity, ignoring its clear factual inaccuracy and semantic incoherence. This suggests the tool does not perform any real fact-checking or semantic validation. Neither the students nor the teachers could understand why (Mühlhoff and Henningsen, 2024).

Concerns about the reliability of automated grading systems are well documented. Studies of automated essay scoring have shown that algorithmic grading models can produce inconsistent or easily manipulated results, raising questions about their suitability for high-stakes assessment (Perelman, 2014).

None of the systems explained their rationale.

This opacity isn't just inconvenient; it's unjust. Educational research has long emphasised that feedback is most effective when it is specific, timely and transparent. Studies show that students learn best when feedback is clearly linked to learning goals, delivered promptly and provides actionable guidance on how to improve (Ambrose, 2010; Huynh, 2024). Without a clear understanding of what led to a recommendation, students lose the opportunity to reflect and develop.

There are ways to address this. Scholars like Chaudhry, Cukurova and Luckin (2022) have proposed a transparency index that maps out how AI tools in education (outlined in Table 4.1) can and should make their decisions interpretable at every stage, from data input to outcome. That includes making it clear which features influenced an evaluation (e.g., coherence, sentence structure, use of evidence), how confident the system was and what rubric it was following.

Some institutions are moving in this direction. The University of Sydney's Cogniti project is one example. Rather than letting AI generate feedback autonomously, teachers feed the model their marking criteria and assignment goals. The result is co-produced feedback that students can trust, because they know the teacher had a hand in shaping it (Huynh, 2024)

Recent empirical work also supports this approach. A study by Zhang et al. (2025) found that students were more likely to trust feedback when they knew it had been created in partnership with a human. Fully automated responses, once revealed as such, quickly lost credibility.

At the heart of this issue is the question of justice. When AI systems are used in education, students must be able to understand how and why a judgement has been made. Otherwise, they are being asked to participate

TABLE 4.1 Transparency in relation to other dimensions of ethical AI in ed-tech systems. Adapted from Chaudhry, Cukurova and Luckin, 2022

Transparency Dimension	Key Question
Safety	What safety measures and precautions were taken to deter the harmful effects of the AI system?
Explainability	How does the AI system work? Based on which inputs is an AI system making decisions/predictions?
Fairness	What are the contextual limitations of this AI system? What biases exist in the system and for whom?
Accountability	Who will be responsible for the mistakes of an AI system?
Interpretability	Are the explanations provided by an AI system understandable for stakeholders?

in a system where learning outcomes are shaped by forces they can neither see nor question. In a just educational environment, that's unacceptable.

Automation and Epistemic Integrity

AI's ability to generate plausible-sounding answers or compose complete texts has raised earlier concerns about authenticity and authorship. Ethically, this touches on more than plagiarism or academic integrity. It raises questions about *epistemic labour*: Who is doing the work of thinking, writing and synthesising? When AI takes on that role, even in part, we risk misrepresenting what a student knows or understands. Educational ethics requires that what we assess and what we celebrate reflects the learner's own intellectual effort, not the fluency of a predictive model.

This issue becomes more pronounced when we consider that epistemic labour (the cognitive effort involved in understanding, interpreting and constructing knowledge) is central to the educational enterprise. Learning is not simply the accumulation of accurate information, but the development of reasoning skills, critical judgement and conceptual understanding. When automation is introduced into this process, it does not merely assist the learner; it has the potential to displace the learner's active engagement.

In practice, students who use AI to draft essays or solve assignments may present work that appears coherent and well-structured. Yet, the underlying knowledge work, which is the process of discovery, struggle and revision, is missing. This disparity between product and process results in epistemically shallow submissions. They may be polished, but yet hollow. The ethical concern centres not simply on misrepresentation but on pedagogical loss or the forfeited opportunity for genuine insight and growth.

Furthermore, handing over the core tasks of thinking and reasoning to AI raises the broader issue of intellectual responsibility. If a student relies on AI-generated argumentation or reasoning, who is accountable for logical flaws or factual errors? Traditional moral agency, attributed to the learner, becomes obscured. As automation becomes normalised in assignments, institutions risk valuing performance over understanding, efficiency over depth and appearance over inquiry.

The risks of epistemically shallow work and obscured intellectual responsibility highlight the need for institutions to move beyond prohibition or punitive measures when addressing student use of generative AI.

Simply banning tools or relying on detection systems fails to address the deeper pedagogical concern: that learning is being replaced with performance.

MINI CASE STUDY: IMPLEMENTING THE AI ASSESSMENT SCALE AT BRITISH UNIVERSITY VIETNAM

British University Vietnam (BUV), a school with around 2,500 students, delivers a UK-based curriculum and operates within a transnational academic framework. While the medium of instruction is English, the majority of students are non-native speakers. In early 2023, BUV, like many higher education institutions, encountered a dramatic rise in student use of GenAI tools such as ChatGPT. By July 2023, about 70% of academic integrity issues were linked to GenAI misuse. Existing policy, centred on prohibition and AI-detection tools, proved inadequate and disproportionately punitive, prompting institutional leadership to seek an ethical and pedagogically grounded alternative.

CHALLENGE

The primary challenge BUV faced was maintaining academic integrity while preparing students to ethically and effectively use GenAI tools in their academic and future professional work. Banning AI tools created enforcement challenges, fostered distrust, and failed to recognize the technology's potential to support learning. Additionally, GenAI detection tools produced inconsistent results, particularly disadvantaging students whose writing diverged from normative native-English patterns.

SOLUTION

BUV adopted the AI Assessment Scale (AIAS), a five-level framework (shown in Table 4.2) designed to integrate GenAI use into assessments with clarity, flexibility, and ethical transparency. Approved in September 2023 and rolled out in October, the AIAS provided a structured method for educators to align assessments with GenAI capabilities and for students to understand acceptable usage parameters.

The AIAS rollout was accompanied by policy documentation addressing three pillars: Ethics & Transparency, Security & Privacy, and Limitations & Bias. Faculty received training on AIAS-aligned assessment design, and restrictions on AI levels were implemented selectively to maintain disciplinary rigor and meet external accreditation requirements.

TABLE 4.2 The AIAS Levels

Level	Title	Description
1	No AI	GenAI is entirely prohibited. Used for invigilated exams or tasks assessing unaided performance.
2	AI-Assisted Idea Generation and Structuring	AI supports brainstorming or outlining. Final submission must be AI-free.
3	AI-Assisted Editing	AI may assist with refining student-generated content. Original versions must be submitted for comparison.
4	AI Task Completion, Human Evaluation	AI is used for task elements. Students must critically assess and reflect on AI outputs.
5	Full AI	AI is used throughout the task. No obligation to specify AI-generated content.

IMPLEMENTATION

During the October 2023 semester, the AIAS was formally implemented across all faculties. Academic staff were encouraged to utilize Levels 3–5 to foster critical engagement with GenAI, while Level 1 was restricted to assessments requiring invigilation or externally validated competencies. Students were briefed on the AIAS and provided with guidance on how to use GenAI ethically in line with their assessment level.

RESULTS

The pilot implementation yielded promising outcomes:

- **Academic Integrity**: In April 2023, 2.84% of student submissions (116 cases) were penalized for GenAI-related misconduct. Following the October 2023 implementation, there were no reported cases of GenAI-related academic misconduct. While this may partly reflect revised policy enabling grade adjustments instead of formal penalties, it also signals improved transparency and ethical alignment in GenAI use.
- **Student Performance**: Student grades improved by an average of 5.9% between the September 2022 and September 2023 semesters. Furthermore, the module pass rate increased by 33.3%, suggesting that students, particularly those facing language barriers, were better able to demonstrate learning through AI-supported, multimodal tasks.

- **Pedagogical Shifts**: Faculty reported widespread adoption of GenAI in teaching and assessment. Innovative assessments emerged, particularly at Levels 4 and 5, encouraging student creativity through video, design, and code-based submissions. These shifts enabled students to leverage GenAI for ideation, production, and critique, fostering deeper engagement with learning outcomes.

CONCLUSION

The AI Assessment Scale (AIAS) enabled BUV to shift from a reactive and punitive model of AI governance to a proactive, integrative, and student-centered framework. By embedding GenAI use within pedagogical practice, the AIAS reduced misconduct, improved student performance, and cultivated a culture of ethical AI engagement. The pilot demonstrates how institutions can maintain academic standards while preparing students for AI-infused academic and professional environments. Further research is required to test the AIAS across broader contexts and to adapt it to the evolving capabilities of GenAI technologies.

Source: *"The AI Assessment Scale (AIAS) in Action: A Pilot Implementation of GenAI Supported Assessment"* by (Furze et al., 2024)

Redefining Learning and the Ethics of Process

Previously, we've also noted AI's tendency to favour polished outputs over reflective processes. From an ethical standpoint, this shift challenges the value we place on formative struggle, revision and growth. If the use of AI shortcuts becomes normalised, the learning process itself is flattened, and students may be rewarded for efficiency rather than engagement. Ethics in this context means ensuring that systems do not simply reward what is easiest to measure, but what is most meaningful to learn.

The core of this dilemma lies in what educational philosopher Noddings (2005) calls *the ethic of care* in pedagogy, in which meaningful learning is not merely a transactional outcome but a developmental experience. When GenAI tools intervene at the level of idea formation or revision, they can bypass the discomfort that typically accompanies learning. This includes the stumbles, uncertainties and the slow refinement of thought. While such discomfort is rarely pleasant, it is often essential. It is where understanding is forged, not merely performed (Lee, 2025; Roberts, Hesse and McArdle, 2025).

AI-integrated assessment systems often risk prioritising efficiency and surface-level correctness over the deeper, formative aspects of learning. When learners use AI to simulate mastery, the crucial processes of experimentation, reflection and feedback are diminished. This is not merely a pedagogical shortfall. It also raises ethical concerns by masking the true state of a learner's development and misrepresenting their readiness for future inquiry. As discussed earlier in this book, such distortions are amplified by standardised assessment regimes, which already privilege scalable outputs over authentic engagement. Bearman, Ryan and Ajjawi (2023) highlight this persistent tension between institutional metrics and meaningful assessment practices, a tension that AI, when used uncritically, only intensifies.

To address this, ethics must be embedded in the design of assessments and the norms around AI use. That means prioritising assignments that capture interim thinking in the form of idea mapping, annotations and metacognitive commentary, and rewarding evidence of conceptual evolution over final polish. It also involves transparency where students must be invited into the conversation about what counts as learning, how AI fits into that process and where the line lies between augmentation and avoidance.

Reclaiming the ethics of process requires a shift in focus from what learners can produce to how they arrive at understanding. In this vision, AI is not prohibited but positioned as a partner in inquiry, used to provoke questions, test assumptions and reflect on thought, rather than to conceal or compress it. Such strategies will be presented in Chapter 6: AI and the Top 5.

Educator Deskilling and Professional Responsibility

Finally, we previously raised the issue of educator deskilling where AI begins to displace core professional practices such as feedback, differentiation or planning. Ethically, this matters not only because it may diminish teacher agency, but because it redistributes responsibility in problematic ways. When AI tools give flawed or biased outputs, who is accountable? When human judgement is reduced to oversight rather than authorship, the pedagogical relationship is altered. Ethical educational practice depends on teacher presence, interpretation and care. These are roles that no system can supplant.

BOUNDARIES THAT BUILD TRUST

Technology always arrives with promise. It also arrives with pressure; sometimes subtle, sometimes seismic. In education, the integration of AI tools is no longer a question of *if*, but *how*. And that *how* hinges on the guardrails we build; not just technical, but ethical, pedagogical and institutional.

Let's be clear, guardrails aren't constraints to innovation. They're the structures that keep innovation meaningful. When we talk about introducing AI into teaching and learning, we have to talk about what holds it accountable. Who is responsible when a tool misjudges a student's work? What happens when feedback lacks context, or when data flows where it shouldn't? These aren't peripheral issues. They're central to how trust is built in the learning space.

At the core, ethical guardrails begin with transparency. Students need to know when AI is being used, what it's doing and how decisions about their learning are being made. Hidden algorithms that *nudge* a student or assign grades based on invisible parameters risk eroding not only fairness but the relational fabric of the classroom. In contrast, visible, explainable systems support student agency. They give learners the ability to ask, "Why?" and receive an answer that makes sense.

Privacy guardrails are just as vital. Education systems collect extraordinary amounts of student data, including writing samples, behavioural logs and engagement metrics. When AI enters the picture, that data becomes training material, fuel and the feedback loop. But where does it go? Who sees it? And who profits? Minimising data collection, encrypting storage and refusing third-party monetisation aren't just technical best practices; they're ethical lines in the sand.

Security guardrails protect more than servers. They protect students' intellectual and emotional safety. Before we roll out the next chatbot or adaptive feedback system, we need to ask hard questions. *Has the tool been audited for bias? Is it resilient against misuse? Does it reinforce stereotypes in subtle ways?* Schools can't afford to outsource these questions to vendors alone. Educators must be involved in the vetting process, not just as users but as informed stewards of learning.

And then there's the classroom itself. Pedagogical guardrails ensure AI remains a *support*, not a substitute. A feedback tool might suggest clearer phrasing or better structure, but it can't understand the nuance of a student's struggle or the context behind a missed concept. Only a teacher can do that. AI can help us scale feedback, track progress and even flag misconceptions. But it shouldn't close the loop. Students still need conversations. They need the messy, human part of learning. The part that doesn't fit neatly into a prompt or output field.

The role of the educator, then, doesn't shrink with AI. It sharpens. Guardrails remind us that education is a human endeavour, even in a digital age. When designed with intention, they don't block innovation. They make space for it to be ethical, equitable and ultimately transformative.

Ethical Guardrails

The use of AI in education carries opportunities and risks. Establishing clear ethical guardrails ensures that the benefits of AI do not come at the expense of student autonomy, privacy or equity. Four core practices can guide responsible use:

Transparency Notices

Students should never be left uncertain about whether an AI system is shaping their learning experience. Transparency involves not only disclosing the presence of AI but also clarifying what it does, what data it uses and how its outputs are applied. This can be implemented through syllabus statements, short notices within digital platforms or project guidelines. For example, a syllabus might include: "*This course uses AI-based plagiarism detection software. The system analyses writing style and compares submissions with external databases. It does not retain your full papers beyond the semester.*" Transparency builds trust and prepares students to critically engage with AI rather than passively accept its authority.

Consent Mechanisms

Whenever AI tools handle sensitive data or contribute to assessments, students should have meaningful choices about participation. An opt-in model might be used for formative writing assistants that provide grammar and style feedback, allowing students to decide whether they wish to receive algorithmic guidance. Conversely, for required institutional systems (e.g., anti-plagiarism checks), an opt-out option might not be feasible, but alternative submission processes should be provided for students with ethical concerns. The key principle is respecting student agency by making participation visible and, where possible, voluntary.

Bias Auditing

AI systems, particularly large language models, can reproduce or amplify social biases. Regular audits are therefore essential. An instructor might periodically test an AI feedback system with identical assignments submitted under different student identities (e.g., names coded as male/female, or linked to different cultural backgrounds) to identify discrepancies in grading or feedback. Auditing should not be a solitary activity: involving diverse stakeholders such as equity officers, teaching assistants and students themselves broadens the range of perspectives on potential harms. Where biases are detected, educators should document findings and either adjust how the tool is used or escalate concerns to institutional leaders.

Ethics Checkpoints

Before deploying new AI tools, educators should conduct a structured ethical impact assessment. This need not be lengthy; a one-page checklist can surface critical issues. Example prompts include:

- *Who is the intended beneficiary of this tool (e.g., students, instructors, administration)?*
- *Who might experience harm (e.g., students from marginalised groups, those without reliable internet access)?*
- *What values are advanced or compromised (e.g., efficiency vs. academic integrity, personalisation vs. fairness)?*
- *What safeguards can mitigate risks (e.g., anonymising data, supplementing AI feedback with human review)?*

By institutionalising these checkpoints, schools and universities foster a culture of ethical reflexivity where technological adoption is never divorced from its human consequences.

REFLECTION POINT: ANTICIPATING THE ETHICAL RISKS OF INTRODUCING AI TOOLS INTO YOUR CLASS

This checklist will assist you in anticipating ethical risks and safeguarding student rights when introducing AI tools into teaching and learning.

1. Transparency and Disclosure
   - Have I clearly communicated to students that this AI tool is being used?
   - Have I explained what data it uses, how outputs are generated and where results will appear?
   - Is there a written notice (syllabus statement, platform message or project brief) documenting this?
2. Consent and Agency
   - Do students have a meaningful choice to opt in or out of the tool's use?
   - If opting out is not possible (e.g., plagiarism detection), have I provided an alternative pathway?
   - Does the tool respect student autonomy and avoid coercive use?
3. Bias and Equity
   - Have I tested or reviewed the tool for biased outputs (e.g., gender, cultural, linguistic)?
   - Are diverse stakeholders (students, colleagues, equity officers) involved in periodic audits?
   - Could any group of students be disproportionately disadvantaged by this tool?
4. Privacy and Data Protection
   - What data does the tool collect (student writing, voice, demographics)?
   - Where is this data stored, and who has access?
   - Does the tool comply with institutional policies and relevant privacy regulations (e.g., GDPR, FERPA)?
5. Values and Potential Harm
   - Who primarily benefits from this tool (students, instructors, administrators)?
   - Who could be harmed, and how?
   - What academic values (e.g., integrity, fairness, inclusivity) might be at stake?
   - What safeguards or contingency plans will I put in place if harms emerge?
6. Decision Point
   - Based on this assessment, do the benefits outweigh the risks?
   - If yes: What ongoing monitoring will I implement (e.g., semesterly bias audits, student feedback)?
   - If no: What ethical concerns prevent adoption at this time?

Pedagogical Guardrails

AI tools should never displace the professional judgement of educators or the active engagement of students. Their role is to enhance teaching and learning, not automate it. Pedagogical guardrails ensure that AI is used in ways that respect human oversight, promote critical thinking and align with authentic learning.

Human-in-the-Loop Feedback

AI can generate formative comments on student work at scale, but without human review, such feedback risks being inaccurate, insensitive or pedagogically shallow. Educators should position themselves as moderators who filter, contextualise and refine AI outputs. For instance, when an AI provides suggestions on a draft essay, the instructor might validate useful points, flag misleading ones and add personalised insights that the AI cannot capture (e.g., a student's progress over time). This human-in-the-loop approach ensures that students receive feedback that is both efficient and empathetic.

REFLECTION PROMPTS

AI feedback becomes more valuable when students are encouraged to engage critically with it rather than treating it as authoritative. Pairing AI use with reflection tasks reinforces metacognitive skills. A simple scaffold might include three prompts:

1. *Which AI suggestions do you find most helpful, and why?*
2. *Which do you disagree with, and what is your reasoning?*
3. *What specific revision will you make in response to this feedback?*

For example, in a creative writing course, after AI suggests sentence-level grammar corrections, students might reflect on whether those corrections alter their intended style or tone. Such structured reflection trains learners to evaluate feedback critically instead of outsourcing judgement.

Override Mechanisms

AI tools should never dictate final academic decisions. Educators must retain control over grading, curriculum design and learning outcomes. This ensures that AI augments professional judgement rather than undermining it. For example, in an AI-assisted grading system, the instructor might review a sample of student submissions where the AI flagged plagiarism or unusual phrasing, and then decide whether those concerns are valid. This safeguard prevents overreliance on automated judgements.

Pedagogical Fit Tests

The adoption of an AI tool should be guided by instructional purpose, not novelty. Educators should explicitly map each AI application to targeted learning outcomes. A useful exercise is to complete a "fit test" by asking:

- *Which learning goal does this AI tool directly support (e.g., improving argumentation, enhancing peer feedback, fostering coding fluency)?*
- *What pedagogical role does it play (e.g., tutor, feedback provider, resource recommender)?*
- *Does this tool risk narrowing the learning experience (e.g., focusing only on grammar while ignoring higher-order reasoning)?*

For example, if the learning outcome is "*students will construct evidence-based arguments*," then an AI tool that merely highlights sentence clarity would have limited fit. By contrast, a tool that prompts students to evaluate the strength of evidence in their drafts could directly reinforce the targeted skill.

When systematically applied, these guardrails help educators resist pressures to adopt AI indiscriminately, ensuring that every tool aligns with intentional teaching practice.

REFLECTION POINT: DOES AI ALIGN WITH YOUR LEARNING AND TEACHING OBJECTIVES

This checklist will help you determine whether an AI tool aligns with course objectives, respects learner needs and supports sound pedagogical practice.

1. Alignment with Learning Outcomes
    - Which specific learning outcome(s) does this tool support?
    - Does the tool reinforce higher-order skills (e.g., analysis, evaluation, creativity), or only lower-order skills (e.g., grammar correction, fact recall)?

- Can I justify its inclusion in terms of instructional value, not novelty?

Example: If the learning outcome is *"students will construct evidence-based arguments,"* does the tool provide prompts or feedback that help students evaluate evidence quality?

2. Role in Pedagogical Design
    - What role does the tool serve? (Tutor, coach, feedback provider, recommender, simulator, etc.)
    - Does the tool complement, rather than replace, my instructional responsibilities?
    - How will students' critical engagement be maintained (e.g., through reflection prompts, peer discussion or instructor moderation)?
3. Risks and Safeguards
    - Could the tool unintentionally narrow the scope of learning (e.g., focus only on surface-level correctness)?
    - What mechanisms exist for me to override or correct AI outputs?
    - How will I monitor and address errors, biases or misalignments with course goals?
4. Student Experience
    - Does the tool enhance student autonomy, or risk overreliance?
    - Will students understand its role and limitations (through transparency notices)?
    - How will I ensure accessibility for all students (e.g., those with limited internet, language differences or disabilities)?
5. Decision Point
    - Based on this analysis, will I adopt the tool?
    - If yes: What instructional scaffolds (e.g., human-in-the-loop feedback, reflection prompts) will I add to ensure effective use?
    - If no: Why does the tool not fit my pedagogical context at this time?

Technical Guardrails

Ethical and pedagogical safeguards rely on a strong technical foundation. Without robust data protections and accountability structures, even well-intentioned use of AI can expose students and institutions to unnecessary risks. The following technical guardrails provide educators with a framework for safe and responsible deployment.

Data Minimisation

AI tools should operate on the smallest possible dataset necessary for the learning task at hand. Educators should avoid uploading entire student profiles, personal identifiers or unrelated records unless there is a clear instructional justification and institutional approval. For example, if an AI writing assistant is used to provide feedback on a single essay, only the essay text, and not demographic data, grades or prior submissions, should be uploaded. Where possible, anonymisation techniques (removing names, IDs or sensitive context) should be applied to protect student privacy.

Secure Access and Encryption

Tools must comply with national and international data protection standards such as the General Data Protection Regulation (GDPR) in the EU or the Family Educational Rights and Privacy Act (FERPA) in the United States. At minimum, secure logins (multi-factor authentication) and encrypted storage should be required. For example, a classroom using a cloud-based AI tutor should ensure that student submissions are stored only on encrypted servers located within approved jurisdictions, with role-based access limiting who can view or modify the data. Educators should verify that vendors provide clear compliance documentation before adopting a tool.

DID YOU KNOW?

Privacy and protection information can be found on the websites of reputable tools. For example, these policies for Microsoft's Copilot can be found here https://learn.microsoft.com/en-us/copilot/privacy-and-protections and OpenAI's here https://openai.com/security-and-privacy/.

However, despite the apparent transparency of these companies' privacy and security policies, there are many who remain suspicious. For example, in a University of Sydney opinion piece, Professor Uri Gal warns that ChatGPT poses significant privacy risks (Gal, 2023). It's built on roughly 300 billion words scraped from the internet, much of it personal and used without consent, raising concerns about contextual integrity, lack of individual control over data and GDPR compliance. OpenAI offers no means for individuals to check or delete their data, and the model may reproduce copyrighted or sensitive content without compensation or permission.

Audit Trails

Accountability requires traceable records of how AI systems are used. Audit trails should capture which tools were used, when, for what purpose and what outputs were generated. This is especially critical in contexts where AI contributes to assessment. For instance, if an AI system flags a student submission for possible plagiarism, a time-stamped record of the output and the instructor's decision should be stored. Such trails protect both students and educators by providing evidence for appeal processes or academic integrity reviews. Institutions might consider centralised dashboards where instructors can review AI activity logs.

Model Versioning and Traceability

AI models evolve rapidly, and updates can subtly alter their outputs. Educators need to know which version of a model is in use and when it was last updated to make sense of changes in behaviour. For example, if a grading assistant suddenly begins giving systematically harsher feedback, the instructor should be able to check whether the vendor updated the model mid-semester. Transparent versioning information, similar to software release notes, helps educators trace inconsistencies, document issues and communicate clearly with students. Where possible, educators should archive example outputs from each version for comparison over time.

Together, these guardrails position educators not merely as users of AI, but as responsible stewards of data security and system accountability.

Institutional Guardrails

The responsibility for ethical and pedagogical AI use cannot rest solely on individual educators. Institutions must create structures that guide adoption, ensure accountability and empower all stakeholders. Institutional guardrails distribute responsibility across the community, making AI governance a shared and sustainable practice.

AI Literacy Training

Educators require more than surface-level familiarity with AI; they need critical literacy. Mandatory training programs should address not only how AI tools function but also their limitations, risks and ethical implications. For example, a training module might include:

- A primer on how large language models are trained and where biases originate.
- Case studies of AI misuse in education (e.g., overreliance on automated grading).
- Hands-on activities where teachers critique AI-generated feedback on student work.

Such training ensures educators can evaluate claims made by vendors, contextualise AI outputs and communicate transparently with students.

Review Committees

No single role has sufficient expertise to evaluate AI tools. Cross-functional review committees should include teachers, IT staff, ethics advisors, administrators and students. Their task is to vet AI applications before deployment, considering technical security, pedagogical fit and ethical implications. For instance, a committee reviewing an AI proctoring system might weigh efficiency benefits against risks to student privacy and test anxiety. Importantly, committees should establish documentation practices so that decision rationales are transparent and revisitable.

Policy Frameworks

Institutions need clear, enforceable policies that define acceptable AI use and outline escalation procedures when problems arise. Such policies might address:

- Privacy expectations: What data can and cannot be collected from students.
- Prohibited uses: For example, banning AI from making final grading decisions.
- Accountability processes: Steps for students or staff to report misuse or malfunction.

For example, a school district might publish a policy stating: "*AI-assisted grading tools may be used for formative feedback but cannot determine final grades. All AI tools must comply with FERPA standards, and concerns should be reported to the Academic Integrity Office.*" Written frameworks provide consistency across classrooms and prevent ad hoc or uneven adoption.

Student Co-Creation

Students are not passive recipients of AI systems as they directly experience the benefits and harms. Involving them in the design, testing and review of tools helps institutions identify blind spots that adults may miss. For example, during pilot testing of an AI writing coach, students might report that feedback often ignores cultural variations in expression or favours a particular writing style. Co-creation could take the form of student advisory panels, feedback surveys or participatory design workshops. This practice not only improves tool selection but also fosters digital agency and trust.

Institutional guardrails transform AI adoption from isolated experimentation into a coordinated practice grounded in transparency, inclusivity and accountability.

MINI CASE STUDY: TEACHER OVERRELIANCE ON AI GRADING

CONTEXT

In a recent experimental study, teachers were asked to review student work that had been incorrectly scored "5/10." Some were told the score came from an AI system, while others were told it came from a human grader.

CHALLENGE

When informed that the grade was AI-generated, teachers were significantly less likely to challenge the error. Instead of exercising their professional judgment, many deferred to the AI's authority.

OUTCOME

Teachers corrected the flawed score **22% less often** when it was labeled as AI-generated compared to human-generated. This created a measurable fairness gap, especially disadvantaging students subjected to overly harsh AI assessments.

LESSONS LEARNED

- Educators may subconsciously over-trust AI systems, even when outputs are objectively wrong.

- AI grading tools should never operate without clear **human-in-the-loop review**.
- Institutional policies should emphasize that AI is advisory only, never determinative of student outcomes.

Source: Bankwest Curtin Economics Centre, 2023, "Flawed Oversight: Teachers Don't Catch AI's Grading Mistakes When AI is Harsh"

UNRESOLVED ISSUES AND EMERGING RISKS

While ethical, pedagogical, technical and institutional guardrails provide a framework for responsible use of AI in education, they do not eliminate the deeper tensions that accompany its adoption. Beyond questions of policy and implementation lie broader systemic, relational and epistemic challenges that shape how AI redefines what it means to teach and to learn. These issues, which range from bias and data sovereignty to the erosion of trust, the normalisation of surveillance and the shifting definition of knowledge itself, cannot be solved through technical fixes alone. Instead, they demand sustained critical reflection, collaborative oversight and a willingness to confront the ways in which AI both amplifies and disrupts existing inequities in education.

Systemic Issues

While individual educators can adopt ethical and pedagogical guardrails, many of the challenges posed by AI operate at a systemic level, beyond classroom control. These issues highlight the need for collective action, regulatory oversight and institutional vigilance.

Algorithmic Bias and Discrimination

Bias is not only a technical flaw but also a universal hazard. When AI grading or feedback tools replicate gendered, racial or linguistic stereotypes, the harm is distributed across entire groups of students rather than isolated individuals. The Fobizz case in Germany, where nonsensical texts were rewarded more highly than student essays, illustrates how unchecked algorithms can systematically privilege form over substance, undermining both fairness and credibility (Mühlhoff and Henningsen, 2024). Similarly, large-scale investigations have shown that AI grading systems can return widely divergent scores for identical work, further destabilising trust (Mok et al. 2024).

Data Sovereignty and Ownership

AI tools often require vast quantities of student data, much of which is stored on third-party servers located outside national jurisdictions. This raises urgent questions about sovereignty: who owns the intellectual and behavioural data generated in learning? In contexts where servers are hosted abroad, schools may have limited recourse if data is breached or exploited. As Gal (2023) argues, individuals currently lack the ability to see, delete or control their data in large-scale generative models, rendering ownership ambiguous and privacy precarious.

Commercial Exploitation

AI in education is increasingly delivered through private companies whose business models are driven by data monetisation. Students' writing, queries and even behavioural traces risk becoming resources for commercial training pipelines or targeted advertising (Williamson and Hogan, 2020). This introduces a conflict between the public mission of education and the private motives of profit. Without systemic guardrails, schools risk becoming data suppliers rather than protectors of student welfare.

Lack of Regulatory Oversight

Finally, education often lags behind formal regulatory frameworks. While laws such as GDPR and FERPA offer some protections, they were not designed for large-scale GenAI. The result is a governance vacuum in which powerful technologies enter classrooms with limited accountability. Without broader legal and institutional frameworks, the risks of harm (bias, exploitation, opacity) fall disproportionately on students and teachers (Selwyn, 2022).

Relational Issues

Beyond systemic concerns, AI reshapes the relational fabric of education: how students relate to teachers, to one another and to the learning process itself.

Erosion of Trust and Human Connection

When students suspect that feedback is machine-generated, they may perceive it as generic or impersonal, weakening the trust that underpins learning relationships. Recent research confirms that students are more likely to value and act upon feedback when they know it has been shaped by a human teacher, even if AI contributed to its production (Zhang et al., 2025). Trust is not a byproduct of efficiency. It emerges from care, presence and dialogue.

Informed Consent and Student Autonomy

Many students and even some educators remain unaware of what AI tools actually do with their data, or how outputs are produced. Informed consent requires more than a checkbox; it demands genuine understanding of risks and rights. Without this, student autonomy is compromised, and classrooms risk slipping into what legal scholars call "forced participation" in opaque systems (Chaudhry, Cukurova and Luckin, 2022).

Surveillance Culture

Proctoring software and learning analytics dashboards exemplify how AI can normalise surveillance. While intended to ensure integrity, these tools often create climates of suspicion. Students describe feeling criminalised, monitored not as learners but as potential violators (Feathers and Rose, 2021). The risk is that surveillance becomes normalised, shifting classrooms away from curiosity and towards compliance.

Digital Inequity

Finally, the uneven distribution of AI tools exacerbates existing inequalities. Well-resourced schools may deploy secure, pedagogically aligned systems, while under-resourced institutions are left with free or unvetted tools that compromise privacy or accuracy. The result is a widening digital divide where access to ethical, high-quality AI support becomes a privilege rather than a right (Williamson and Hogan, 2020).

Epistemic and Pedagogical Issues

Fundamentally, education is not just about transmitting information but cultivating the processes of knowing, reasoning and reflecting. AI challenges this epistemic foundation in profound ways.

Opacity of AI Decision-Making

When AI systems act as black boxes, students and teachers alike are denied insight into how judgements are formed. This undermines the principle of transparency that is central to education. Without the ability to question, critique or understand feedback, learners are asked to trust what they cannot interrogate, which is a direct contradiction of critical pedagogy (Chaudhry, Cukurova and Luckin, 2022).

Shifting Definitions of Knowledge and Learning

GenAI raises the unsettling question: what counts as knowledge? If a polished essay can be produced with minimal cognitive effort, is the output equivalent to learning? As previously discussed, educational institutions already struggle with metrics that privilege efficiency over reflection. AI risks accelerating this shift, normalising outputs that conceal rather than reveal the process of intellectual growth.

Misalignment with Pedagogical Intentions

AI systems are typically optimised for efficiency, correctness or pattern recognition. Yet, meaningful learning often involves struggle, failure and revision. These qualities are ones which AI tends to obscure or shortcut. This creates a misalignment between what technology values and what education values. Left unchecked, AI could reshape pedagogy to prioritise what machines measure easily rather than what learners need most (Noddings, 2005; Lee et al., 2025).

Overreliance and Deskilling

Just as students risk losing critical thinking skills through overdependence on AI, educators risk professional deskilling. If grading, feedback or planning is continually outsourced, teachers may become overseers of automation rather than active shapers of learning. This is not merely a loss of professional identity; it represents a redistribution of epistemic responsibility that weakens the human dimension of education (Selwyn, 2022).

WHO HAS LEARNED WHAT?

The incorporation of AI in education brings about questions that extend far beyond technical performance. At the systemic level, issues of bias, ownership and governance demand sector-wide oversight. At the relational level, AI challenges trust, autonomy and equity within the classroom. At the epistemic level, it forces us to confront what learning is and how it should be assessed.

Across these domains, one principle stands out: guardrails are not constraints on innovation but conditions for meaningful innovation. Ethical, pedagogical, technical and institutional guardrails ensure that AI enhances rather than erodes the values of education, including equity, care, transparency and intellectual integrity.

The unresolved questions remain pressing:

- What obligations do educators have when AI intervenes in formative feedback?
- When does efficiency compromise epistemic integrity?
- How should consent and transparency be safeguarded in opaque algorithmic environments?
- Who is accountable when AI decisions influence outcomes that matter?

These questions have not yet been answered for three interrelated reasons. First, AI technologies themselves are evolving too rapidly for stable frameworks to keep pace; what is ethical today may be inadequate tomorrow. Second, educational contexts differ widely across institutions, disciplines and cultures, meaning no single policy or guardrail can apply universally. Third, the values of equity, autonomy and trust which are at stake are not purely technical matters but contested ethical commitments, subject to debate and reinterpretation. In this sense, the questions cannot be definitively answered, but must be continually revisited as part of an ongoing ethical conversation within education.

In the chapters that follow, we turn from these dilemmas towards possibility and reimagine pedagogy itself in AI-mediated classrooms. The task is not to settle every question in advance, but to cultivate a culture of inquiry where teachers, students and institutions are equipped to navigate the uncertainties of a shifting technological landscape.

REFLECT AND REFRAME

1. Have I communicated clearly to my students when and how AI tools are used in my teaching?
2. How can I increase students' understanding of the rights they have in AI-mediated learning environments?
3. Have I reviewed the privacy policies of the tools I use, and are they compliant with local data protection laws?
4. In my current practice, where do I see a tension between efficiency and educational integrity?
5. What would ethical AI governance look like at my institution, and who should be involved in shaping it?

REFERENCES

Ambrose, S. A., 2010. *How learning works: Seven research-based principles for smart teaching.* Jossey-Bass.

Bearman, M., Ryan, J., and Ajjawi, R., 2023. Discourses of artificial intelligence in higher education: A critical literature review. *Higher Education*, 86(2), 369–385. https://doi.org/10.1007/s10734-022-00937-2

Chaudhry, M. A., Cukurova, M., and Luckin, R., 2022. A transparency index framework for AI in education. *arXiv*. https://doi.org/10.48550/arXiv.2206.03220

Dietvorst, B. J., Simmons, J. P., and Massey, C., 2015. Algorithm aversion: People erroneously avoid algorithms after seeing them err. *Journal of Experimental Psychology: General*, 144(1), 114–126. https://doi.org/10.1037/xge0000033

Feathers, T., and Rose, J., 2021. Students are rebelling against eye-tracking exam surveillance tools. *VICE*. https://www.vice.com/en/article/students-are-rebelling-against-eye-tracking-exam-surveillance-tools/

Furze, L., Perkins, M., Roe, J., and MacVaugh, J., 2024. The AI Assessment Scale (AIAS) in action: A pilot implementation of GenAI-supported assessment. *Australasian Journal of Educational Technology, [online]* 40(4), 38–55. https://doi.org/10.14742/ajet.9434

Gal, U., 2023. ChatGPT is a data privacy nightmare. *University of Sydney News & Opinion*, 8 February. https://www.sydney.edu.au/news-opinion/news/2023/02/08/chatgpt-is-a-data-privacy-nightmare.html

Huynh, M., 2024. How generative AI can make personalised feedback at scale more consistent and efficient. *Teaching@Sydney*. https://edu.ational-innovation.sydney.edu.au/teaching@sydney/how-generative-ai-can-make-personalised-feedback-at-scale-more-consistent-and-efficient/

Lee, H. -P. H., Sarkar, A., Tankelevitch, L., Drosos, I., Rintel, S., Banks, R. and Wilson, N., 2025. The impact of generative AI on critical thinking: Self-reported reductions in cognitive effort and confidence effects from a survey of knowledge workers. *Microsoft Research*. https://www.microsoft.com/en-us/research/publication/the-impact-of-generative-ai-on-critical-thinking-self-reported-reductions-in-cognitive-effort-and-confidence-effects-from-a-survey-of-knowledge-workers/

Lee, J., 2025. UCLA grad brazenly shows off ChatGPT that did his assignments for him — and critics aren't happy: 'We're so cooked'. *New York Post*, 26 June. https://nypost.com/2025/06/26/tech/ucla-grad-brazenly-shows-off-chatgpt-that-did-his-assignments-for-him-and-critics-arent-happy-were-so-cooked/

Mok, R., Akhtar, F., Clare, L., Li, C., Ida, J., Ross, L., and Campanelli, M., 2024. Using AI large language models for grading in education: A hands-on test for physics. *arXiv preprint arXiv:2411.13685.*

Mühlhoff, R., and Henningsen, M., 2024. Chatbots im schulunterricht: Wir testen das fobizz-tool zur automatischen bewertung von hausaufgaben. arXiv preprint arXiv:2412.06651.

Noddings, N., 2005. *The challenge to care in schools: An alternative approach to education*. 2nd ed. Teachers College Press.

Roberts, M., Hesse, M., and McArdle, M., 2025. How AI is depriving students of basic human skills. *The Washington Post*, 19 May. https://www.washingtonpost.com/opinions/2025/05/19/impromtpu-podcast-ai-education-citizenship/

Selwyn, N., 2022. Education and technology: Key issues and debates. *ResearchGate* [Preprint]. https://www.researchgate.net/publication/364165885_Neil_Selwyn_Education_and_technology_Key_issues_and_debates

Perelman, L., 2014. When "the state of the art" is counting words. *Assessing Writing*, 21, 104–111.

Williamson, B., and Hogan, A., 2020. Commercialisation and privatisation in/of education in the context of Covid-19. *Education International Report*. https://www.researchgate.net/publication/343510376_Commercialisation_and_privatisation_inof_education_in_the_context_of_Covid-19

Zhang, A., Gao, Y., Suraworachet, W., Nazaretsky, T., and Cukurova, M., 2025. Evaluating Trzust in AI, human, and co-produced feedback among undergraduate students. *arXiv preprint arXiv:2504.10961*.

CHAPTER 5

Process over Product

When assessment focuses primarily on the end product, be it a report, a solution or an essay, without regard to the cognitive journey that produced it, GenAI can act as a shortcut that bypasses understanding entirely.

CHAPTER AIMS

The aim of this chapter is to introduce key themes explored in this book in relation to:

1. *the pedagogical implications of generative AI for assessment design,*
2. *the shift from product-focused to process-oriented evaluation in higher education and*
3. *frameworks that support transparent, secure and authentic demonstration of student learning.*

BEYOND THE FINAL ANSWER

In cultivating deep learning, educators have long turned to constructive alignment, ensuring that learning outcomes, teaching strategies and assessment tasks work in concert to support conceptual understanding (Biggs, Tang and Kennedy, 2022). When designed well, assessment does more than measure learning; it shapes it. It directs attention, rewards

DOI: 10.1201/9781003624981-5

effort and signals what matters most in a learning environment. Yet, in an age of GenAI, the fidelity of this alignment is under pressure.

Historically, assessment in education emphasised *process* through oral examinations, iterative projects and dialogic feedback that foregrounded how learners developed understanding over time. However, with the rise of mass education and the need for scalable, comparable metrics, assessment practices shifted decisively towards *product*. Final examinations, graded essays and summative outputs became dominant, largely because they were administratively efficient and easy to quantify. Yet, this evolution brought its own problems. Even in 2002, Knight was already diagnosing summative assessment in higher education as a system in "disarray," arguing that grades had become detached from meaningful indicators of student learning. He noted that what was being assessed was often not what was most educationally valuable. In effect, assessment became a proxy for learning, not a reflection of it (Knight, 2002). The arrival of GenAI has made this misalignment more visible (and more urgent) by enabling the production of convincing outputs without the underlying cognitive engagement that authentic learning requires.

AI tools such as ChatGPT and Copilot offer students unprecedented access to polished, plausible answers often indistinguishable from those written by humans. While this can support learning under the right conditions, it also risks hollowing out the very processes that deep learning depends on: sustained engagement, productive struggle and the incremental building of structured knowledge. When assessment focuses primarily on the end product, be it a report, a solution or an essay, without regard to the cognitive journey that produced it, GenAI can act as a shortcut that bypasses understanding entirely.

This shift is not merely a matter of academic dishonesty or tool misuse. It reveals a deeper vulnerability in how we assess learning. If a student can meet task requirements without genuinely engaging with the task, the assessment fails as a pedagogical instrument. It becomes performative rather than diagnostic. Worse still, it may reinforce surface learning by rewarding outputs that conceal rather than reveal thinking.

Traditional assessments, particularly summative tasks such as essays, take-home exams and coding assignments, are now susceptible to automation. GenAI systems can generate plausible responses with minimal human input, making it increasingly difficult to determine whether a student has personally developed an idea or merely curated it from a prompt.

DID YOU KNOW?

In October of 2025, the University of Cape Town (UCT) will discontinue the use of AI detection tools, such as Turnitin's AI Score, due to concerns about their reliability and the risk of unfair academic outcomes. The university will instead implement an AI in Education Framework that supports AI-resilient assessment practices and promotes ethical AI literacy among both staff and students. (Walji, 2025)

Assessment, then, is less about *catching* AI and more about designing for trustworthy evidence of learning. Regulators and quality agencies now emphasise redesign over detection: shift assessment modes, normalise disclosure and assure learning through robust, secure checkpoints rather than forensic text analysis alone (QAA, 2023; TEQSA, 2024, 2025).

Take, for example, an undergraduate art class. Previously, students might have been assessed through a 1,500-word written artist statement explaining the conceptual development of their final piece, with the text run through AI-detection software to flag possible generative content. Under a redesigned approach, students instead present their artwork alongside a short oral presentation detailing their creative process, material choices and conceptual evolution. They also submit a reflective log that includes any use of AI tools, which is then discussed during an in-class critique session. This method aligns with the policies suggested by QAA (2023) and TEQSA (2024, 2025).

For educators, the challenge is not to reject GenAI, but to reimagine assessment in its presence. What needs to be evaluated is not only what students produce, but how they got there, including their strategies, decisions, revisions and reflections. Assessing process over product demands a shift in both mindset and method. It calls for transparency, traceability and a renewed focus on formative moments within the learning arc.

This chapter explores how assessment can be reframed to maintain integrity, foster deep learning and meaningfully engage with the realities of AI-assisted education.

LEVELS, LANES AND TRAFFIC LIGHTS

Across institutions, a pragmatic vocabulary has emerged that allows course teams to label each task's permitted AI use and its security requirements. Before we can meaningfully explore how AI might be integrated into the process of learning itself, we first need to examine the acceptable levels of its involvement. Establishing clear boundaries and shared language around when, how and to what extent AI may be used ensures that both educators and students engage with these tools transparently and responsibly. These frameworks provide a foundation for trust, clarity and alignment before any deeper pedagogical integration can take place.

Explicit Permission Levels

Explicit permission levels establish a shared vocabulary for signalling exactly how, and to what extent, students may use GenAI in a given task. Rather than relying on ad-hoc statements, each assessment is tagged with a clearly defined category that sets boundaries (what is and is not permitted), spells out the required process evidence (e.g., drafts, prompt logs, version history) and specifies accountability for accuracy and attribution. This approach reduces ambiguity for students and markers, aligns expectations across a program and shifts practice from post-hoc detection to transparent, declared use (see Table 5.1).

As summarised in Table 5.1, UCSF's School of Pharmacy adopts a clear AI-permission scale from AI-1 (Disallowed) to AI-4 (Unregulated). Crucially, the middle settings of AI-2 (Restricted) and AI-3 (Documented) make disclosure and verification part of the assessed work. Here, students are required to provide prompt histories, drafts and brief attestations, integrating process evidence into the brief rather than treating it as an afterthought (UCSF School of Pharmacy, 2023).

A Ladder of Assistance

A ladder of assistance articulates, in plain terms, the *type and degree* of AI support permitted at each stage of a task. Instead of a binary "allowed/not allowed," it offers calibrated rungs from no assistance, to light-touch editing, to planning and design support, through to fully AI-integrated work, each tied to clear expectations for attribution, verification and process evidence (drafts, prompt logs, version history). The point is pedagogical as much as regulatory: to scaffold responsible use, align the permitted assistance with the learning outcomes and make expectations transparent for both students and markers (see Table 5.1).

As summarised in Table 5.1, UNSW operationalises this through a student-facing Levels of AI Assistance framework that ranges from *No assistance* and *Simple editing* to *Planning/design*, *Assistance with*

TABLE 5.1 Permission Levels (task-by-task AI use) This table outlines explicit AI-permission levels used to define what kinds of GenAI assistance are acceptable per task, along with required artefacts and examples of application

Level Label (Example)	What Students May Use AI for	What Remains Strictly Human	Evidence/Artefacts Required	Typical Use Cases	Notes/Exemplar Policies
AI-0: None	No AI use permitted	All idea generation, drafting, coding, analysis and citations	Invigilation or viva; draft checks may be requested	High-stakes assurance (capstones, licensure-adjacent tasks)	Maps to "Disallowed" (UCSF); "No assistance" (UNSW)
AI-1: Restricted	Limited sub-tasks (e.g., brainstorming, grammar tidy, pseudocode) explicitly named on brief	Core reasoning, structure, argument, code design	Short prompt summary; annotated draft showing human changes	Early coursework; scaffolding tasks	Matches "Restricted" (UCSF) and "Simple editing" (UNSW)
AI-2: Documented	Any AI may be consulted, but student curates, verifies and rewrites	Final accountability for accuracy, originality and citations	Prompt log/ summary; version history; data/ citation trail	Projects, labs, design reports	"Documented" (UCSF); "Planning/design" or "Assistance with attribution" (UNSW)
AI-3: Open	AI is integral to the task (e.g., prompt engineering, model comparison)	Reflection on methodology and limits	Methods note explaining how AI shaped the work; reproducible steps	AI-literacy outcomes; studio or portfolio tasks	"Unregulated/with disclosure" (UCSF) or "Gen-AI software-based assessment" (UNSW)

attribution and *GenAI software-based assessment*. Crucially, the intermediate rungs specify when students must retain drafts and how they should acknowledge AI input, thereby folding disclosure and verification into normal assessment practice rather than treating them as afterthoughts (UNSW, n.d.).

Traffic-Light Models

Traffic-light models provide a fast, highly legible shorthand for signalling AI expectations on briefs and rubrics. Using a Red–Amber–Green (RAG) palette, instructors can indicate at a glance what kinds of AI support are permitted, under what conditions and which artefacts must evidence the student's own contribution. In practice, Red denotes no AI use; Amber allows tightly specified uses with documentation; and Green encourages broader use paired with reflection and verification. This colour grammar reduces ambiguity, supports moderation and aligns security expectations across subjects and programs (see Table 5.2).

As summarised in Table 5.2, several universities now use this RAG shorthand. Warwick (IATL) adopts Red for prohibition, Amber for limited, named uses with documentation, and Green for full use accompanied by a record of how AI was employed (University of Warwick, 2024).

TABLE 5.2 Traffic-light Categories (Fast Labels for Briefs) This Table Introduces a Red–Amber–Green (RAG) System for Quickly Signalling AI Use Policies within Assignment Briefs, Including Conditions and Expectations for Each Colour Category

Category	What's Allowed	What to Submit	Good for	Watch-outs
Red	No AI use	Nothing AI-related; may require in-room or viva	Licensing-adjacent knowledge; threshold concepts	Overuse can under-prepare students for AI-pervasive practice
Amber	Specified AI uses only (listed on brief)	Prompt summary/log; annotated draft indicating human vs AI	Mixed-mode tasks; staged learning	Be explicit: which stages? What tools? How verified?
Green	Broad AI use encouraged with critical reflection	Methods note; full prompt log; reproducible workflow	AI literacy; design and research projects	Require verification and reflection to avoid superficial outsourcing

The University of Leeds applies an institution-wide traffic-light scheme with parallel guidance for staff and students on categorisation and acknowledgement (University of Leeds, 2025). Macquarie University provides a concise, one-page GenAI Traffic Light Guide that course teams can attach to task sheets, clarifying permitted tools, required disclosures and verification expectations (Macquarie University, 2024). Across these models, the emphasis is not merely on permission but on evidence, including prompt summaries or logs, annotated drafts and/or reflective method notes, so that declared AI use is transparent and accessible rather than an afterthought.

These schemes do two things well: (1) they normalise disclosure and process evidence; and (2) they give staff a clear grammar for matching *permission level* to *task security.* (See also CMU and Duke clause banks that map neatly onto this spectrum.)

PROGRAM-LEVEL PATTERNS: SECURE VERSUS OPEN

Many universities now design assessment at the program level, so students both demonstrate attainment under secure conditions and learn to use AI responsibly.

For example, the University of Sydney's two-lane model (see Table 5.3) sets AI as permitted by default from Semester 1, 2025, for most assessments, with invigilated exams and tests excluded. From Semester 2, the model is formalised across programs, combining a secure lane of in-person, contemporaneous assessments used to assure learning outcomes and an open lane that scaffolds and assesses responsible AI use, with explicit alignment to TEQSA's assessment-reform principles (University of Sydney, 2024; Bridgeman and Liu, 2024).

The University of Melbourne's approach to assessment includes a formal requirement to assure learning through secure evaluation practices. According to this policy, at least 50% of a subject's total marks must be derived from secure assessments such as invigilated exams, interactive oral tasks or observed performances and placements. Alternatively, if this threshold is not met within individual subjects, an equivalent strategy must be embedded programmatically across the degree to ensure assessment security and integrity throughout the curriculum (University of Melbourne, 2025).

These frameworks collectively advance a shift from reactive detection to proactive design. Rather than attempting to eliminate AI from

TABLE 5.3 Program Lanes (Where AI is Permitted vs. Assured) This Table Presents a Two-lane Programmatic Model that Separates Secure, Invigilated Tasks from Open, AI-Inclusive Tasks Emphasising Where Learning Must be Assured and Where AI Use is Developed Responsibly

Lane	Assessment Security Profile	Typical Formats	AI Use	Evidence/Verification	Purpose
Secure lane	High assurance; contemporaneous or observed	Invigilated exams; interactive orals; in-class build-and-defend; observed performance/ placement	Usually **AI-0/AI-1**	Identity check; viva; artefact provenance; supervisor observation	Certify attainment of core outcomes without external assistance
Open lane	Authentic, extended tasks	Take-home projects; studios; peer review; fieldwork; code repos	**AI-1–AI-3**, declared and evidenced	Prompt summaries/ logs; drafts; commits; data provenance; reflection	Build *responsible* AI practice and real-world workflow competence

assessment, they advocate for a principled balance: reserving high-security methods for verifying core competencies while enabling open, transparent AI use in tasks that build professional and reflective capabilities. The goal is not uniform restriction but strategic differentiation which matches assessment security to learning purpose. By embedding clear expectations for disclosure, authorship and accountability, institutions can maintain academic integrity without abandoning authenticity or innovation.

Documenting AI Use: The Audit as Evidence of Learning

As higher education shifts from detection to design, many universities now require students to audit and disclose their use of AI tools within assessments. This practice recognises that transparency is itself a pedagogical act. One that cultivates ethical reasoning, accountability and critical reflection. Rather than penalising students for engaging with generative systems, these frameworks invite them to demonstrate *how* they used AI, *why* they used it and *what they learned* through that process.

To support this emerging expectation, the *AI Use Disclosure Pro Forma* that follows takes its lead from several institutional exemplars that have integrated disclosure into their assessment frameworks. Each model balances innovation with integrity, requiring documentation of prompts, drafts, reflections and attestations of authorship as outlined in Table 5.4.

Together, these approaches make visible the process of AI-assisted learning. They converge on four shared principles:

1. **Transparency** – Students declare what AI tools were used and why.
2. **Vcrification** Students evidence how outputs were checked, rewritten or validated.
3. **Reflection** – Students articulate the impact of AI use on their learning and ethics.
4. **Accountability** – Students attest to authorship and take responsibility for all final content.

TABLE 5.4 University Frameworks Requiring AI Audits

Institution	Framework/Policy	Core Student Requirements
University of New South Wales (UNSW)	*Levels of AI Assistance Framework* (n.d.)	Students indicate permitted level of AI use (None to GenAI Software Based); submit a prompt summary or screenshots; provide annotations identifying AI-assisted sections; and include a reflection explaining verification steps and learning impact.
University of California, San Francisco (UCSF) School of Pharmacy	*Policy on Use of Artificial Intelligence (2023)*	Under AI-2 (Documented) and above, students provide prompt logs, version histories and a brief attestation confirming accountability for originality, accuracy and citations.
University of Adelaide	*Artificial Intelligence in Assessment Guidelines v2.2 (2025)*	Students must attach an AI Disclosure Appendix detailing tools used, prompts and outputs, verification methods and a reflection on reliability and bias. Transparency and authorship evidence are mandatory in AI-assisted settings.
University of Sydney	*AI Assessment Policy (2024)*	All open-lane tasks require an AI Disclosure Appendix listing tools, describing their contribution, offering critical commentary on limitations and including a signed authorship statement.
Macquarie University	*Generative AI Traffic Light Guide (2024)*	Under *Amber* and *Green* categories, students provide a short disclosure note ("AI tools were used … ") plus a prompt log; reflection and verification are encouraged to avoid superficial outsourcing.

The AI Use Disclosure Pro Forma

The following pro forma translates the institutional expectations in Table 5.4 into a single, practical document that students can attach to any submission. It is deliberately simple: a one-page record that prompts transparent reporting, reflective commentary and evidence of process. A downloadable version of this form is available at www.the-ai-educator.com.

AI USE DISCLOSURE PRO FORMA

(To be submitted with any assessment where AI tools have been used)

Student Name: ____________________ **Student ID**: ________________

Course/Assignment Title: ________________ **Date**: ________________

1. **Tools Used**

   List every AI or automation tool you used. Include simple tools (e.g., Grammarly) as well as generative ones (e.g., ChatGPT, Copilot, Midjourney).

Tool Name	Version/Date Accessed	Purpose of Use (e.g., drafting, grammar check, idea generation)
Example: ChatGPT	April 2025 version	*Used to suggest section order for my data ethics report; I wrote and expanded all content myself.*
Example: Grammarly	Chrome plugin (May 2025)	*Accepted grammar fixes; rejected style suggestions that changed meaning.*

2. **Prompts and Outputs Summary**

   Show how you interacted with AI and how you evaluated the results.

Prompt/Query (abridged)	AI Output Summary	How I Used/ Edited It	Verification Step
Example: "Give me three possible titles for an essay on AI and privacy"	Suggested generic titles ("AI and the Future of Privacy," etc.)	Combined two ideas and rewrote into "*Privacy by Prompt: Ethical AI in Data Work*"	Checked against academic sources to confirm terminology accuracy

3. **Reflection and Learning Impact**

   Answer in 2–3 sentences each. Use these examples as a guide.

   - **How did AI assist your learning or workflow?**

     Example: "It helped me organise my ideas early in the drafting stage and reduced time spent outlining."

- **What did you verify or correct after receiving the AI output?**
  Example: "The AI misinterpreted one case study, so I replaced its example with one from the course readings."
- **What limitations or biases did you notice?**
  Example: "The language was overly confident and lacked citations; I learned to fact-check and tone it down for academic writing."

4. **Evidence of Process**
   Tick all that apply and attach where possible.
   ☐ Prompt log (screenshot or transcript)
   ☐ Tracked drafts showing edits
   ☐ Annotated AI outputs (highlighted changes)
   ☐ Storyboard/notebook/version history
   Example: Attached – two draft versions with tracked changes showing how AI-generated bullet points were expanded into full paragraphs; screenshot of ChatGPT conversation (prompt + response).
5. **Authorship Statement**
   I declare that any AI tools used in preparing this work are listed and described above.
   I take full academic responsibility for verifying the accuracy, originality and integrity of the submitted content.

Personal Declaration (1–2 sentences):

Example: "AI tools were used for brainstorming and proofreading only. All analysis, interpretation and writing are my own."

____

____

Signature: ____________________ **Date**: ____________

By embedding this form within assessment briefs, educators align with international good practice while fostering a culture of openness and metacognitive awareness. The audit ceases to be an administrative add-on; it becomes a learning artefact which is a tangible demonstration of how students plan, verify and ethically integrate AI into their scholarly and creative work.

PROCESS MATTERS

Shifting from product to process requires not only redesigning tasks but also rethinking how learning is evaluated. Traditional assessment often privileges final outputs like essays, projects and reports, over the intellectual, creative or technical journey that produces them. Yet, in an AI-pervasive environment, process becomes the more reliable indicator of genuine learning. Evaluating process means making student thinking visible. This can be done by tracing how ideas evolve, how decisions are made and how tools, including AI, are used, critiqued and integrated.

Thinking About Thinking, and Why It Matters

It's one thing to require students to show their process; it's another to teach them to understand it. This is where metacognition (thinking about thinking) becomes essential. It's not just a buzzword. It's a cornerstone of deep learning. When students plan their approach, monitor their decisions and revise based on feedback or tool output, they're doing more than completing a task. They're engaging in self-aware, strategic learning. They're building cognitive endurance.

For example, a student might begin a design project with a vague idea and turn to an AI tool for structure. After reviewing the output, they might discard it, realising it's too generic, and instead craft a new outline from scratch. That moment of rejection is not a failure; it's a metacognitive win. It reveals the student's capacity to evaluate external input critically, regulate their own process and make an informed choice. These are the muscles we want students to flex.

Alongside that cognitive work sits an equally important partner: ethical reasoning. As GenAI weaves itself into academic life, students must also decide not just how to use it, but whether to. This is more than following the rules. It's about cultivating integrity. If a student asks ChatGPT to generate three options for a report title, evaluates them and chooses to create their own instead, that decision shows ethical awareness. They've weighed the convenience of automation against the value of original thought.

These kinds of moments should be visible in the work. That's why we ask for draft histories, prompt logs and reflective notes. Not to punish, but to understand. To support students in developing not just knowledge, but judgement. And in the age of AI, judgement, both cognitive and ethical, might be the most important outcome of all.

Evaluating Process

There are multiple ways to evaluate learning processes without compromising rigour. Educators can require artefacts that evidence progression, such as version histories, draft annotations or planning documents. Reflective commentaries and methods notes can illuminate the reasoning behind key decisions, revealing both metacognitive insight and ethical awareness. Oral presentations, interactive vivas and in-class build-and-defend tasks provide real-time demonstrations of understanding and authorship. Peer feedback loops and group task boards surface contributions over time, anchoring collaborative work in observable practices.

Importantly, process evaluation should not be reserved only for high-stakes contexts. When embedded early and often, it fosters habits of transparency, iteration and critical reflection. It also cultivates a deeper sense of ownership where students learn not just to complete tasks, but to account for *how* they completed them. As assessment priorities shift towards transparency and integrity, the evaluation of process becomes not only feasible but essential.

To meaningfully evaluate process, educators need structured ways to capture and interpret how students work through tasks. Table 5.5 is a list of process evidence types, each accompanied by a brief description and an example of how it can be implemented across disciplines. These could be used in addition to the previously presented proforma.

TABLE 5.5 Process Evidence Types and Cross-disciplinary Examples. This Table Lists Various Types of Process-based Evidence Educators Can Require, with Descriptions and Sample Applications to Support Transparency, Critical Engagement and Authorship Verification

Evidence Type	Description	Example
Version History	A record of iterative development or drafting stages, showing changes over time	A student submits multiple drafts of a literature review with tracked edits and comments
Prompt Log	A transparent account of prompts entered into AI tools and the outputs received	For a design task, a student includes screenshots of prompts used in Midjourney or ChatGPT
Methods Note	A short reflective explanation of how the task was approached, including tool use	After completing a data analysis, the student submits a note explaining data choices, AI use
Annotated Draft	A draft annotated to indicate what was student-written, AI-generated or revised	In a business report, the student uses margin notes to identify AI-assisted sections
Planning Document	A mind map, outline or workflow that shows early-stage thinking	A game development student submits a storyboard and logic flowchart created before coding

(*Continued*)

TABLE 5.5 (Continued)

Evidence Type	Description	Example
Reflective Commentary	A personal reflection on the decision-making process, challenges and insights	A student reflects on how they chose among competing AI outputs when planning an essay
Build-and-Defend	In-class task where students extend or explain submitted work orally or in writing	Students explain a feature they added to their codebase under supervision in a lab session
Task Board/ Sprint Log	A visual or written timeline showing who contributed what and when in group tasks	A peer-reviewed shared Kanban board documents group progress in a collaborative design task

These artefacts are not only evaluative tools but also learning instruments. They guide students towards greater intentionality, ethical engagement and critical self-awareness. By integrating such evidence into the assessment process, educators foster transparency, deepen intellectual accountability and reduce opportunities for superficial or AI-outsourced submissions.

As process becomes central to demonstrating authentic learning in AI-supported environments, educators need clear, equitable criteria for evaluating how students approach, develop and reflect on their work. Assessing process is not simply about checking effort; it is about recognising the intellectual and ethical decisions students make along the way. This includes how they plan, iterate, justify choices and integrate tools like GenAI transparently and responsibly.

The rubric in Table 5.6 builds upon the *Structure of Observed Learning Outcomes (SOLO) taxonomy* developed by Biggs and Collis (2014), providing a structured means of evaluating the *depth* and *complexity* of student learning processes. By situating process evaluation within this framework, the rubric moves beyond checklist-style grading to recognise progressive levels of understanding, from surface engagement to relational and extended abstraction. It supports both formative and summative assessment, enabling educators to diagnose where students are positioned in their development and to guide them towards higher-order integration and transfer of learning. When used alongside process artefacts such as prompt logs, version histories, planning documents or method notes, the rubric foregrounds the student's learning trajectory and critical engagement with tools like generative AI, rather than relying solely on the polish of the final product.

TABLE 5.6 A Rubric Evaluation Process. This Rubric Provides Structured Criteria for Assessing Planning, Iteration, AI Use, Decision-making, Reflection and Authorship, with Illustrative Examples to Calibrate Evaluation Across Performance Levels

Criterion	Pre-structural (No Clear Evidence of Learning Process)	Uni-structural (Simple or Isolated Evidence of Process)	Multi-structural (Several Aspects Evident but Unconnected)	Relational (Integrated, Connected Understanding of Process)	Extended Abstract (Generalised Insight; Innovation Or Transfer Beyond Task)
Planning and Organisation	No plan or sequencing evident. **Example**: Started coding or writing without an outline or timeline.	Minimal planning; one stage or goal identified. **Example**: Created a basic to-do list but did not link it to project stages.	Several planning elements shown but unconnected. **Example**: Drafted an outline and collected sources but without logical sequence.	Logical, well-sequenced plan linking stages to learning goals. **Example**: Produced a storyboard or Gantt chart showing when research, drafting and testing would occur and updated it as work progressed.	Sophisticated planning that adapts dynamically and informs future work. **Example**: Iteratively revised plan based on feedback; documented what worked for use in later projects.
Iteration and Development	Single submission; no revision. **Example**: Submitted final essay without drafts or edits.	Minor surface edits only. **Example**: Fixed typos after grammar-checker suggestions.	Multiple drafts but limited commentary or reflection. **Example**: Uploaded three drafts but did not explain why changes were made.	Meaningful cycles of revision guided by evaluation and feedback. **Example**: Adjusted report structure after peer review; modified AI-generated code following testing.	Iteration demonstrates experimentation and conceptual growth. **Example**: Documented an evolution from prototype to user test to refined model with rationale and reflection.

Decision-Making and Justification	Decisions arbitrary or unexplained. **Example**: Selected dataset or design style "because it was easiest."	Some rationale given but little awareness of alternatives. **Example**: Used ChatGPT output without comparing to other sources.	Multiple decisions described though not linked to goals. **Example**: Explained several design choices separately but not how they interact.	Clear reasoning for key decisions; connects acceptance/ rejection of AI output to objectives. **Example**: Chose to rewrite AI-generated introduction to better match discipline tone and explained reasoning in methods note.	Decisions show ethical and critical reasoning transferable beyond task. **Example**: Compared multiple AI tools, discussed bias and proposed selection criteria for future projects.
Transparency of AI Use	AI use hidden or unacknowledged. **Example**: Submitted work partly written by AI without mention.	Mentions AI tool but provides no detail. **Example**: "Used ChatGPT" stated once in passing.	Lists tools and prompts but lacks context. **Example**: Included copy of prompt log without explaining what was kept or changed.	Full disclosure of tools, prompts, edits and verification steps. **Example**: Table showing each prompt, AI output, revisions and verification notes.	Transparent documentation with critical analysis and innovation. **Example**: Created an annotated prompt log evaluating output quality and proposed best-practice workflow for peers.

(Continued)

TABLE 5.6 (Continued)

Criterion	Pre-structural (No Clear Evidence of Learning Process)	Uni-structural (Simple or Isolated Evidence of Process)	Multi-structural (Several Aspects Evident but Unconnected)	Relational (Integrated, Connected Understanding of Process)	Extended Abstract (Generalised Insight; Innovation Or Transfer Beyond Task)
Critical Reflection	No reflection or only descriptive comment. **Example**: "This assignment was easy."	Basic awareness of success or difficulty. **Example**: "AI helped me finish faster."	Reflects on multiple aspects but lacks synthesis. **Example**: Describes feedback received but not how it changed approach.	Analytical reflection linking choices, learning and outcomes. **Example**: Discusses how AI summaries improved clarity but reduced originality; explains adjustments made.	Deep metacognitive insight and transfer of learning. **Example**: Articulates how understanding of AI bias will shape future research practice or teaching philosophy.
Evidence of Authorship	No supporting artefacts. **Example**: Only final submission uploaded.	Single artefact with minimal traceability. **Example**: Attached final document plus one screenshot.	Several artefacts present but weak linkage. **Example**: Drafts uploaded but lack timestamps or explanation.	Strong evidential chain: drafts, logs and notes show genuine authorship. **Example**: Provides tracked-change files, prompt logs and commit history aligned with development timeline.	Authorship evidence interpreted critically and generalised to others. **Example**: Analyses version history to propose criteria for verifying authorship in AI-supported tasks.

Notes:

- This rubric can accompany artefact-based submissions such as process journals, method notes or reflective appendices.
- Weightings can be adjusted depending on whether the assessment is formative, summative or part of a secure/open design.
- Rubric language aligns with descriptors used in program assurance and academic integrity guidelines.

To illustrate how this rubric can be applied in practice, the following example presents excerpts from a student's submission at different performance levels. The artefact includes both the student's recorded process and evaluative comments aligned to the rubric criteria. Together, they demonstrate what competent work might look like, offering practical guidance for educators in recognising depth, transparency and critical engagement with GenAI.

Student Artefact Excerpt: Reflective Report with Annotations
Task: Reflect on your contributions to the group project, explaining your design decisions, use of AI tools and key learning moments. Submit with prompt logs and a version history.

1. **Planning and Organisation**

   "I was responsible for writing the introduction to the report. I didn't make a plan, but I looked at examples online and started drafting right away."

   Evaluator Comment: Evidence aligns with the **Uni-structural** level. The student demonstrates awareness of their role but provides little evidence of structured planning or sequencing. No planning artefacts, such as outlines or workflow diagrams, are supplied.

2. **Iteration and Development**

   "I wrote the introduction in one sitting. After feedback from the group, I changed a few sentences to make them shorter."

   Evaluator Comment: This reflects **surface-level iteration** consistent with the **Uni-structural** level. Edits appear mechanical and lack documentation of substantive revision or conceptual growth. No version trail is included.

3. **Decision-Making and Justification**

   "I used ChatGPT to check my grammar and make the sentences sound more formal."

   Evaluator Comment: The student demonstrates basic decision-making characteristic of the **Multi-structural** stage – acknowledging AI use but offering limited critical justification or awareness of alternatives. Discussion of ethical or methodological reasoning is absent.

4. **Transparency of AI Use**

   AI Prompt Log: "Fix grammar and make this more formal."

   Evaluator Comment: Transparency remains at the **Uni-structural** level. Only one prompt is listed, with no contextualisation or reflection on the AI's output, limiting the ability to assess verification or critical engagement.

5. **Critical Reflection**

   "I think the introduction was fine overall. Using AI saved me time and made it sound better."

   Evaluator Comment: Reflection is **Pre-structural to Uni-structural** as it identifies superficial outcomes (speed, polish) but does not connect experience to learning, ethics or future application.

6. **Evidence of Authorship**
   - Submitted Word document
   - No tracked changes or draft history
   - One AI prompt copy-pasted into appendix

   Evaluator Comment: Authorship evidence remains at the **Pre-structural** level. Minimal documentation makes it difficult to verify ownership or reconstruct the learning process.

Overall Evaluation (SOLO-aligned):
The submission demonstrates a **Multi-structural** level of process engagement overall. The student shows isolated understanding of the stages involved in planning, revising and using AI, but these remain unconnected and lack reflective synthesis.

Feedback Summary:
To progress towards the **Relational** level, the student should integrate their planning, decision-making and AI use into a coherent workflow, supported by evidence such as version histories, annotated drafts and prompt logs. Advancing to the **Extended Abstract** level would involve demonstrating transferable insight, critically evaluating the limitations of AI assistance and applying those reflections to future collaborative or disciplinary contexts.

What High-Security looks like in Practice

Many institutional design notes converge on the same pattern: embed high-security checkpoints at moments where attainment must be assured, then offset them with more open, lower-security work elsewhere in the subject or program. In practice, this looks like sequencing an invigilated quiz or an interactive oral immediately after a take-home task; requiring students to rebuild or defend a submitted artefact in class; or mandating authorship trails, such as drafts, version histories, prompt summaries and data provenance, so that products are anchored to observable processes. The guiding principle is proportionality. The closer a task sits to threshold outcomes or accreditation standards, the tighter the security (e.g., contemporaneous performance, identity verification, observation). Conversely, where the aim is to cultivate responsible AI practice, designers deliberately allow AI, but insist on transparency and verification through method notes, reproducibility steps and short viva-style checks (see Table 5.3 for the secure/open lane logic).

Charles Sturt University's guidance is unusually concrete on how to operationalise this balance. It begins with a vulnerability audit of existing tasks, pinpointing items that invite superficial outsourcing (generic essays, isolated case write-ups, standardised lab reports, boilerplate coding exercises) and then offers like-for-like mitigations. For written tasks, this includes interactive orals that sample key claims, staged drafts with targeted feedback checkpoints and case work tied to locally verifiable artefacts (briefs, datasets, field notes) so that students must show how their argument arose. For empirical and design tasks, the guidance emphasises verified data provenance (supplying or generating data in controlled conditions, logging transformations), reproducible workflows (scripts, notebooks, commit histories) and in-class build-and-defend activities that test whether students can explain or adapt what they submitted. For programming, it recommends scaffolded repositories with commit cadence expectations, live walk-throughs of critical functions and small parameter-randomised extensions that students complete under light supervision to demonstrate personal competency. Collectively, these moves do not *ban AI*; they re-centre assessment on demonstrable authorship and judgement, with clear, evidence-based pathways for students to show how AI, if used, was directed, checked and integrated (Charles Sturt University, 2025).

The University of Adelaide's approach closely mirrors the middle tiers of UCSF's AI-permission scale, particularly AI-2 (Restricted) and AI-3 (Documented), by normalising the disclosure and evaluation of AI use as a routine part of assessment (UCSF School of Pharmacy, 2023). Their AI in Assessment Guidelines (2025) adopt a four-tiered model that includes AI-Assisted Editing and AI-Assisted Ideas, where students may use GenAI for restructuring, brainstorming or improving drafts, but are held accountable for transparency, source verification and critical engagement. These settings do not prohibit AI, but instead embed structured expectations for documentation, student responsibility and evidentiary authorship. This parity in approach underscores a sector-wide shift: disclosure and process transparency are becoming essential components of academic integrity in AI-enabled contexts.

The example, shown in Table 5.7, illustrates how a vulnerability audit can be used to redesign a course's assessment suite using the Charles Sturt method of targeted mitigation. The *Before* column surfaces where tasks invite superficial outsourcing or unverifiable authorship; the *After* column shows concrete changes that either raise task security (e.g., invigilated quizzes, interactive orals, in-class build-and-defend) or preserve authenticity while demanding process transparency (drafts, prompt logs, version history, data provenance). Read across any row to see the principle of proportionality at work: higher-stakes outcomes are checked contemporaneously, while open, AI-inclusive tasks are retained but scaffolded with explicit disclosure and verification. The result is a balanced pattern that certifies attainment without defaulting to bans, and that teaches students to use GenAI responsibly under clear, assessable conditions.

In parallel, the University of Adelaide reinforces this approach with a self-review tool that complements the vulnerability audit model. Titled *Evaluating the Validity of Your Assignments* (shown in Figure 5.1), it supports educators in critically analysing existing assessments across five

TABLE 5.7 Generic Assessment Redesign Using Vulnerability Audit Using the Charles Sturt Method. This Table Contrasts Legacy Assessment Designs with Revised Versions that Incorporate Mitigation Strategies, Security Checkpoints and Process Evidence Aligned to GenAI Considerations

Task Type	Before (Legacy Design)	After (Redesign/ Mitigation)	Evidence of Authorship
Short Written Task	Broad essay or review with generic prompt	Locally anchored case brief; interactive oral or annotated defence	Annotated bibliography; oral notes
Technical Build Task	Take-home code/ design with common spec	Scaffolded repo with commit cadence; in-class "extend and explain"	Commit logs; extension artefact
Data/Analysis Task	Report on open/ public dataset	Supplied dataset with checksum; notebook pipeline; in-class replication step	Data provenance; replication transcript
Collaborative Project	One shared group deliverable	Sprint reviews; rotating roles; individual walkthroughs of modules	Task board history; walkthrough recordings
Quiz/Test	Untimed online quiz	Invigilated, time-boxed quiz with variant pools; scratchpad collected	Proctoring log; scratchpad
Capstone/Final Task	Take-home exam or portfolio	In-person practical with rotating tasks; viva on design decisions	IDE history; viva rubric
Reflective Note	Optional or post-hoc reflection	Required methods note across tasks with explicit AI disclosure	Prompt summaries; version trails

dimensions: alignment with learning outcomes, authenticity, AI relevance, security and practical feasibility. By guiding course designers through targeted reflection, such as whether a task fosters real-world skills or if AI use should be encouraged, restricted or disclosed, it enables the systematic refinement of assessment architecture. When used alongside design patterns like Charles Sturt's mitigation model, the tool strengthens the evidentiary basis for authorship claims and ensures assessments remain resilient, ethical and meaningful in AI-enabled contexts (University of Adelaide, 2025).

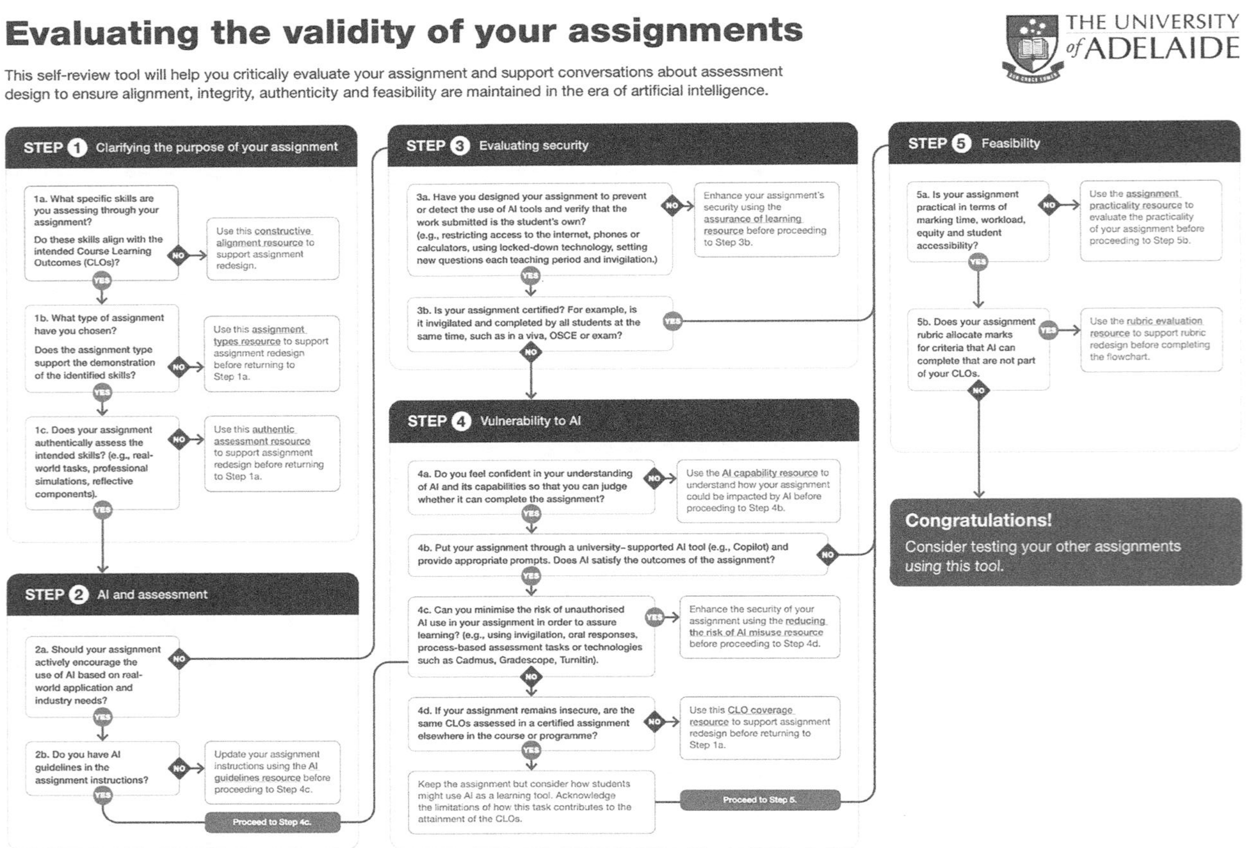

FIGURE 5.1 The University of Adelaide's self-evaluation tool for determining assessment security (Smith et al., 2025).

The following worked examples show how several traditional assessment methods can be redesigned with security in mind while helping embed the use of GenAI into a student's professional practice.

Worked Examples

To translate principles into practice, this section presents a series of worked examples that demonstrate how vulnerable assessments can be redesigned to support both academic integrity and authentic learning in AI-pervasive contexts. Each example begins with a vulnerability audit, followed by targeted mitigations and revised weightings that align assessment design with the dual aims of evidencing authorship and cultivating responsible AI use. These exemplars show how proportional security, transparent disclosure and process-based evaluation can be embedded across diverse task types without sacrificing pedagogical intent.

Worked Example 1: Redesigning a Reflection Essay

Step 1 Vulnerability Audit of Current Assessment

Task: Individual Reflection Essay (30%)

Original aim: Students demonstrate a foundational understanding of ethical principles in data science (bias, transparency, privacy) by reflecting on real-world examples and identifying key ethical issues.

Vulnerabilities:

- High risk of GenAI drafting or refining reflective essays.
- Students could easily prompt AI with queries such as "Write a reflection on bias and privacy in data science" and receive fluent, plausible submissions.
- Difficult to authenticate whether a student's reflection genuinely represents their thinking, unless tied to verifiable lived experience or contemporaneous performance.

Step 2 Targeted Mitigation

Charles Sturt University's framework emphasises proportionality rather than blanket bans. Assessments most at risk of outsourcing are reinforced with secure checkpoints (in-person, oral or practical), while open elements can still allow AI use, provided that students must evidence their process and human judgement.

This redesign aligns with the University of Adelaide's AI-3 setting (AI-Assisted Ideas), where students are permitted to use AI for drafting or structuring ideas, but must clearly document and evaluate its role. The disclosure appendix aligns with Adelaide's emphasis on validating outputs and maintaining student accountability for all content submitted.

Redesigned Task – Hybrid Reflection (30%)

- **Checkpoint element**: In-class reflective writing on a surprise topic, completed under exam conditions. This secures a sample of the student's authentic voice and reasoning.
- **Open element**: Extended take-home reflection where AI use is permitted, but students must attach an AI Disclosure Appendix detailing prompts, outputs and a short critique of the AI's response.

Mitigation rationale: The checkpoint captures personal authorship and authentic voice; the open component scaffolds AI literacy by requiring transparency, critique and reflective judgement.

Step 3 Redesigned Assessment Weighting

Assessment Task	Open/Secure Split	Mitigation Strategy
Reflection Essay (30%)	20% take-home (open, AI allowed with disclosure) + 10% in-class (secure)	Captures authentic personal reflection through supervised writing; develops AI literacy through transparent disclosure and critique of AI use

How this Redesign Works in Practice

By reading across this redesign, we see proportionality in action. The in-class checkpoint anchors the student's authentic reflective style, while the take-home extension acknowledges that students may experiment with AI tools. Rather than penalising this, the disclosure appendix makes AI use accessible and transparent. The result is an assessment that both certifies attainment (secure lane) and teaches responsible AI practice (open lane).

Worked Example 2: Redesigning a Group Project

Step 1 Vulnerability Audit of Current Assessment

Task: Group Project (40%)

Original aim: Students collaborate to research a historical, cultural or philosophical issue, co-author an analytical essay and deliver a group presentation discussing differing perspectives.

Vulnerabilities:

- Some students contribute minimally while others carry the analytical or writing load.
- Sections of interpretation or background synthesis can be produced by AI tools, making it difficult to identify original thought.
- A polished, collective essay conceals individual argumentation, voice and critical engagement.

Step 2 Targeted Mitigation

Group work is retained to preserve the collaborative exchange of ideas that characterises humanities scholarship, but additional checkpoints and reflective artefacts are introduced to verify authorship and intellectual engagement.

Each student submits an Individual Process Commentary in the form of a short reflective document outlining their specific contributions, the interpretive decisions made and any use of AI for drafting, summarising or editing. This mirrors Adelaide's AI-4 level (AI-Assisted Creation, Human Evaluation), where students are expected to engage critically with AI outputs and take responsibility for curating and defending the intellectual quality of their contributions.

Redesigned Task: Collaborative Project with Individual Accountability (40%)

- **Checkpoint elements**: Mid-semester discussion workshops and short oral progress presentations where students articulate their interpretive stance, sources and evolving argument.
- **Open elements**: The co-authored group paper and presentation are retained, accompanied by each student's Individual Process Commentary disclosing their analytical role, AI use and reflective insights on collaboration.

Mitigation Rationale

Live workshops provide contemporaneous evidence of individual interpretation and argumentation. The process commentaries make authorship transparent while fostering critical reflection on how generative tools may assist or distort textual analysis.

Step 3 Redesigned Assessment Weighting

Assessment Task	Open/Secure Split	Mitigation Strategy
Group Project (40%)	25% group deliverable (open, AI allowed with disclosure) + 15% secure checkpoints (in-class discussions and oral progress reviews)	Workshops and oral checkpoints confirm authorship and understanding; individual commentaries disclose AI use, interpretive choices and reflective insights.

How this Redesign Works in Practice

The redesign preserves the collaborative essence of humanities inquiry for dialogue, interpretation and argument, while embedding transparency and authorship assurance. The oral checkpoints allow educators to witness each student's reasoning process, reducing the risk of invisible outsourcing. The Individual Process Commentaries transform disclosure into a reflective learning task, encouraging students to evaluate how AI tools might shape their interpretive voice, argument structure and ethical engagement with texts. In doing so, the assessment balances fairness with authenticity, fostering both collaborative scholarship and personal intellectual accountability.

Worked Example 3: Redesigning a Technical Build Task

Step 1 Vulnerability Audit of Current Assessment

Task: Technical Build (20%)

Original aim: Students create a small software prototype (e.g., web app, design artefact).

Vulnerabilities:

- Students can submit AI-generated boilerplate code or reuse templates.

- Hard to detect provenance of a code repository without a process trail.
- Take-home builds risk wholesale outsourcing.

Step 2 Targeted Mitigation

A technical build remains essential, but it's scaffolded with provenance checks and an in-class extension.

This structure reflects both AI-2 (Editing) and AI-4 (Creation) in the Adelaide model. Commit logs and AI disclosure documents ensure clarity around the role of AI in development, while the in-class extension ensures students can independently explain and evaluate their code, meeting the expectation of human oversight and critical reflection on AI outputs.

Redesigned Task – Scaffolded Build + Extension (20%)

- **Checkpoint element**: In-class "extend and explain" exercise where students modify their own repo (new feature, bug fix) and talk through their design decisions.
- **Open element**: Take-home repo development, with required commit cadence and AI Disclosure Appendix (prompts, outputs, rationale for use).

Mitigation rationale: The commit history and disclosure show process; the in-class extension proves authorship and understanding.

Step 3 Redesigned Assessment Weighting

Assessment Task	Open/Secure Split	Mitigation Strategy
Technical Build (20%)	10% take-home repo (open, AI allowed with disclosure) + 10% in-class extension (secure)	Commit cadence and disclosure log demonstrate process; extension task provides observed authorship evidence

How this Redesign Works in Practice

Instead of discarding coding tasks as "too easy to outsource," this redesign secures them with a mix of provenance and performance. Students show they can work with AI responsibly at home, and also demonstrate understanding in class.

Worked Example 4: Redesigning a Case Study Analysis

Step 1 Vulnerability Audit of Current Assessment

Task: Case Study Analysis (30%)

Original aim: Students analyse a real-world patient scenario to apply ethical principles (e.g., consent, confidentiality, duty of care) and propose a management plan.

Vulnerabilities:

- Students could outsource the written analysis to AI, which can generate fluent clinical-style essays.
- Over-reliance on generative tools risks producing generic or decontextualised management strategies.
- Difficult to confirm whether the analysis reflects the student's own clinical reasoning without observable performance.

Step 2 Targeted Mitigation

Rather than banning AI entirely, the task is restructured to include both secure checkpoints and open elements.

This redesign aligns with Adelaide's AI-3 setting, as it encourages students to use AI tools for idea generation and language refinement, provided they document this process and verify the outputs. The AI Methods Note functions as both a learning scaffold and an integrity checkpoint.

Redesigned Task – Layered Case Analysis (30%)

- **Checkpoint element (10%)**: In-class worksheet where students annotate a patient case with ethical red flags and potential decisions. This is completed under supervision in a tutorial.
- **Open element (20%)**: Extended take-home analysis where students expand on their notes into a structured essay or report. AI use is permitted but must be documented in an AI Methods Note, explaining how (or if) AI assisted their reasoning and evaluating the reliability of outputs.

Mitigation rationale: The supervised annotation secures a baseline of authentic clinical reasoning; the take-home task develops depth, critical thinking and AI literacy.

Step 3 Redesigned Assessment Weighting

Assessment Task	Open/Secure Split	Mitigation Strategy
Case Study Analysis (30%)	20% extended analysis (open, AI allowed with disclosure) + 10% in-class annotated worksheet (secure)	In-class notes provide authentic baseline; extended analysis builds depth and transparency in AI use

How this Redesign Works in Practice

This redesign safeguards a task where unverified take-home writing is highly vulnerable to AI outsourcing. By embedding a secure checkpoint in the form of supervised case annotations, instructors capture authentic evidence of each student's reasoning process. The open, extended analysis remains essential for developing professional communication skills and the ability to integrate multiple perspectives. Requiring students to document and critique any AI assistance both limits the risk of uncritical outsourcing and turns AI into an object of critical reflection.

Worked Example 5: Redesigning a Creative Portfolio

Step 1 Vulnerability Audit of Current Assessment

Task: Creative Portfolio (40%)

Original aim: Students produce a portfolio of artworks or media pieces (e.g., photography series, short film, design prototypes) accompanied by an artist's statement.

Vulnerabilities:
- Students could submit AI-generated images, video or design assets with minimal personal input.
- Text-based artist statements could be drafted entirely by AI.
- Difficult to verify whether the portfolio process represents the student's creative development.

Step 2 Charles Sturt Method: Targeted Mitigation

The task is redesigned to capture process and ensure observable authorship, while still allowing AI tools in transparent, critical ways.

This is consistent with AI-4 in Adelaide's framework, where students are expected to critically engage with AI-generated content and retain full responsibility for curating, evaluating and integrating it into their creative output. The process journal reinforces the Adelaide emphasis on citation, understanding and explainability.

Redesigned Task – Process-Driven Portfolio (40%)

- **Checkpoint element (15%)**: In-class studio session where students must create a draft artefact under observation (e.g., sketch, storyboard or raw footage) and briefly present their design intent.
- **Open element (25%)**: Final portfolio submitted with a Creative Process Journal documenting iterations, influences and any use of AI tools (with screenshots, prompts or version histories).

Mitigation rationale: The in-class draft secures evidence of authentic creative practice; the process journal scaffolds transparency and critical evaluation of AI's role in the workflow.

Step 3 Redesigned Assessment Weighting

Assessment Task	Open/Secure Split	Mitigation Strategy
Creative Portfolio (40%)	25% final portfolio + process journal (open, AI allowed with disclosure) + 15% in-class draft creation (secure)	In-class draft provides observable baseline; process journal documents iterations, influences and AI use

How this Redesign Works in Practice

This redesign reframes the portfolio as a process-rich rather than purely product-oriented task. The in-class draft establishes each student's authentic creative starting point and verifies that they can generate work without external assistance. The open portfolio component, meanwhile, reflects professional creative practice where iteration, collaboration and tool use are normal. By requiring a process journal with explicit AI disclosure, the design acknowledges that students may experiment with generative tools but ensures this is documented and critically evaluated.

Evidence of Authorship Beats Detection

Across the frameworks, the common currency is *process evidence*: prompt logs or summaries, draft/version histories, code traces and commit logs, data provenance and, in higher-stakes settings, oral defence. Notably, the documented or amber/green categories explicitly require disclosure and record-keeping of AI use (UCSF School of Pharmacy, 2023; University of Warwick, 2024; University of Leeds, 2025; UNSW, n.d.).

This signals a pivot in assessment logic from detection to authorship. Rather than investing in technical arms races to *catch* AI-generated text, institutions are converging on mechanisms that make authorship visible through process. This approach reflects two realities. First, that detection tools remain unreliable and prone to false positives, threatening fairness. Second, that GenAI is already embedded in professional practice, and graduates will need to demonstrate not avoidance, but *responsible integration.*

For educators, the implication is a structural redesign of assessment tasks. The focus shifts towards formative and process-rich modes where the student's journey is observable. Oral presentations, interactive vivas and seminar defences enable students to narrate and justify their decisions. Iterative design journals, sketchbooks or lab notebooks capture development stages, making it difficult to present AI-generated products without evidence of human mediation. Collaborative projects that incorporate peer feedback and visible task boards create distributed authorship trails, further anchoring the work. In these settings, the evidentiary burden is shifted to where students must *show their work* rather than simply submit a polished product.

As Messina and Panciroli (2025) argue, assessment frameworks must now value the *how* as much as the *what*, recognising meta-learning, reflexivity and process literacy as outcomes in their own right. This aligns with wider shifts in pedagogy that emphasise authenticity and transparency. A student who can explain their reasoning orally, show their version history and critically reflect on their engagement with AI tools demonstrates a form of competence that goes well beyond the static correctness of a final submission.

The guiding principle is thus proportionality in which the higher the stakes, the more contemporaneous and observable the evidence of authorship required. Low-stakes or exploratory work can remain open to AI use, scaffolded by disclosure requirements, while threshold outcomes are certified through secure, process-based verification. In this way, evidence of authorship does not merely replace detection; it reframes assessment integrity around learning as process, not product.

A Simple Synthesis You Can Apply Tomorrow

For each assessment item, specify four things: a *permission level*, a *security setting*, the *evidence you will collect* and the *process/ideas you will evaluate.*

1. **Permission level** (one line on the brief; adapted from UCSF/UNSW/RAG models)
    - **AI-0 (None).** No AI permitted; misconduct if used.
    - **AI-1 (Restricted).** AI permitted only for named sub-tasks (e.g., brainstorming/outline); submit a brief prompt summary.
    - **AI-2 (Documented).** Any AI permitted; submit prompt log and drafts/version history; student remains responsible for accuracy.
    - **AI-3 (Open).** AI encouraged as part of outcomes; submit a short methods note describing how AI informed the work.
2. **Security setting** (decided at subject/program level)
    - **Secure.** Invigilated or contemporaneous tasks; interactive orals; observed performance/placement; in-class build-and-defend.
    - **Open.** Take-home projects; studios and critiques; peer-reviewed artefacts with AI-inclusive workflows. (Aligns with Sydney's two-lane model and Melbourne's secure-assessment principles.)
3. **Evidence of authorship** (state explicitly)
    - A completed AI Use Disclosure Proforma
    - Drafts/version history
    - Prompt logs or summary statements
    - Data/citation trails
    - Viva/Q&A on demand (Reflected in UCSF/UNSW/Warwick/Leeds requirements.)
4. **Process and ideas** (how the student's thinking is measured)
    - **Idea development**: Look for originality, contextualisation and adaptation of AI outputs rather than surface polish.

- **Decision-making trail**: Ask students to explain why they chose one approach over another, and what alternatives they considered.
- **Critical reflection**: Evaluate how well students critique the limitations of AI outputs, note biases and reconcile them with disciplinary standards.
- **Iteration and growth**: Assess the movement from early drafts/sketches to final artefacts, noting evidence of refinement and responsiveness to feedback.

Taken together, these design choices provide a flexible but rigorous framework for assessment in an AI-pervasive environment: specify what kind of AI use is permitted, secure key checkpoints where attainment must be assured, collect explicit evidence of authorship and evaluate the student's process and ideas rather than just their final product. Yet assessment design does not operate in isolation. It sits within broader pedagogical traditions that shape how students engage with learning. To see how these principles can be practically applied across the curriculum, we now turn to five of the most influential approaches to teaching and learning, and consider how GenAI might be integrated within each.

From Redesign to Reconnection

This chapter has argued that GenAI does not require the abandonment of assessment integrity but rather its reorientation. By shifting focus from product to process, and from detection to design, educators can safeguard deep learning while embracing the evolving realities of AI-assisted education. Through frameworks such as permission levels, traffic-light models and proportional security patterns, assessment can become both more transparent and more resilient. Crucially, the emphasis on authorship evidence that can include prompt logs, version histories, reflective notes, reinstates the learning journey as a central object of evaluation, not merely its output.

Yet, assessment does not stand alone. It is deeply intertwined with how we teach, what we value and how students engage. Chapter 6 turns to the pedagogical foundations that shape these engagements, exploring how GenAI can be thoughtfully embedded within five widely used teaching approaches. Rather than seeing AI as a disruption, we consider how it might be aligned with existing pedagogical intentions to enhance, rather than displace, authentic learning.

REFLECT AND REFRAME

1. Which part of your assessment design is most vulnerable to superficial outsourcing?
2. How do you currently evaluate the student learning journey, not just its endpoint?
3. To what extent are your students equipped to think about their own thinking?
4. What small change could you implement tomorrow to centre process in your assessment?

REFERENCES

Biggs, J. B., and Collis, K. F., 2014. *Evaluating the quality of learning: The SOLO taxonomy (Structure of the Observed Learning Outcome)*. Academic Press.

Biggs, J., Tang, C., and Kennedy, G., 2022. *Teaching for quality learning at university*. 5th ed. McGraw-Hill Education (UK).

Bridgeman, A., and Liu, D., 2024. *Aligning our assessments to the age of generative AI. Teaching@Sydney*. The University of Sydney. https://edu.ational-innovation.sydney.edu.au/teaching@sydney/aligning-our-assessments-to-the-age-of-generative-ai/

Charles Sturt University, 2025. *Assessment and generative artificial intelligence*. Division of Learning and Teaching. https://www.csu.edu.au/division/learning-teaching/assessments/assessment-and-artificial-intelligence/assessment-and-generative-artificial-intelligence

Walji, S., 2025. UCT drops AI cheating detection tools over accuracy concerns. *MyBroadband*, 20 August. https://mybroadband.co.za/news/ai/606707-one-of-south-africas-biggest-universities-drops-ai-cheating-detection.html

Knight, P. T., 2002. Summative assessment in higher education: Practices in disarray. *Studies in Higher Education*, 27(3), 275–286. https://doi.org/10.1080/03075070220000662

Macquarie University, 2024. *Generative artificial intelligence: Traffic light guide*. Macquarie University. https://ishare.mq.edu.au/prod/file/7f8b0aba-f392-4fb8-91ea-e6de42d8fe30/1/GAIT%20Traffic%20Light%20Guide.pdf

Messina, S., and Panciroli, C., 2025. Rethinking teaching with GenAI: Theoretical models and operational tools. *Journal of Inclusive Methodology and Technology in Learning and Teaching*, 5(1), 1–10. https://cris.unibo.it/handle/11585/1015174

Quality Assurance Agency for Higher Education, 2023. *Reconsidering assessment for the ChatGPT era: QAA advice on developing sustainable assessment strategies*. QAA. https://www.qaa.ac.uk/docs/qaa/members/reconsidering-assessment-for-the-chat-gpt-era.pdf

Smith, R., Moss, P., Rathnappulige, S., Correas, C., Palmer, E., Barbieri, W., Lee, D., and Wanner, T., 2025. Designing AI-resilient assessment: A practical validity tool for higher education [conference presentation]. *HERGA Conference*, Adelaide, SA, Australia, 1 October.

TEQSA (Tertiary Education Quality and Standards Agency), 2024. *Gen AI strategies for Australian higher education: Emerging practice*. TEQSA. https://www.teqsa.gov.au/guides-resources/resources/corporate-publications/gen-ai-strategies-australian-higher-education-emerging-practice

TEQSA (Tertiary Education Quality and Standards Agency), 2025. *Gen AI knowledge hub*. TEQSA. https://www.teqsa.gov.au/guides-resources/higher-education-good-practice-hub/gen-ai-knowledge-hub

University of California, San Francisco, School of Pharmacy, 2023. *Policy on use of artificial intelligence (AI) in assessments and deliverables*. UCSF School of Pharmacy. https://pharm.ucsf.edu/current/policies/ai

University of Adelaide, 2025. *Artificial intelligence in assessment guidelines: Version 2.2*. University of Adelaide. Internal document.

University of Leeds, 2025. *AI and assessments*. University of Leeds. https://generative-ai.leeds.ac.uk/ai-and-assessments/

University of Melbourne, 2025. *Assuring learning at Melbourne*. University of Melbourne. https://about.unimelb.edu.au/education-melbourne/assuring-learning-at-melbourne

University of New South Wales, n.d. *Using AI in university: Levels of AI assistance*. University of New South Wales. https://www.unsw.edu.au/student/managing-your-studies/academic-skills-support/toolkit/ai

University of Sydney, 2024. University of Sydney's AI assessment policy: Protecting integrity and empowering students. *University of Sydney News & Opinion*, 27 November. https://www.sydney.edu.au/news-opinion/news/2024/11/27/university-of-sydney-ai-assessment-policy.html

University of Warwick, IATL, 2024. *IATL UG student handbook 2024–25*. University of Warwick. https://warwick.ac.uk/fac/cross_fac/iatl/study/currentstudents/iatl_ug_student_handbook_2024-25_final.pdf

CHAPTER 6

AI and the Top 5

What was once an opportunity to wrestle with complex ideas becomes a button-click exercise in outsourcing thought.

CHAPTER AIMS

The aim of this chapter is to introduce key themes explored in this book in relation to:

1. *Investigate the integration of generative AI into pedagogical design through the lens of generativism.*
2. *Discuss the development of meta-AI literacy as a multidimensional capacity essential for ethical and adaptive learning.*
3. *Exemplify the strategic use of AI-based provocations to cultivate critical reflection, epistemic awareness and learner agency.*

DEEP LEARNING IN THE AGE OF GENERATIVE AI

In the spirit of cultivating deep learning, as advocated by Biggs, Tang and Kennedy (2022), educators strive to build environments where students engage meaningfully with content, develop well-structured knowledge frameworks and learn conceptually rather than through rote memorisation. These principles are supported not only by student dispositions but also by the deliberate and thoughtful strategies employed by teachers. These strategies scaffold understanding, confront misconceptions and

DOI: 10.1201/9781003624981-6

align assessment with intended learning outcomes. However, the rise of GenAI tools presents both opportunities and subtle threats to this pedagogical ideal.

From the student's perspective, one of the core pillars of deep learning is the intention to genuinely engage with a task. This intention often springs from curiosity or a drive to master the subject. But with tools like ChatGPT or Copilot offering instantaneous answers, that intrinsic motivation risks being displaced by a far more superficial goal: getting the task done with minimal cognitive effort. What was once an opportunity to wrestle with complex ideas becomes a button-click exercise in outsourcing thought.

Deep learning also depends on a student's ability to build and navigate a well-organised conceptual knowledge base. When GenAI is used as a crutch rather than a companion, students may never fully internalise the content, and instead, they receive the *what* but not the *why*. Instead of working from first principles, they are handed polished conclusions, often devoid of the nuance or struggle that fosters true understanding. Even more concerning is the subtle shift in preference in that students may come to favour answers that sound good over those they have worked to understand, and the risks don't end with students. On the teaching side, GenAI can inadvertently disrupt carefully constructed learning sequences. Teachers who aim to explicitly reveal the structure of a topic, build upon prior knowledge or provoke active student engagement may find their efforts diluted when students sidestep these activities by relying on AI-generated explanations. Worse still, many AI outputs are plausible-sounding but structurally incorrect or conceptually flawed (at the time of writing and they can only get better), thus embedding new misconceptions rather than resolving existing ones.

As extensively discussed throughout, assessment becomes particularly vulnerable. A cornerstone of Biggs and Tang's approach is the alignment of assessment with structural understanding. Yet, GenAI tools are adept at producing fluent, even impressive-sounding answers that mask shallow or non-existent understanding. This creates a pedagogical smoke screen where students can appear to meet outcomes without genuinely achieving them. The integrity of assessment, and by extension, the integrity of learning, is compromised.

There are also broader implications for the learning environment. Where classrooms once thrived on trust, openness and a willingness to learn through failure, the spectre of AI misuse can foster anxiety and mistrust. Students may fear being penalised, while teachers may second-guess the authenticity of student submissions. The classroom shifts from being a safe space for exploration to a guarded space of surveillance.

GenAI, then, is not inherently at odds with deep learning, but its application needs to be guided by pedagogical intention. Used thoughtfully, these tools can support reflection, prompt critical inquiry and provide scaffolds that promote learning. But without structure and ethical framing, they risk becoming vehicles for surface learning.

The challenge for educators is clear. Design learning experiences that make GenAI an ally in the journey of deep learning, rather than a shortcut around it. In this chapter, we will examine the use of GenAI in some of the most popular pedagogical approaches before introducing some new approaches with a GenAI foundation.

Integrating AI in the Top 5 Pedagogies

The integration of GenAI into educational settings introduces a significant philosophical tension: traditional pedagogy often emphasises certainty and structured knowledge, whereas GenAI operates within realms of ambiguity and probabilistic reasoning. This dichotomy becomes particularly pronounced in disciplines such as history, ethics and art, where interpretation and nuanced understanding are paramount.

In the field of digital humanities, Guo (2024) highlights concerns regarding the incorporation of GenAI tools like ChatGPT. While these tools can democratise access to data analysis and interpretation, they also risk oversimplifying complex humanistic inquiries. Guo notes that reliance on pattern-based approximations may dilute the depth and nuance essential to academic practice in the humanities.

These concerns are echoed more broadly in recent scholarship advocating for a reaffirmation of traditional humanistic inquiry. For instance, Wang et al. (2025) argue that the accelerated deployment of AI in fields such as translation and transcultural communication threatens to erode the interpretive rigour and cultural depth that humanistic disciplines cultivate. They caution against substituting AI-generated fluency for the slower, context-rich processes of human understanding, warning that a failure to preserve these qualities risks producing a culturally shallow educational environment.

Educators must therefore resist the temptation to outsource critical thinking to AI. Instead, they should foreground human judgement, encourage debate and design learning experiences that demand context-aware decision-making practices that GenAI cannot yet replicate.

The disruption of traditional pedagogies is not merely a technological shift but a paradigmatic one. As GenAI tools become embedded in educational practice, the assumptions, values and structures underpinning pedagogy must evolve. This is not a call to abandon established methods but an invitation to reimagine them in light of a new educational reality.

While the *top* pedagogical approaches can vary depending on context (discipline, age group, learning environment), research over the last decade consistently shows the highest impact on student engagement, retention and skill transfer from the following five in higher education and adult learning contexts. We will therefore examine how GenAI can be embedded into the learning and teaching activities of each, with several worked examples and illustrated uses.

Active Learning

Active learning is one of the most well-researched and widely celebrated approaches in higher education. At its heart, it shifts students away from being passive listeners and places them in the role of active participants who *do* something with the content. Instead of only absorbing information, they discuss it, argue over it, apply it to problems and reflect on what it means. Research has consistently shown that this style of learning improves engagement, retention and overall performance. In fact, a large meta-analysis by Freeman et al. (2014) found that students in active learning environments not only scored higher on assessments but were also far less likely to fail their courses.

Active learning can take many forms: quick "think-pair-share" activities, small group problem-solving, case study analysis or hands-on experimentation. The common thread across all of these is interaction, including students with each other, with the teacher and with the ideas themselves.

Where GenAI Fits In: GenAI can give active learning an extra dimension by adding immediacy, variety and even a touch of unpredictability. For example, while students are working on a problem in groups, they can quickly test their thinking against what an AI suggests. This doesn't replace their reasoning or the group discussion, but gives them another voice to react to, sometimes being supportive, sometimes challenging. AI can also surface alternative perspectives or prompt angles students may not have considered, keeping the discussion lively and pushing beyond the obvious.

The key is to treat AI not as the answer machine but as a conversation starter. It can stimulate new directions and highlight blind spots, but the heavy lifting, interpreting, debating and making judgements still sit with the students.

Building Critical Thinking with AI: One of the strengths of active learning is how it encourages higher-order thinking. Adding AI makes this even stronger. Students don't just have to come up with an answer; they also have to evaluate whether the AI's answer makes sense, where it falls short or what it misses altogether. This comparison naturally nudges them towards metacognition, where they're not only thinking about the problem but also reflecting on *how* they're reasoning and whether their process stands up against other approaches.

Because AI responses are probabilistic rather than definitive, they often introduce ambiguity. This is actually an advantage. It forces students to grapple with multiple possibilities and weigh competing arguments, which is precisely the kind of thinking that deepens understanding.

Worked Examples:

EXAMPLE 1: THINK-PAIR-SHARE WITH AN AI TWIST

1. **Think**: Students respond individually to a complex question, such as "What are the ethical trade-offs of using biometric data in urban surveillance?"
2. **Pair**: Before comparing with a peer, each student asks a GenAI system for its perspective. They then weigh their own ideas against the AI's, noting overlaps and differences.
3. **Share**: In small groups, students debate which arguments hold up best, with the teacher helping to highlight nuance and context.

Here, AI becomes a "third partner" in the conversation. It gives students something to push against or refine, without displacing the centrality of human dialogue.

STEP-BY-STEP INTERACTIONS

1. **Introduce the question.**
   The instructor poses a discipline-specific, debatable question (e.g., "What are the ethical trade-offs of using biometric data in urban surveillance?").
2. **Think (individual response).**
   Students write a short answer in 3–5 minutes, highlighting key arguments.
3. **AI consultation:**
   Prompt to AI:

> *Provide 3–4 perspectives on the following question:*
> *"What are the ethical trade-offs of using biometric data in urban surveillance?"*
> *For each perspective, give one supporting argument and one counterpoint.*
> *Keep responses under 200 words total.*

4. **Pair (compare ideas).**
   Students compare their own answer with the AI's, noting agreements, disagreements or entirely new perspectives.
   Follow-up prompt (optional):

> *Here is my argument: [paste].*
> *Compare it with the perspectives you generated earlier.*
> *Identify one strength and one limitation in my reasoning.*
> *Keep feedback constructive and under 100 words.*

5. **Share (small group discussion).**
   Groups discuss:
   1. Which perspectives seem most compelling and why?
   2. Where did AI add nuance or miss the mark?
   3. What contextual factors (historical, cultural, disciplinary) shape their judgements?

6. **Instructor wrap-up.**
   Teacher highlights strong examples of critical evaluation and reinforces that AI provides starting points but cannot replace human interpretation.

EXAMPLE 2: CASE STUDY WITH AI BRAINSTORMING

In a public health course, students are asked to design an intervention for a community dealing with a waterborne illness outbreak. As groups outline their strategies, they use AI to generate additional suggestions on communication methods, treatment prioritisation or logistical planning. Students then evaluate these AI contributions, filtering out impractical ones and adapting useful elements into their final plan.

The exercise shows students that while AI can throw ideas on the table, it is their contextual knowledge, ethical reasoning and critical evaluation that shape a workable solution.

STEP-BY-STEP INTERACTIONS

1. **Present the case**.
   The instructor shares a short scenario: "A rural community is experiencing a waterborne illness outbreak. Resources are limited. Design an intervention plan to contain the outbreak and protect public health."
2. **Group brainstorm (initial ideas)**.
   Students outline possible interventions (e.g., water treatment, public education, supply chain logistics).
3. **AI brainstorming**.
   Prompt to AI:

> *A rural community is experiencing an outbreak of waterborne illness.*
> *Resources are limited.*
> *Suggest 5 possible interventions across prevention, treatment and public communication.*
> *List pros and cons for each in a table format.*
> *Keep responses practical and concise.*

4. **Compare and critique**.
   Groups compare AI's ideas with their own, selecting those that are realistic and discarding those that are impractical.
   Follow-up prompt to AI:

> *Here is our proposed plan: [paste].*
> *Critique it from the perspective of feasibility in a low-resource setting.*
> *Suggest one improvement we could make.*

5. **Revise the plan.**
   Groups integrate useful AI suggestions while justifying why they accept or reject others.
6. **Instructor checkpoint.**
   Teacher asks:
   1. "Which AI suggestion added the most value, and why?"
   2. "What contextual factors did AI miss?"

7. **Present solutions.**
   Groups share their final intervention plans, focusing on critical reasoning and context-sensitive decision-making.

Final Reflections: Active learning thrives on participation and the exchange of ideas. GenAI can't replace those human interactions, but it can add sparks that make them richer. The real gains come when AI is used to provoke deeper questioning and reflection, helping students test their thinking in ways that a traditional classroom might not allow on its own.

Problem-Based Learning

Problem-Based Learning (PBL) is built around the idea that students learn best when they are tackling authentic, complex problems rather than working through neatly packaged exercises. Instead of being handed content first and applying it later, students begin with the problem and draw in the knowledge and skills they need along the way. Barrows and Tamblyn (1980), who pioneered PBL in medical education, argued that this approach more closely mirrors how professionals actually work: they encounter messy situations, identify what they need to know and collaborate to find viable solutions. Since then, PBL has spread widely, particularly in health, engineering and business education, where its focus on real-world application is especially valued.

In practice, a PBL cycle often begins with a scenario, like a patient presenting symptoms, a client with a project brief or a social issue needing intervention. Students work in groups to define the problem, identify knowledge gaps and divide tasks. The teacher becomes a facilitator, nudging inquiry without dictating solutions. The power of PBL lies in its capacity to foster self-directed learning, collaboration and problem-solving skills that extend beyond any single discipline.

Where GenAI Fits In: GenAI can add significant value to the PBL process, particularly in the early stages of problem scoping and brainstorming. Students can use AI to generate possible hypotheses, identify overlooked angles or surface background information quickly. This helps them map the problem space more efficiently, freeing up time to dig deeper into analysis and evaluation.

AI can also simulate stakeholders, offering perspectives that challenge student assumptions. For instance, in a business PBL task, AI could role-play as a sceptical investor or a concerned customer, allowing students to stress-test their proposals. However, as with Active Learning, the risk lies in students outsourcing too much of their thinking. Educators must design tasks where AI's role is clearly bounded: it can suggest, provoke or model perspectives, but it cannot decide the solution.

Building Critical Thinking with AI: The essence of PBL is inquiry and judgement. By introducing AI into the process, students gain an opportunity to practice discernment by deciding which AI-generated ideas are worth pursuing and which are superficial or misleading. This mirrors professional practice, where information from consultants, stakeholders or reports must be critically weighed rather than accepted at face value.

AI also introduces uncertainty, since its suggestions may not be contextually accurate or feasible. Students must therefore evaluate credibility, align ideas with disciplinary standards and justify their choices. These are the very capacities of critical thinking (analysis, evaluation and synthesis) that PBL is designed to strengthen.

Worked Examples:

EXAMPLE 1: MEDICAL PBL WITH AI HYPOTHESIS GENERATION

Students in a medical course are given a patient case presenting multiple overlapping symptoms. After brainstorming their initial hypotheses, they query an AI system to see what differential diagnoses it suggests. The students then compare their reasoning with the AI's output, identifying missing conditions or ruling out irrelevant ones. This not only deepens their medical reasoning but also trains them to treat AI as a supplementary resource rather than an authority.

STEP-BY-STEP INTERACTIONS

1. **Launch the case**.
   The instructor shares a short vignette (vitals, key symptoms, brief history).
   Teacher cue: "Your first task is to list differential diagnoses you consider most plausible and why."
2. **Individual hypothesis generation**.
   Students spend 5 minutes writing differentials with brief justifications.
   Student note template: Diagnosis, key supporting signs red flags to rule out.
3. **Group compare and consolidate**.
   Small groups merge lists and agree on top 5 candidates.
4. AI consultation: generate and justify differentials.
   Student prompt to AI:

> *You are a clinical reasoning assistant for medical students.*
> *Case: [paste vignette with vitals, onset, key positives/negatives, meds, risk factors].*
> *Task:*
>
> 1. *Produce a ranked differential diagnosis list (top 10) with brief pathophysiological rationale.*
> 2. *For each item, list key discriminating findings and initial tests.*
> 3. *Flag immediate red flags that require urgent action.*
> 4. *Format as a table. If uncertain, state the uncertainty explicitly.*

5. **Cross-check and gap analysis**.
   Students compare their group list with the AI list.
   Follow-up prompt to AI:

> *Here is our current differential: [paste].*
> *Identify any high-yield diagnoses we may have missed and justify why they belong or not, given the case data.*
> *Keep to <150 words.*

6. **Plan diagnostics**.
   Students draft an initial testing plan, then pressure-test it.

Prompt to AI:

> *Given this prioritised differential [paste] and this setting (urban emergency department with basic labs and imaging), propose a cost-conscious initial testing sequence.*
> *Explain how each test will discriminate among the top 5 possibilities.*

7. **Bias and safety check**.
   Prompt to AI:

> *Identify common cognitive biases that could mislead our workup on this case.*
> *Suggest two debiasing strategies we can apply now.*

8. **Instructor checkpoint**.
   Teacher circulates with two quick questions:
   1. "Which single piece of data would most change your plan, and why?"
   2. "What diagnosis are you most at risk of missing?"

9. **Decision and documentation**.
   Students finalise the plan and produce a brief **S**ubjective, **O**bjective, **A**ssessment, **P**lan (SOAP) entry.
   Prompt to AI for formatting only:

> *Review this note for structure and clarity only.*
> *Do not alter clinical content.*
> *Suggest headings and formatting improvements.*

10. **Metacognitive reflection**.
    Each student writes 120–150 words: What did AI add? What did it miss? What evidence most influenced your decision?
    Artefacts produced: prioritised differential table, testing plan with rationales, SOAP note, reflection.

EXAMPLE 2: ENGINEERING PBL WITH AI AS A STAKEHOLDER SIMULATOR

Engineering students are asked to design a renewable energy solution for a small rural community. Alongside their group discussions, they use AI to simulate responses from different stakeholders: a local government official, a community leader and an environmental activist. These perspectives force the students to refine their proposal, balancing technical feasibility with social and political realities. The activity underscores the importance of empathy and context in engineering practice.

STEP-BY-STEP INTERACTIONS

1. **Scenario brief.**
   Instructor provides community profile: population, load estimates, budget ceiling, grid access, terrain, regulatory constraints.
2. **Team scoping and roles.**
   Students assign roles: systems engineer, community liaison, environmental analyst, project manager. They define success criteria.
3. **Option generation.**
   Prompt to AI:

> *Context: Remote community energy project.*
> *Parameters: [paste quantitative constraints].*
> *Produce 3–4 feasible system architectures (e.g., solar + storage, wind + diesel backup),*
> *each with pros, cons, indicative capacities and key risks.*
> *Present in a concise comparison table.*

4. **Stakeholder simulation.**
   Prompt to AI:

> *Role-play three stakeholders responding to Option B:*
>
> 1. *Local council finance officer prioritising cost stability.*
> 2. *Community elder prioritising reliability and minimal disruption.*
> 3. *Conservation biologist prioritising habitat protection.*
>
> *Provide a short statement from each and 2–3 non-negotiable concerns.*

5. **Design iteration based on feedback.**
   Teams revise their preferred option to address concerns.
   Prompt to AI:

> *Given these stakeholder concerns [paste],*
> *suggest specific design modifications or operational policies that address each concern.*
> *Indicate expected impact on CAPEX, OPEX, reliability and environmental risk.*

6. **Preliminary sizing sanity check.**
   Prompt to AI:

> *Using these peak and average loads [paste], insolation/wind data [paste or cite source] and budget [value], propose rough-order sizing for generation and storage.*
> *State all assumptions. If data are missing, list what is needed.*

7. **Risk register and mitigation.**
   Prompt to AI:

> *Generate a risk register for our revised design.*
> *Include risk, likelihood, impact and mitigation actions.*
> *Limit to the top 8 risks.*

8. **Trade-off analysis.**
   Teams construct a simple decision matrix.
   Prompt to AI:

> *Build a multi-criteria comparison of Options A, B-revised and C across cost, reliability, maintainability, environmental impact and social acceptability.*
> *Provide a 0-5 score with one-sentence justifications.*
> *Do not pick a winner; the team will decide.*

9. **Equity and community impact check.**
   Prompt to AI:

> *Identify potential equity issues in our plan (tariff structures, land use, maintenance training).*
> *Suggest measures to ensure fair distribution of benefits and burdens.*

10. **Executive summary and defense.**
    Teams draft a two-page brief for the council.
    Prompt to AI for editing only:

> *Edit this executive summary for clarity and cohesion.*
> *Do not invent data or citations.*
> *Highlight any claims that require sources.*

11. **Reflection.**
    Each student writes a short memo on how stakeholder inputs changed the design and where AI advice was accepted or rejected, with reasons.
    Artefacts produced: comparison table of options, revised architecture with sizing assumptions, risk register, decision matrix, executive summary, reflection memos.

Final Reflections: Problem-Based Learning thrives on authentic, open-ended challenges. GenAI, when carefully integrated, can broaden the horizons of inquiry and add richness to the perspectives students encounter. The key lies in positioning AI as a catalyst for exploration, not a shortcut to the "answer." When used this way, it enhances the very qualities that make PBL so powerful: collaboration, critical thinking and the ability to navigate complexity in real-world contexts.

Inquiry-Based Learning

Inquiry-Based Learning places curiosity at the centre of the classroom. Rather than starting with content and moving towards questions, students begin with questions and follow lines of inquiry that lead them to knowledge. The approach has deep roots in Dewey's educational philosophy, which emphasised learning through experience and reflection (Dewey, 1986). In practice, inquiry can take different forms, such as structured, guided or open activities, depending on how much control the teacher gives students over the process.

At its best, inquiry-based learning develops intellectual curiosity, independence and a sense of ownership over knowledge. Students learn not just to answer questions but also to ask better ones. This iterative cycle of questioning, investigating and reflecting aligns well with scientific reasoning and also with the interpretive practices of the humanities and social sciences.

Where GenAI Fits In: GenAI can serve as a catalyst for inquiry by generating initial questions, providing multiple perspectives or surfacing counterpoints students might overlook. It can help students refine broad or vague inquiries into sharper, researchable ones. During the investigation phase, AI can simulate different schools of thought, suggest resources or highlight common pitfalls. However, the danger lies in students allowing AI to become the *source* of inquiry rather than the *support* for inquiry. To preserve rigour, educators must position AI as a tool for sparking and scaffolding student-driven exploration.

Building Critical Thinking with AI: Inquiry-based learning is inherently about critical engagement. By using AI-generated responses as a springboard rather than an endpoint, students practice evaluating credibility, identifying bias and situating knowledge within disciplinary frameworks. Comparing AI's perspectives with peer and scholarly sources encourages metacognitive reflection: What counts as evidence? Why does one interpretation carry more weight than another? This iterative evaluation process strengthens critical thinking by requiring students to judge not just the *answers* but also the *questions* that drive inquiry.

Worked Examples:

EXAMPLE 1: GENERATING AND REFINING RESEARCH QUESTIONS

Students are given a broad theme, such as "climate change and society," and must refine it into a focused research question. After developing their own drafts, they consult an AI system to brainstorm possible questions and critique their wording. The students then revise their questions, compare them with peers and justify why their version is the most promising line of inquiry.

STEP-BY-STEP INTERACTIONS

1. **Theme introduction**.
   The instructor presents the broad topic (e.g., "climate change and society").
2. **Initial brainstorming**.
   Students list 3–5 potential questions individually.
3. **AI brainstorming**.
   Prompt to AI:

> *Suggest 10 possible research questions on the theme "climate change and society."*
> *Provide a mix of descriptive, analytical and evaluative questions.*
> *Label each with the type of inquiry it represents.*

4. **Refinement step**.
   Students select one of their own questions and compare it with the AI list.
   Follow-up prompt:

> *Here is my draft research question: [paste].*
> *Critique it in terms of scope, clarity and researchability.*
> *Suggest two refinements that would make it stronger.*

5. **Group compare.**
   In small groups, students share their refined questions, discuss overlaps and identify which inquiries seem most promising.
6. **Instructor checkpoint.**
   Teacher highlights examples of well-scoped vs. overly broad or vague questions, reinforcing criteria for strong inquiry.

EXAMPLE 2: EXPLORING MULTIPLE PERSPECTIVES ON A HISTORICAL EVENT

Students are asked to investigate how different groups interpreted the fall of the Berlin Wall. They brainstorm possible stakeholders, then use AI to generate short summaries of their perspectives. From there, students identify sources to validate or challenge the AI-generated accounts, deepening their understanding of historical interpretation.

STEP-BY-STEP INTERACTION WITH PROMPTS

1. **Case introduction.**
   The instructor introduces the event and explains that the task is to examine multiple perspectives.
2. **Student hypotheses.**
   Students brainstorm which groups (e.g., East German citizens, West German politicians, Soviet officials, U.S. media) might have interpreted the event differently.
3. **AI perspective generation.**
   Prompt to AI:

> *Provide 4 contrasting perspectives on the fall of the Berlin Wall, each representing a different stakeholder (East German citizens, West German politicians, Soviet officials, U.S. journalists).*
> *For each, summarise their likely interpretation in under 100 words.*

4. **Critical comparison.**
   Students discuss in groups: Which perspectives align with what they already knew? Which seems surprising?

5. **Research follow-up.**
   Prompt to AI:

> *Suggest 5 primary or secondary sources (books, articles, archives) that could help verify or challenge each of the perspectives listed. Provide full citations where possible.*

6. **Independent validation.**
   Students select one perspective and research it further using scholarly sources, comparing AI's summary with what historians have argued.
7. **Reflection.**
   Each student writes a short commentary on how the AI's initial framing helped or hindered their inquiry.

Final Reflections: Inquiry-Based Learning is about cultivating curiosity and empowering students to drive their own learning journeys. GenAI can enrich this process by offering starting points, scaffolds and alternative viewpoints, but its role must remain secondary to student-led questioning and evaluation. When framed this way, AI supports the heart of inquiry: the pursuit of deeper, better questions that open pathways to discovery.

Collaborative Learning

Collaborative learning emphasises students working together to construct understanding, solve problems or create products. Unlike simple group work, where tasks may be divided and completed individually, collaboration requires interdependence: students must negotiate meaning, share perspectives and co-create knowledge. Johnson and Johnson's (1999) research on cooperative learning identified key conditions for success, including positive interdependence, individual accountability, promotive interaction and group processing. When these are present, collaborative learning has been shown to improve achievement, foster deeper understanding and build communication skills.

The approach can be structured in various ways: small-group projects, peer teaching, collaborative writing or problem-solving tasks. Regardless of the format, the goal is to use dialogue and joint effort to achieve outcomes that individuals could not accomplish alone.

Where GenAI Fits In: GenAI can strengthen collaborative learning by acting as a neutral third-party contributor that sparks discussion, challenges group assumptions or provides multiple perspectives for teams to debate. For example, it can generate draft ideas that groups critique together, simulate stakeholder voices for role-play activities or provide structured feedback on group outputs. At the same time, educators must ensure AI doesn't become the silent group member doing the cognitive heavy lifting. Its role should be to catalyse conversation and provide material for critique, not to replace the collaboration itself.

Building Critical Thinking with AI: Collaboration already nurtures critical thinking as students must evaluate ideas, weigh trade-offs and justify their reasoning to peers. Adding AI raises the level of challenge: groups now critique both each other's contributions and those of a machine. This forces explicit articulation of standards; what makes an idea credible, relevant or contextually appropriate. When students disagree with AI outputs, they sharpen their ability to defend their reasoning and identify flaws in probabilistic responses.

Worked Examples:

EXAMPLE 1: COLLABORATIVE POLICY DRAFTING

Students in a political science course are tasked with drafting a policy brief on regulating social media platforms. They work in small groups, using AI to generate multiple draft sections that they then revise, critique and integrate into a coherent final document.

STEP-BY-STEP INTERACTIONS

1. **Task launch.**
   Instructor assigns the group project: "Draft a policy brief recommending how governments should regulate misinformation on social media."

2. **Initial brainstorming**.
   Groups list possible approaches (e.g., government oversight, platform self-regulation, public education).
3. **AI draft generation**.

> *Generate three possible policy positions on how to regulate misinformation on social media platforms.*
> *For each, provide:*
>
> 1. *A brief description (50 words max),*
> 2. *One strength,*
> 3. *One potential drawback.*
>
> *Present as a table.*

4. **Group critique**.
   Students compare their brainstormed ideas with AI's suggestions. They debate which to adopt, adapt or reject.
5. **Drafting sections**.
   Each group member writes one section of the policy brief, then uses AI for constructive feedback.

> *Here is a draft section of our policy brief: [paste text].*
> *Review it for clarity, coherence and logical flow.*
> *Suggest no more than three specific improvements, keeping the original voice and intent.*

EXAMPLE 2: COLLABORATIVE CASE ROLE-PLAY

In a business course, students are given a case study on an international company facing a supply chain crisis. Each group member assumes the role of a different stakeholder (CEO, logistics manager, government regulator, community representative). AI is used to generate prompts and counterarguments for each role, fuelling deeper role-play discussions.

STEP-BY-STEP INTERACTIONS

1. **Case introduction.**
   Instructor provides a scenario: "A multinational company faces severe supply chain disruptions due to political unrest in a supplier country."
2. **Role assignment.**
   Students adopt different stakeholder perspectives.
3. **AI role briefings.**

> *Provide a short (150 words max) role briefing for each of the following stakeholders responding to a supply chain crisis:*
>
> 1. *CEO,*
> 2. *Logistics manager,*
> 3. *Government regulator,*
> 4. *Community representative.*
>
> *Each should outline their top priority and one major concern.*

4. **Role-play discussion.**
   Students debate strategies from their roles, referencing AI-generated briefs as starting points.
5. **AI counterarguments.**

> *Here are four proposed strategies from our group: [list].*
> *Generate counterarguments for each strategy from the perspective of one opposing stakeholder.*
> *Keep responses under 75 words each.*

6. **Group resolution.**
   Students negotiate a shared plan, documenting compromises and trade-offs.
7. **Reflection.**
   Students write individually: "How did AI's role-briefings and counterarguments shape our negotiation? Which ideas were most useful, and which did we reject?"

Final Reflections: Collaborative learning thrives when students must articulate, defend and revise ideas in dialogue with peers. GenAI enriches this process by offering multiple perspectives, draft materials and structured provocations that groups can test against their own reasoning. As long as AI's role is carefully framed, it strengthens rather than dilutes the collaborative process, ensuring that students, not the machine, remain the primary co-constructors of knowledge.

Flipped Classroom

The flipped classroom reverses the traditional teaching sequence. Instead of using class time for lectures and homework time for problem-solving, students first engage with content outside of class through readings, videos or tutorials, then use class sessions for active problem-solving, application and discussion. This approach frees classroom time for higher-order activities, where students can ask questions, practice skills and get immediate feedback from peers and instructors.

Bishop and Verleger's (2013) review of flipped classroom research emphasises its two essential elements: interactive group learning inside the classroom and direct computer-based instruction outside of it. When implemented well, the model has been shown to increase student engagement, improve learning outcomes and foster a more student-centred environment.

Where GenAI Fits In: GenAI can enhance both sides of the flipped model. Before class, AI can act as a personalised tutor, helping students clarify difficult concepts, generate practice questions or provide alternative explanations in simpler language. In class, it can serve as a stimulus for group work by providing scenarios, counterarguments or variations on problems for students to analyse. Importantly, AI should never replace the instructor's carefully designed learning materials but can act as a supplement to reinforce comprehension and extend inquiry.

Building Critical Thinking with AI: The flipped classroom is designed to free class time for analysis, synthesis and evaluation. AI can help scaffold this by posing follow-up questions, generating alternative perspectives and offering immediate but fallible responses for critique. Students learn not only by applying concepts but also by questioning and refining what

AI provides. This iterative cycle of explanation, critique and improvement strengthens metacognition and disciplinary reasoning.

Worked Examples:

EXAMPLE 1: PRE-CLASS CONCEPT EXPLORATION WITH AI TUTORING

Students in an economics course are assigned a video lecture on supply and demand to watch before class. Afterward, they use AI as a practice tutor to test their understanding, clarify misconceptions and prepare for in-class activities.

STEP-BY-STEP INTERACTION WITH PROMPTS

1. **Pre-class content.**
   Students watch a 15-minute lecture video on supply and demand principles.
2. **Self-check questions.**
   Students answer 3–5 multiple-choice questions created by the instructor.
3. **AI tutoring session.**

> *I've just watched a lecture on supply and demand.*
> *Ask me 5 practice questions that test both definitions (e.g., equilibrium price, elasticity) and application (e.g., predicting effects of a price ceiling).*
> *After each of my answers, tell me if I'm correct and explain why in less than 100 words.*

4. **Misconception correction.**
   If students miss a question, they prompt AI for clarification.

> *I answered this question incorrectly: [paste question and wrong answer].*
> *Explain where my reasoning went wrong and give me a hint for remembering the correct concept.*

5. **Class preparation.**
   Students come to class with a clearer understanding and specific questions to raise in group discussions.

EXAMPLE 2: IN-CLASS PROBLEM APPLICATION WITH AI VARIATION

During class, engineering students work in teams to solve a problem on bridge design. After completing the instructor's version, they use AI to generate alternative scenarios and test their understanding by adapting their solutions to new conditions.

STEP-BY-STEP INTERACTION WITH PROMPTS

1. **Instructor problem.**
   Teams calculate load-bearing requirements for a bridge design under given conditions.
2. **Initial group solution.**
   Students present their answers and explain their reasoning to peers.
3. **AI-generated variation.**

> Here is our bridge design problem: [paste original problem statement].
> *Create two new variations of this problem that increase complexity slightly (e.g., different materials, environmental constraints).*
> *Provide enough detail for calculation but keep the scope manageable for class discussion.*

4. **Group adaptation.**
   Teams attempt to solve the AI-generated variations, discussing which principles carry over and which need adjustment.
5. **AI critique and feedback.**

> *Here is our solution to the modified bridge problem: [paste solution].*
> *Check the reasoning for logical consistency.*
> *Do not give the correct answer, just flag possible flaws or overlooked considerations.*

6. **Instructor synthesis.**
   The teacher closes the session by highlighting how core concepts apply across contexts and where deeper disciplinary knowledge is required.

Final Reflections: The flipped classroom shifts the focus of class time from content delivery to active problem-solving. GenAI strengthens this model by supporting pre-class preparation with personalised feedback and enriching in-class application with dynamic variations and critiques. Used well, it amplifies the flipped classroom's central promise: to make face-to-face time more engaging, critical and collaborative.

The discussion so far has examined how GenAI can be woven into five of the most established pedagogies in higher education: Active Learning, Problem-Based Learning, Inquiry-Based Learning, Collaborative Learning and the Flipped Classroom. Each is backed by decades of research showing its positive impact on student engagement, retention and critical thinking. By exploring worked examples, we have seen that AI can extend the reach of these approaches by providing fresh perspectives, scaffolding inquiry and provoking deeper reflection while still requiring educators to preserve the human-centred qualities that make these pedagogies effective.

Beyond these well-established models lies a landscape of pedagogies that are newer, less tested and often still evolving. These *emerging pedagogies* frequently grow out of changes in technology, culture or educational philosophy. They may lack the weight of long-term evidence, yet they capture the spirit of experimentation and innovation that characterises contemporary teaching practice. In the context of AI, they open possibilities not just for enhancing traditional methods but for reimagining how learning itself is structured in an increasingly digital and interconnected world.

THE EMERGENCE OF NEW PEDAGOGIES

Emerging pedagogies represent the frontier of educational practice, where innovation often outpaces long-term evaluation. Unlike the well-established approaches we have already examined, these pedagogies are shaped by rapid advances in technology, shifting cultural contexts and evolving theories of how people learn in digital environments. They invite experimentation, encourage flexibility and often blur traditional boundaries between formal and informal learning. While their research base may still be developing, their relevance is undeniable, particularly as GenAI accelerates the transformation of how knowledge is created, shared and experienced. Exploring these pedagogies allows us to imagine futures of teaching and learning that are not simply adjusted to AI but fundamentally reshaped by it.

No longer are students solely dependent on educators to access or interpret information. While tools like Google Search have long provided vast repositories of knowledge, students often encounter difficulty in constructing effective queries and critically interpreting the returned results. In contrast, conversational agents like ChatGPT offer a more guided and intuitive interaction, reducing the friction between question and comprehension.

Research by Niranon and Triyason (2024) showed that students using ChatGPT for self-learning not only performed better on analytical tasks but did so in less time compared to peers using traditional search engines. Similarly, Zhang and Yang (2025) found that students were drawn to ChatGPT's fluent, personalised and seemingly empathic responses, frequently describing it as more like conversing with a helpful tutor than searching a database. This rapport fosters a sense of trust and engagement, even when students remain aware of the tool's fallibility.

As a result, many students are more likely to explore topics in greater depth with ChatGPT than they would with search engines, simply because the AI feels accessible and responsive. Yet, this shift in interaction raises important pedagogical concerns. With AI tools capable of generating multiple plausible answers, contrasting viewpoints and sophisticated explanations, the conventional role of the educator, as the gatekeeper of correct information, begins to shift. This prompts deeper questions: What is the role of the teacher in an AI-augmented classroom? How do we assess learning when knowledge can be generated on demand?

Meta-AI Literacy

The cultivation of meta-AI literacy (Carolus et al., 2023) encourages students to approach AI not as a magic oracle, but as a collaborator in thought. Understanding how students and teachers perceive and engage with AI is critical in an age where AI technologies increasingly shape both professional and everyday contexts. Traditional definitions of AI literacy, often focused on knowledge, application and ethical awareness, are no longer sufficient for comprehensively capturing what it means to be AI literate in practice. In response to this gap, Carolus et al. (2023) developed the Meta AI Literacy Scale (MAILS), a psychometrically validated instrument that not only measures core AI competencies such as understanding, detecting, using and ethically evaluating AI, but crucially expands the construct to include *psychological meta-competencies* such as self-efficacy, problem-solving, emotion regulation and persuasion literacy.

This broader framing is particularly important for educators seeking to prepare students for a future shaped by rapid technological change. Unlike earlier instruments, MAILS distinguishes between possessing factual knowledge about AI and having the self-regulatory and emotional tools to *persist*, *adapt* and *critically reflect* when working with intelligent systems. For students, this means that simply being taught how AI works is not enough; they must also be equipped to manage their own confidence, learning strategies and emotional responses when using or being influenced by AI technologies.

In educational contexts, such a measure enables instructors and researchers to assess not only what students know about AI, but how prepared they are to navigate it in complex, real-world situations. For instance, a student who understands AI theoretically but lacks the self-efficacy to experiment with AI tools, or who is easily swayed by persuasive AI interfaces, may struggle to use these systems responsibly and effectively. By identifying these psychological dimensions, MAILS provides a powerful lens for tailoring instruction, interventions and support services that foster sustainable and ethical engagement with AI. A methodology for measuring student meta-ai literacy, adapted from the 34 self-assessment questions provided in Carolus et al. (2023), is shown in Table 6.1

The pedagogical shift here involves scaffolding iterative thinking and reflective practices rather than delivering static content.

As the MAILS framework demonstrates, a comprehensive understanding of AI literacy must extend beyond technical knowledge and ethical awareness. It must incorporate the metacognitive and affective capacities students need to navigate an AI-mediated world: self-efficacy, emotion regulation, persuasion literacy and adaptive learning strategies. These are not ancillary skills; they are foundational to student agency, critical engagement and ethical AI use.

This expanded conception of AI literacy has clear implications for educational design. It demands more than curriculum revision; it requires a

TABLE 6.1 Methodology for Measuring Student Meta-AI Literacy Using MAILS

Component	Sub-Dimensions	Sample Items (Self-Assessment Prompts)
1. AI Literacy		
Use and Apply AI	Practical usage of AI in everyday contexts	"I can use AI applications to make my everyday life easier."
Understand AI	Knowledge of AI concepts and implications	"I know the most important concepts of the topic 'artificial intelligence.'"
Detect AI	Ability to identify AI systems	"I can distinguish if I interact with an AI or a real human."
AI Ethics	Awareness of ethical implications	"I can weigh the consequences of using AI for society."
Create AI (*optional*)	Ability to develop AI applications	"I can develop new AI applications."
2. Meta-Competencies	Confidence in AI-related learning and problem-solving	"I can handle most problems in dealing with artificial intelligence well on my own."
AI Self-Efficacy	Confidence in AI-related learning and problem-solving	"I can handle most problems in dealing with artificial intelligence well on my own."
AI Learning	Ability to stay current with AI	"Although there are often new AI applications, I manage to always be 'up-to-date.'"
3. AI Self-Competency		
Persuasion Literacy	Awareness of AI influence on decision-making	"I realise if artificial intelligence is influencing me in my everyday decisions."
Emotion Regulation	Managing emotions in AI use	"I can handle it when everyday interactions with AI frustrate or frighten me."

structural recalibration of how we define and assess student readiness in an AI-integrated society. The existing accreditation frameworks, grounded largely in traditional cognitive domains, must evolve to include meta-AI competencies as core graduate attributes.

Just as GenAI is reshaping what it means to learn, teach and assess, it also compels a reassessment of institutional benchmarks for program quality. We must ask: How well do our graduates manage uncertainty, critique algorithmic outputs and sustain inquiry in conversation with AI? Can they identify when their own reasoning has been nudged by persuasive interfaces or undermined by cognitive fatigue in AI-mediated tasks?

These questions cannot be answered through content mastery alone; they require instruments like MAILS, which evaluate learners' dispositions and capacities to think with, through and against intelligent systems.

This shift sets the stage for Generativism, a pedagogical paradigm that positions AI not as an object of instruction but as a dialogic partner in learning. As the next section will argue, the future of education lies in designing co-constructed learning environments where human and AI intelligences interact in ways that prioritise sense-making, critical reflection and the iterative construction of knowledge. The inclusion of meta-AI literacy in accreditation metrics is therefore not a peripheral concern; it is a prerequisite for building educational systems that are resilient, adaptive and ethically grounded in the age of GenAI.

Generativism

Generativism is a pedagogy proposed by Pratschke (2023) that explicitly treats GenAI as a co-designer, co-deliverer and co-assessor of learning. Drawing on constructivist, social and experiential traditions, Generativism emphasises knowledge as something produced in collaboration with AI rather than consumed from it. Where traditional approaches tend to treat AI as an enhancement to existing teaching, Generativism makes the human–AI partnership its defining feature.

Generativism meets the criteria that define a pedagogy.

1. **Philosophical and theoretical grounding**. Generativism builds on constructivism (Piaget, 2013, Vygotsky, 1978), social learning (Bandura & Walters, 1977), experiential learning (Kolb, 1984) and connectivism (Siemens, 2005), but reframes them for the Web 4.0 era. Its central epistemological claim is that learning occurs through *symbiotic interaction* with generative systems, where students act as both interpreters and co-authors of knowledge.

2. **Core principles and values**. Generativism assumes that students are active agents who codesign their learning in partnership with AI. The teacher's role shifts from authority to facilitator, while AI functions as collaborator, challenger and guide. The goal is not simply knowledge acquisition but iterative meaning-making in a dynamic human–AI ecosystem.

3. **Characteristic practices.** In practice, Generativism is defined by:
   - o **Codesign** of tasks and learning experiences with AI, where prompts, scaffolds and scenarios are co-created.
   - o **Codelivery** of activities, where AI operates as tutor, role-player or provocateur in real time alongside peers.
   - o **Coassessment**, where reflection on the dialogue with AI forms part of the evaluative process.

4. **Assessment stance.** Generativism emphasises *assessment as learning*, where the process of interacting with AI by asking, critiquing, iterating and revising is as important as any final output. This marks a shift from product-oriented grading to process-oriented evaluation that captures how students engage critically and creatively with machine partners.

5. **Theory–practice loop.** Though still new, Generativism is already visible in practice. The worked examples we explored in earlier sections of AI-enhanced Active Learning, AI-supported PBL and others all embody the spirit of Generativism. They illustrate that even when educators believe they are "adding AI" to an existing pedagogy, they are in fact already participating in Generativist practice.

In this sense, Generativism sits both *within* and *beyond* the Top 5. It is visible in their AI-infused adaptations, yet it also stands apart as a pedagogy in its own right: one that makes the human–AI relationship central rather than incidental. This dual positioning suggests that Generativism may become the defining pedagogical orientation of the GenAI era, a framework that both reframes existing approaches and offers a foundation for entirely new ones.

Worked Examples

EXAMPLE 1: CO-DESIGNING A RESEARCH QUESTION

Students in a sociology seminar are tasked with exploring how AI influences civic participation. Rather than beginning with a teacher-assigned question, the class codesigns the inquiry with GenAI, iteratively refining the scope and focus. This process highlights Generativism's principle that learning is co-constructed with AI.

STEP-BY-STEP INTERACTION WITH PROMPTS

1. **Initial brainstorming.**
   Students draft tentative questions on AI and civic participation.
2. **AI expansion of options.**

> Generate 10 possible research questions about the relationship between AI and civic participation.
> Include a mix of descriptive (what is happening), analytical (why it happens) and evaluative (what should be done) questions.

3. **Comparison and refinement.**
   Students compare their own drafts with AI's list, noting overlaps and novel angles.
4. **Collaborative refinement with AI.**

> Here is our draft research question: [paste].
> Critique it for scope, clarity and researchability.
> Suggest two refinements that make it more precise and academically rigorous.

5. **Class selection.**
   Groups present their refined questions, and the class votes on which to pursue.
6. **Co-assessment.**
   Students reflect on how AI shaped their thinking and submit a short commentary on what they retained, revised or rejected.

EXAMPLE 2: AI AS CO-ASSESSOR IN A CREATIVE PROJECT

In a media studies course, students create short podcasts critiquing representations of AI in popular culture. After producing their draft episodes, they invite AI into the assessment process as a feedback partner, aligning with Generativism's emphasis on coassessment.

STEP-BY-STEP INTERACTION WITH PROMPTS

1. **Project creation.**
   Students produce 5–7 minute podcasts analysing films or TV series that feature AI.
2. **AI peer review.**

> Here is the transcript of our podcast: [paste].
> Evaluate it using three criteria: clarity of argument, use of evidence and critical engagement with cultural context.
> Provide feedback in bullet points, no more than 100 words per criterion.

3. **Student response.**
   Students discuss which pieces of AI feedback are valid, which miss the mark and why.
4. **Revision cycle.**

> Here is our revised transcript.
> Compare it with the original and identify the most significant improvements.
> Suggest one further change to strengthen the analysis.

5. **Final reflection.**
   Students submit their final podcast along with a brief essay explaining how both peer and AI feedback shaped their revisions.

These examples demonstrate how Generativism differs from the Top 5 pedagogies: the AI is not just a supplement but an active participant in codesign, codelivery and coassessment. Students are evaluated not only on their final product but also on the quality of their interaction with AI; what they chose to keep, adapt or reject.

Designing Courses through Generativism

Designing courses in alignment with generativism requires a shift from content delivery to dialogic learning experiences in which students engage with GenAI as both a cognitive tool and a collaborative partner. The ABC

Learning Design Framework (Young et al., 2019) provides a robust structure for this transformation.

The application of generativism through the ABC Learning Design Framework (Young et al., 2019) allows educators to operationalise the theory in tangible ways across diverse instructional contexts. By aligning GenAI capabilities with each of the six activity types, Acquisition, Investigation, Discussion, Collaboration, Practice and Production, educators can scaffold meaningful student engagement that balances cognitive, social and metacognitive dimensions of learning. Table 6.2 provides a structured overview of how each ABC activity can be reimagined through a generativist lens, illustrating the role of GenAI, associated pedagogical strategies and practical examples of implementation. This framework supports intentional design that not only integrates AI tools but also cultivates critical, reflective and ethically grounded learner practices.

In the *Acquisition* phase, traditional lectures and reading materials are augmented by custom GPTs, document-based chatbots and interactive explainers. This allows students not only to access core content but to question, probe and personalise their understanding in real time. For *Investigation*, learners are guided to conduct critical AI-assisted research using tools like semantic search engines, agent-based retrieval systems and hypothesis-testing through simulated models, all while reflecting on the epistemological limits of AI-generated knowledge.

In the *Discussion* and *Collaboration* phases, GAI functions as a dialogic partner that can mediate, moderate or extend student conversation. For example, AI personas representing conflicting scholarly viewpoints can be used to scaffold debate, provoke argumentation or challenge assumptions. Students can co-construct knowledge with peers and bots alike, refining ideas through iterative questioning and response. In *Practice*, AI becomes a rehearsal space, where students can test language fluency, debug code or revise argumentative essays with instant feedback and reflective prompts. Finally, in *Production*, learners synthesise their understanding through generative tasks: designing AI prompts, curating learning artefacts or creating comparative outputs that juxtapose human and AI-generated work. Across each activity type, the educator's role becomes one of orchestration, designing learning environments that prioritise metacognitive awareness, encourage critical AI interaction and assess not just the outcomes, but the *process* of knowledge construction.

TABLE 6.2 Designing Courses with Generativism Using the ABC Framework

ABC Activity Type	Role of GenAI	Generativist Strategy	Sample Implementation
Acquisition	Interactive explainer and tutor	Personalised content inquiry	Students use a custom GPT trained on course readings to explore key concepts through dialogue.
Investigation	Research assistant and semantic search engine	Critical analysis and sense-making	Learners compare AI-generated literature reviews with human-authored sources, reflecting on biases and validity.
Discussion	Dialogic provocateur and peer avatar	Argumentation and reflection	AI personas representing differing theoretical views engage students in structured debates and Socratic questioning.
Collaboration	Co-constructor of knowledge	Co-design and peer engagement	Students and AI co-author a project proposal, with peer review cycles facilitated by AI-generated feedback prompts.
Practice	Feedback generator and simulation tool	Iterative learning and self-monitoring	Learners rehearse skills (e.g., language, coding, argumentation) with GAI, receiving scaffolded prompts and reflections.
Production	Creative partner and critical comparator	Knowledge synthesis and transformation	Students generate artefacts (e.g., essays, videos, code) using GenAI, then critique and improve them through human analysis.

In many ways, Generativism illustrates how pedagogical innovation and conceptual frameworks work in tandem. As a pedagogy, it provides a philosophical stance and practical activities that centre learning on co-construction with AI.

While generativism provides the pedagogical architecture for designing collaborative, dialogic and sense-making experiences with GenAI, it also invites a deliberate shift in how we conceptualise learner agency. Central to this approach is not only the co-construction of knowledge but also the cultivation of critical distance; an ability to question the outputs of AI, challenge dominant narratives and reflect on one's own epistemic stance. This is where the strategic use of *provocations* becomes essential. As a complementary strategy to generative learning, provocations function as intentionally dissonant design elements that deepen engagement, disrupt passivity and prompt ethical interrogation. In what follows, we explore how provocations can be deployed to surface ambiguity, foster critique and position AI as a site of inquiry rather than certainty.

Provocations

In the context of GenAI, *provocations* serve as structured disruptions to passive learning, intentionally designed to challenge assumptions, surface bias and activate critical reflection (Drosos et al. 2025). As a pedagogical strategy, provocations use GenAI not merely to deliver content or automate tasks, but to create friction. This means productive moments of uncertainty or contradiction that invite learners to pause, interrogate and respond. Drawing from constructivist and dialogic learning traditions, this strategy reframes AI not as a neutral assistant but as a catalyst for deeper engagement with both disciplinary knowledge and the epistemic risks of automation.

In practice, provocations might involve presenting learners with subtly flawed AI-generated texts, ethically dubious prompts or conflicting interpretations of data, and asking them to identify, evaluate or reconcile these tensions. For example, an AI-generated policy brief on climate migration may omit socio-political variables, inviting students to critique its framing and propose alternatives. In literature or history courses, AI-written narratives could deliberately introduce anachronisms or cultural biases to prompt close reading and source triangulation. The goal is not to "catch the AI out" but to develop students' capacity to engage in epistemic vigilance: the ability to assess credibility, trace provenance and defend their own interpretations.

Such provocations can also extend to metacognitive reflection. When students co-write with AI, they may be asked to compare early drafts with final outputs, analysing how their own cognitive processes shifted through the interaction. Who led the writing? Whose voice dominates the final product? Where did critical engagement fade into compliance? These are not only pedagogical questions but foundational to the emerging ethics of human–AI collaboration. Provocation, then, is a generativist strategy that supports both cognitive dissonance and ethical deliberation, helping students develop resilient, adaptive and reflexive modes of learning in the age of artificial intelligence.

The following worked examples illustrate how provocations can be used in a classroom setting.

WORKED EXAMPLE 1: EPISTEMIC TENSION AS A CLASSROOM STRATEGY

Context: Undergraduate History Course; "Global Conflict and Memory"

Provocation Type: Epistemic Tension

Pedagogical Objective: Develop source evaluation and argumentation skills by analysing AI-generated outputs that present contradictory interpretations of a historical event.

Design and Implementation: The instructor prompts a GenAI to produce two historical narratives of the Rwandan Genocide. One version emphasises ethnic divisions and colonial legacies as the primary cause; the other foregrounds international political inertia and media silence. Both texts are generated with scholarly tone and plausible citations, but each omits key contextual factors.

Students are divided into groups and assigned one AI narrative to analyse critically. They are asked to:

1. Identify underlying assumptions, omissions and potential bias in the AI-generated account.
2. Compare their narrative with peer groups' opposing versions.
3. Reconstruct a more balanced, evidence-informed synthesis based on both texts and independent historical sources.

Assessment: Students write a short position paper articulating their revised interpretation of the genocide, justifying their analytical decisions and reflecting on how the AI-generated texts shaped their evaluative process.

Learning Outcome: By grappling with epistemic tension, students deepen their historical reasoning, develop critical reading practices and recognise AI as a generator of perspectives, ones that require human judgement to contextualise, challenge or refine.

WORKED EXAMPLE 2: PRODUCTIVE FAILURE AS A CLASSROOM STRATEGY

Context: Undergraduate Computer Science Course; "Introduction to Algorithm Design"

Provocation Type: Productive Failure

Pedagogical Objective: Highlight the importance of human oversight, error diagnosis and iterative problem-solving when working with AI-generated code.

Design and Implementation: The instructor provides students with a Python function generated by a GenAI tool (e.g., ChatGPT or GitHub Copilot) that purports to implement Dijkstra's algorithm. The code is syntactically correct and partially functional, but includes subtle logic errors: it fails to correctly update distances when encountering shorter paths, and does not handle disconnected graphs.

Students are instructed to:

1. **Run and test the AI-generated code** using a variety of graph inputs.
2. **Document and explain** the discrepancies between expected and actual output.
3. **Debug and revise** the code to align with the correct algorithmic logic.
4. **Reflect** on how and why the AI made these mistakes, and what cognitive strategies they used to correct them.

Assessment: Students submit a debug report that includes:

- A corrected version of the code
- A description of the logic errors in the AI output
- A reflection on how debugging improved their conceptual understanding of the algorithm

Learning Outcome: By working through a controlled failure generated by AI, students engage in deeper sense-making and develop resilience in the face of error. The exercise reinforces algorithmic reasoning, promotes computational metacognition and instils a critical stance towards AI outputs in technical domains.

Further provocations that can be used in learning activities are outlined in Table 6.3.

TABLE 6.3 Types of AI-Based Provocations and Their Pedagogical Objectives

Provocation Type	Description	Pedagogical Objective	Example Implementation
Cognitive Mismatch	Presenting plausible but flawed AI output to surface misconceptions	Activate prior knowledge, strengthen analytical reasoning	AI summarises a theory but omits a key principle; students identify and revise.
Ethical Dissonance	Introducing morally ambiguous or biased AI content	Stimulate ethical reasoning and values clarification	AI generates hiring criteria that reproduce gender bias, students critique assumptions.
Epistemic Tension	Offering conflicting AI-generated claims or interpretations	Develop source evaluation and argumentation skills	Two AI outputs present opposing conclusions on a historical event; students adjudicate based on evidence.
Affective Disruption	Using emotionally provocative or unsettling content to spark reflection	Foster emotional intelligence and empathy in AI interactions	AI writes a poem from a war refugee's perspective; students reflect on affective impact and authenticity.
Voice and Authorship Blur	Having students co-write with AI, then interrogate ownership and influence	Encourage metacognitive reflection on collaboration, identity and agency	Students compare their original draft with the final AI-assisted version; who shaped the argument?
Productive Failure	Deliberately prompting AI to produce incorrect or weak responses	Highlight the importance of human oversight and iterative problem-solving	Students prompt AI to solve a complex equation incorrectly, then correct and explain the error.

From Critical Engagement to Intentional Design

As this chapter has shown, GenAI is not merely a tool to be integrated into educational settings. It is a phenomenon that reshapes how learning is conceived, facilitated and experienced. Through the lenses of generativism, meta-AI literacy and strategic provocations, we have explored how educators can design for dialogic, reflective and ethically responsive learning environments. These frameworks foreground not only the *what* of AI-enabled learning but the *how* and *why*, prompting a shift from content delivery to critical co-construction.

Yet, designing such experiences requires more than a theoretical orientation. It demands precision and intentionality in how educators engage with the AI itself. If generativism invites us to think with AI, and provocations train us to think against it, then prompt engineering becomes the practice through which we learn to *shape* it. Chapter 7 turns to this pragmatic dimension, offering educators the tools to craft prompts that elicit meaningful, contextually grounded and pedagogically aligned outputs. It explores how the art and science of prompt engineering can become a literacy in its own right. One that empowers both teachers and learners to direct the flow of AI-enhanced inquiry.

REFLECT AND REFRAME

1. How does Generativism reframe the role of the teacher in AI-integrated learning environments? In what ways does this differ from traditional pedagogies you've used or experienced?
2. Which dimensions of meta-AI literacy (e.g., self-efficacy, emotion regulation, persuasion literacy) are most relevant to your teaching context? How could they be embedded into course outcomes?
3. What criteria would you use to evaluate a student's ability to critically engage with AI outputs (e.g., their ability to detect bias, challenge assumptions or revise conclusions)?
4. How do you differentiate between augmentation and substitution when introducing AI into your courses? How do students understand this distinction?

REFERENCES

Bandura, A., and Walters, R. H., 1977. *Social learning theory* (Vol. 1, pp. 141–154). Prentice hall.

Barrows, H. S. and Tamblyn, R. M., 1980. *Problem-based learning: An approach to medical education*. Springer Publishing Company.

Biggs, J., Tang, C., and Kennedy, G. (2022). *Teaching for quality learning at university* (5th ed.). McGraw-Hill Education.

Bishop, J., and Verleger, M. A., 2013, June. The flipped classroom: A survey of the research. In *2013 ASEE annual conference & exposition* (pp. 23–1200).

Carolus, A., Koch, M. J., Straka, S., Latoschik, M. E. and Wienrich, C., 2023. MAILS-Meta AI literacy scale: Development and testing of an AI literacy questionnaire based on well-founded competency models and psychological change-and meta-competencies. *Computers in Human Behavior: Artificial Humans, 1*(2), 100014.

Dewey, J. (1986). Experience and education. In *The educational forum* (Vol. 50, No. 3, pp. 241–252). Taylor & Francis Group.

Drosos, N., Karvounidis, T., Karvounidis, I, and Douligeris, C. 2025. Provocations in AI-supported education: Rethinking critical engagement. *International Journal of Educational Technology in Higher Education*, 22(1), 1–17.

Freeman, S., Eddy, S. L., McDonough, M., Smith, M. K., Okoroafor, N., Jordt, H, and Wenderoth, M. P., 2014. Active learning increases student performance in science, engineering, and mathematics. *Proceedings of the national academy of sciences, 111*(23), 8410–8415.

Guo, Q., 2024. Prompting change: ChatGPT's impact on digital humanities pedagogy–A case study in art history. *International Journal of Humanities and Arts Computing*, 18(1), 58–78.

Johnson, D. W. and Johnson, R. T., 1999. Making cooperative learning work. *Theory Into Practice*, *38*(2), 67–73.

Kolb, D. A. (1984) *Experiential learning: Experience as the source of learning and development*. Prentice Hall.

Niranon, D, and Triyason, T. 2024. ChatGPT as a learning companion: A comparative study with traditional search tools. *Journal of Educational Computing Research*, 62(4), 765–784.

Piaget, J., 2013. *Origin of Intelligence in the Child: Selected Works vol 3*. Routledge.

Pratschke, B. M., 2023. Generativism: the new hybrid. *arXiv preprint arXiv: 2309.12468*.

Siemens, G., 2005. Connectivism: A learning theory for the digital age. *International Journal of Instructional Technology and Distance Learning*. [Online]. http://www.idtl.org/Journal/Jam_05/article01.html

Vygotsky, L. S., 1978. *Mind in society: The development of higher psychological processes* (Vol. 86). Harvard University Press.

Wang, J. Q., Liu, G., and Lei, Y., 2025. Reaffirming the importance of traditional humanities in the era of AI-enhanced translation and transcultural communication. *International Communication of Chinese Culture*, 12(2), 277–311.

Young, C., Perović, N., & Baume, D. (2019). *ABC Learning Design: A toolkit for rapid course design*. University College London. https://abc-ld.org

Zhang, M, and Yang, X. (2025). Google or ChatGPT: Who is the better helper for university students. *Education and Information Technologies*, 30(4), 5177–5198.

CHAPTER 7

Prompt Engineering for Learning and Teaching

> **CHAPTER AIMS**
>
> *The aim of this chapter is to introduce key themes explored in this book in relation to:*
>
> 1. *Prompt engineering as a new form of digital literacy for teachers and students.*
> 2. *The integration of prompting across preparation, instruction, reflection and assessment, alongside its risks.*
> 3. *The ways prompting reshapes teacher roles, learner agency and ethical engagement with AI.*

PROMPT ENGINEERING AS CURRICULUM

Prompt design is emerging as a central skill in AI-mediated education. In Guo's (Qiuzi, 2024) case study on digital humanities, students learned to extract meaning from complex data through the iterative crafting of prompts. This repositions educators as mentors in inquiry, guiding students not to the *right answer* but through a process of dialogue with the machine. Such practices embody a shift from product-oriented instruction to process-oriented exploration.

DOI: 10.1201/9781003624981-7

Studies by Zhang (2024) and Niranon and Triyason (2024) reinforce this, showing that students with high GenAI literacy and trust in the system tend to interact more deeply with learning tasks. However, this interaction can lead to overreliance unless counterbalanced by critical thinking skills. Thus, emerging pedagogy must blend prompt proficiency with evaluative habits.

For decades, one of the most critical skills students could develop was the ability to ask good questions. In traditional classrooms, this involved learning how to formulate inquiries that probed deeper thinking, clarified misunderstandings or initiated exploration. With the rise of the internet, this skill evolved into mastering the art of searching through knowing what keywords to use, how to phrase a query in Google and how to critically evaluate the relevance and credibility of the results. Educators often spent time explicitly teaching students how to *Google well.* Today, with the advent of GenAI, the search box has transformed into a dialogue box, and the questions we ask have become prompts. Prompt engineering has become the new search literacy, requiring not only clarity and specificity but also an understanding of how to scaffold, sequence and refine instructions to elicit useful, accurate and creative responses from AI tools.

In educational contexts, prompt engineering holds the potential to augment learning by enabling more tailored, responsive and reflective engagement with content. Educators can use prompts to design lesson plans, generate formative feedback and explore alternate explanations of difficult concepts. Students, in turn, can use prompting to extend inquiry, simulate dialogue or rehearse critical thinking. However, the effectiveness of these applications depends not merely on access to AI but on the *quality and intent* of the prompts provided.

This chapter situates prompt engineering within contemporary educational theory and practice. It provides a structured exploration of how educators can design pedagogically sound prompts to support diverse learning outcomes, and how students can be taught to prompt critically and creatively. It also addresses the growing need for *meta-AI literacy* as first presented in Chapter 6: AI and the Top 5.

As artificial intelligence becomes increasingly integrated into digital learning environments, the ability to prompt well is emerging as a cornerstone of 21st-century educational fluency. This chapter aims to equip readers with both conceptual insight and practical strategies to harness the power of prompt engineering for teaching, learning and assessment.

THEORETICAL FOUNDATIONS

The integration of prompt engineering into teaching and learning sits at the intersection of established educational theories and emerging technological paradigms. While the act of crafting a prompt may seem purely functional or technical, it is in fact deeply pedagogical and shaped by how we understand learning, cognition and communication. To use prompt engineering effectively, educators must consider not only what a prompt produces, but how it supports or disrupts meaningful learning.

Constructivism and Learner Agency

Prompt engineering aligns closely with constructivist theories of education, which posit that learners construct knowledge actively through engagement and exploration. A well-designed prompt acts not as a shortcut to knowledge, but as a scaffold that encourages students to think critically, draw connections and reframe information. When students generate their own prompts to guide AI interactions, they exercise metacognitive control over their learning process, deciding what they want to know, how they want to explore it and what constitutes a satisfactory response. This learner agency mirrors the constructivist emphasis on ownership and inquiry in the learning process (Cole, et al., 1978; Piaget & Cook, 1952).

PROMPT INTERACTION EXAMPLE: STUDENT-GENERATED INQUIRY IN A HISTORY SEMINAR

Context: Undergraduate course on *Modern Revolutions*. Students are exploring the causes of the French Revolution.

INITIAL STUDENT PROMPT TO AI

> *"Explain the primary causes of the French Revolution in simple terms."*

- **Constructivist Note**: At this stage, the student sets the scope of inquiry, activating *prior knowledge* and framing a baseline from which to build.

STUDENT REFLECTION AND REFINEMENT

The student realises the answer is too general and wants to focus on competing interpretations.

FOLLOW-UP STUDENT PROMPT TO AI

> *"Compare how Marxist historians and revisionist historians interpret the causes of the French Revolution. Include key figures and points of disagreement."*

- **Constructivist Note**: Here, the student is *reframing* the task, moving from recall-level knowledge towards disciplinary *sense-making*. They are constructing understanding by drawing connections between different schools of thought.

METACOGNITIVE EXPANSION

The student evaluates the answer, noticing missing nuance, and pushes further.

FINAL STUDENT PROMPT TO AI

> *"Critique the limitations of both Marxist and revisionist interpretations. Suggest how a social or cultural history perspective might provide a more balanced view."*

- **Constructivist Note**: At this point, the learner exercises *metacognitive control*, interrogating the limits of existing interpretations and *synthesising* new perspectives. They are not consuming information, but *constructing knowledge through critical comparison and extension*.

  Learning Outcome: Through iterative prompting, the student not only retrieves information but actively constructs understanding, moving from surface-level facts to disciplinary debate, critique and synthesis. This process exemplifies constructivist learning, where knowledge is built through inquiry, reflection and reorganisation of ideas, rather than delivered fully formed.

Cognitive Load and Instructional Scaffolding

Cognitive Load Theory (Sweller, 1988) reminds us that learning is most effective when instructional materials manage the learner's mental effort wisely. Prompt engineering can serve to reduce extraneous load by narrowing the scope of a task or clarifying expectations for the AI's response. Conversely, overly vague or complex prompts may increase cognitive load and result in frustration or misunderstanding. Educators who understand this balance can use prompts to gradually increase task complexity, offer guided practice and create opportunities for productive struggle, which are principles that align with effective scaffolding.

A dominant theme from Wei et al.'s (2024) study is the concept of *student-initiated scaffolding*, where learners utilise ChatGPT to support their problem-based learning (PBL). This scaffolding comprises iterative interactions for inquiry, idea generation, verification and integration of information, thus aiding self-regulated learning.

Student-initiated scaffolding refers to the adaptive, learner-led use of tools, such as GenAI, to guide and support cognitive processes during complex learning tasks. Rather than relying exclusively on instructor-led direction, students actively engage with AI to define learning goals, generate and evaluate ideas, integrate new information and iteratively refine their understanding. This process mirrors the principles of pedagogical scaffolding, where support is incrementally adjusted based on learner needs until independence is achieved. In the context of PBL, GenAI can function as a responsive scaffold, helping students manage complexity and deepen metacognitive engagement. The following five steps exemplify how this type of scaffolding unfolds:

1. **Inquiry Goal Definition**: initiating the task by formulating guiding questions or objectives;
2. **Idea Generation and Clarification**: prompting the AI to explore concepts or propose solutions;
3. **Verification and Real-World Comparison**: cross-checking AI responses using external sources or empirical data;
4. **Integration and Synthesis**: using AI to structure arguments, explanations or models;
5. **Procedural Guidance and Iterative Refinement**: refining prompts and outputs based on evolving understanding.

EXAMPLE 1: STUDENT-INITIATED SCAFFOLDING WITH GENERATIVE AI

Scenario: A student in a business course is given a PBL task: "*Evaluate the ethical implications of using facial recognition technology in retail environments.*"

Step 1: Defining the Inquiry Goal
The student begins by asking ChatGPT:

> *What are the key ethical concerns related to facial recognition in retail?*

ChatGPT provides an overview, including privacy violations, consent issues and data misuse.

Step 2: Idea Generation
The student follows up with:

> *Give examples of companies that have faced backlash for using facial recognition.*

ChatGPT lists several cases, such as those involving Amazon and Rite Aid.

Step 3: Verification and Cross-Referencing
To validate the claims, the student uses external sources (e.g., Google Scholar or news articles) to verify if the examples given are accurate and up-to-date.

Step 4: Integration and Synthesis
The student then asks:

> *Can you help me structure a short essay integrating ethical theories like utilitarianism or deontology with this topic?*

ChatGPT suggests a structure, linking each theory to potential ethical evaluations of the practice.

Step 5: Procedural Guidance and Reflection
Finally, the student prompts:

What questions should I consider to evaluate whether a retailer's use of facial recognition is ethical?

ChatGPT offers reflective questions, such as whether customers were informed, if consent was obtained and whether data was securely managed.

EXAMPLE 2: STUDENT-INITIATED SCAFFOLDING IN MATHEMATICS

Scenario: A high school student is assigned a PBL task: "*Investigate how exponential growth functions can model the spread of a virus and compare it with real-world data.*"

Step 1: Inquiry Goal Definition
The student starts by asking ChatGPT:

How can exponential functions be used to model the spread of infectious diseases?

ChatGPT explains the basics of exponential growth, referencing functions of the form:

$$N(t) = N_0 e^{rt}$$

where N_0 is the initial population, r the growth rate and t time.

Step 2: Idea Generation and Clarification
The student follows up:

Give an example of an exponential function modelling a disease spread with a starting population of 10 and a growth rate of 0.3.

ChatGPT generates the function and plots hypothetical values over a few days.

Step 3: Verification and Real-World Comparison
The student then asks:

> *Where can I find real-world data on COVID-19 spread in its early stages for comparison?*

ChatGPT suggests CDC, WHO and Our World in Data. The student accesses this data and compares it with the model to discuss deviations due to interventions like lockdowns.

Step 4: Integration with Graphical Interpretation
To deepen understanding, the student prompts:

> *Can you help me write a paragraph explaining how the model matches or deviates from real data, including limitations?*

ChatGPT provides a draft considering overfitting, the effect of non-constant growth rates and public health measures.

Step 5: Procedural Guidance and Iterative Refinement
Finally, the student asks:

> *How can I improve my model to better reflect real-world conditions like slowing spread?*

ChatGPT suggests incorporating logistic functions or piecewise models to simulate a plateau phase and reduced growth rate.

The iterative nature of prompt design mirrors the progressive deepening of cognitive engagement described in Bloom's Taxonomy. Just as learners move from remembering and understanding towards analysing, evaluating and creating, prompts can be crafted with increasing levels of complexity to guide students through these stages. A simple recall prompt may activate foundational knowledge, while a more elaborate prompt can scaffold critical comparison or original synthesis. In this way, prompt engineering does not merely extract information from AI but becomes a structured pathway for cognitive growth, aligning directly with Bloom's hierarchy of learning objectives.

Bloom's Taxonomy, Webb's Depth of Knowledge and Prompt Complexity

Prompt engineering can also be mapped to Bloom's Revised Taxonomy (Anderson and Krathwohl, 2001), providing a framework to align the depth of AI interaction with learning objectives. Simple prompts such as "*Define osmosis*" target lower-order cognitive skills like remembering or understanding. More complex prompts, such as "*Compare the impacts of osmosis in plant and animal cells*" or "*Design an experiment to test osmosis in living organisms,*" engage higher-order thinking like analysis, evaluation or creation. By deliberately designing prompts across Bloom's hierarchy, educators can scaffold student thinking and ensure alignment between prompt complexity and cognitive challenge.

Spessard (2025) conceptualises AI prompting not merely as a technical skill but as a pedagogical act aligned with Bloom's Taxonomy and Webb's Depth of Knowledge (DOK). Purposeful prompt design enables educators to create structured opportunities where students interact with AI outputs rather than simply consume them. In this model, the AI generates an initial response to the prompt, and the student's task is to evaluate, refine or extend that output as an activity that mirrors the cognitive demands of the prompt's Bloom level. By deliberately designing prompts across the hierarchy, teachers can scaffold progression from basic recall to creative synthesis. Alignment of prompt types with Bloom's levels is illustrated in Table 7.1, highlighting how educators can embed prompts that provoke deeper thinking and guide students towards increasingly sophisticated engagement (Spessard, 2025).

Webb's DOK framework (Webb, 1997) also provides a way of categorising learning tasks not by difficulty, but by the *cognitive processes* they require. Unlike Bloom's Taxonomy, which focuses on hierarchical levels of knowledge and skills, DOK emphasises the complexity of thinking needed to complete a task. At the lower levels, tasks require simple recall or basic comprehension, while higher levels demand strategic reasoning, synthesis across domains and extended problem-solving over time. In the context of AI-supported learning, DOK is particularly useful for designing prompts that move students beyond surface interactions with generative outputs and into deeper, more sustained engagements. By mapping AI prompting to DOK levels, educators can scaffold student activities from recall and reproduction to extended inquiry, ensuring that interactions with AI are aligned with the depth of thinking expected in disciplinary learning.

TABLE 7.1 Aligning Bloom's Taxonomy with AI Prompting Strategies

Bloom's Level	Example Prompt	Prompt Construction Description	Expected Student Engagement with AI Output
Remembering	"List the key stages of the water cycle."	Use direct, factual questions that require recall of information. Keep language simple and focused on retrieval.	Student checks AI's list against prior knowledge or course materials, correcting errors or filling gaps.
Understanding	"Explain in your own words how photosynthesis works."	Frame the prompt to elicit explanations, paraphrasing or summarising. Encourage rephrasing learned content.	Student evaluates clarity and accuracy of AI's explanation, rephrasing or restructuring it to demonstrate comprehension.
Applying	"Apply Newton's third law to a real-world scenario, such as sports or transportation."	Design prompts to request contextual application of known principles. Real-world connections enhance relevance.	Student critiques AI's example for accuracy and relevance, then adapts or expands it with their own application.
Analysing	"Compare and contrast the causes of World War I and World War II."	Structure prompts to promote comparison, categorisation or identifying relationships. May involve tabular or thematic analysis.	Student identifies gaps or oversimplifications in AI's comparison, reorganises causes into categories and refines analysis with evidence.
Evaluating	"Critique the experimental design of the study: What worked and what could be improved?"	Ask students to judge, critique or defend a position using evidence. Prompts should frame a debate or judgement context.	Student weighs AI's critique against scholarly standards, strengthens weak points and develops an evidence-based judgement.
Creating	"Design a sustainable community plan that integrates green technologies and community welfare."	Use open-ended, synthesis-focused language. Prompt should encourage integration of multiple ideas into a new product or plan.	Student uses AI's initial plan as a draft, then iteratively revises, adds constraints and synthesises ideas into a novel, coherent proposal.

Note: Prompts aligned with higher levels of Bloom's should include open-ended phrasing and, where appropriate, scenarios or constraints to guide depth and creativity. Clear instructional cues (e.g., "create," "design," "evaluate") help students understand the task's cognitive demands (Spessard, 2025; Jackson, 2025; Sasson, et al., 2025)

To illustrate how Webb's framework can be applied in practice, Table 7.2 maps each DOK level to example prompts, construction guidelines and the types of student engagement expected when working with AI-generated outputs. The progression highlights how prompts can be intentionally

TABLE 7.2 Webb's Depth of Knowledge (DOK) and AI Prompting

DOK Level	Example Prompt	Prompt Construction Description	Expected Student Engagement with AI Output
Level 1: Recall and Reproduction	"Define the term 'ecosystem.'"	Focus on direct recall, basic comprehension or following simple procedures.	Student verifies the AI's definition, checks it against course texts and corrects or expands it to ensure precision.
Level 2: Skills and Concepts	"Explain the relationship between predator and prey in an ecosystem."	Require students to make decisions about how to approach a problem using multiple concepts.	Student evaluates AI's explanation for completeness, adds examples or diagrams and refines language to demonstrate conceptual understanding.
Level 3: Strategic Thinking	"Develop a hypothesis for why a population in an ecosystem is declining and propose a testable method."	Encourage reasoning, planning and use of evidence. Prompt should involve complexity and justification.	Student critiques AI's hypothesis, improves experimental design and justifies choices using evidence from research or case studies.
Level 4: Extended Thinking	"Design and implement a long-term study on the effects of urbanisation on biodiversity."	Promote extended time to think, research and synthesise across multiple concepts or subjects.	Student uses AI's draft study plan as a starting point, then expands it with interdisciplinary sources, ethical considerations and long-term methodological detail.

designed to move from straightforward recall tasks towards complex, extended inquiries that demand synthesis and reasoning across domains. In each case, the AI's response is not the end product but a starting point for deeper engagement, with students expected to critique, refine and expand upon what the AI generates in order to meet the cognitive demands of the task.

Taken together, Bloom's Taxonomy and Webb's DOK provide complementary frameworks for aligning AI prompts with cognitive challenge and task complexity. Bloom's hierarchy emphasises the progression from recall to creation, while DOK highlights the depth of reasoning required to complete a task. When applied to prompt engineering, both frameworks shift the focus from generating correct answers to designing interactions where students critically engage with, refine and extend AI outputs. This pedagogical reframing positions prompt design as a central literacy for educators and learners alike. Building on this foundation, the next section turns to the fundamentals of prompt engineering, examining practical techniques for crafting effective prompts that scaffold inquiry, support reflection and enhance learning outcomes.

PROMPT ENGINEERING FUNDAMENTALS

Effective use of GenAI in education begins with understanding the fundamentals of prompt engineering. Much like crafting clear instructions for a student or designing a strong assessment task, writing an effective prompt requires intentionality. At its core, a prompt is not merely a question or command, but a pedagogical tool that shapes the quality, relevance and depth of the AI's response. A vague prompt tends to produce equally vague answers, while a precise and purposeful prompt scaffolds student thinking, encourages deeper exploration and aligns AI interaction with specific learning outcomes.

Components of a Good Prompt

Strong prompts typically share four qualities: clarity, specificity, context and constraints. Clarity ensures that the AI (and the learner working with it) understands exactly what is being asked, avoiding unnecessary ambiguity. Specificity narrows the focus, limiting irrelevant output and increasing coherence. Context provides background information or framing that helps the AI generate responses that are accurate and relevant to the learner's needs. Finally, constraints impose useful limits, such as word count, tone, audience or format, that guide the style and purpose of the AI's output.

For instance, the prompt "*Summarise the causes of World War I in under 100 words for a first-year university history student*" is far more effective than "*Tell me about World War I.*" The former makes clear what is required, who the audience is and how much detail is appropriate. Such scaffolding not only improves the AI's response but also models for students how to frame academic tasks with precision.

Types of Prompts in Education

Educators can draw upon a range of prompt types, each aligned with different pedagogical purposes:

- **Instructional Prompts** direct the AI to explain concepts or processes. Example: "*Explain how photosynthesis works using simple language.*"
- **Exploratory Prompts** invite open-ended analysis or speculation. Example: "*What might happen if gravity suddenly doubled on Earth?*"
- **Comparative Prompts** encourage contrast between ideas, perspectives or methods. Example: "*Compare project-based learning and direct instruction.*"
- **Summarisation Prompts** condense complex material into accessible formats. Example: "*Summarise this article for a busy teacher.*"
- **Role-Based Prompts** situate the AI in a particular persona, enabling simulated dialogue or expertise. Example: "*Act as a science tutor and explain this concept.*"
- **Socratic Prompts** stimulate reflective questioning. Example: "*Why do you think that approach might work?*"

Each type supports different dimensions of learning, from comprehension and recall to higher-order thinking and self-reflection. Teachers can deliberately vary prompt types to balance content delivery with opportunities for inquiry and critique.

Prompt Structures for Learning

Beyond type, the structure of a prompt is equally critical. Three structures are particularly useful in educational contexts:

Zero-Shot Prompts consist of a single instruction without examples. They are best suited for straightforward or well-known tasks. For example:

Student Prompt to AI: "*List three benefits of renewable energy.*"

GenAI's Response:

1. Reduces greenhouse gas emissions by replacing fossil fuels.
2. Provides sustainable and inexhaustible sources of energy, such as solar and wind.
3. Creates economic opportunities through green jobs and new industries.

Student Engagement: The student then checks the AI's list against class materials, adds missing points (e.g., energy security, decentralised access in developing regions) and evaluates whether the examples provided align with the scope of their course.

Few-Shot Prompts provide patterns or examples to guide output. These are particularly valuable in teaching because they model the form or standard expected. By showing AI (and students) what a good output looks like, educators scaffold both the task and the reasoning process behind it. An example of such a prompt used in ChatGPT is illustrated in Figure 7.1.

Student Engagement: The student evaluates whether the AI followed the expected format, critiques the level of detail and refines the summary by adding missing points (e.g., the role of public protests, international diplomacy). This encourages attention to both historical accuracy and structured academic writing.

Similarly, Chain-Of-Thought prompts can guide mathematical reasoning. A student struggling with Pythagoras' Theorem might ask: "*I don't really get Pythagoras' Theorem. Can you explain how it works with an example?*" The AI can then break the problem into incremental steps, showing the relationship between sides of a right triangle and encouraging the student to solve a parallel example independently.

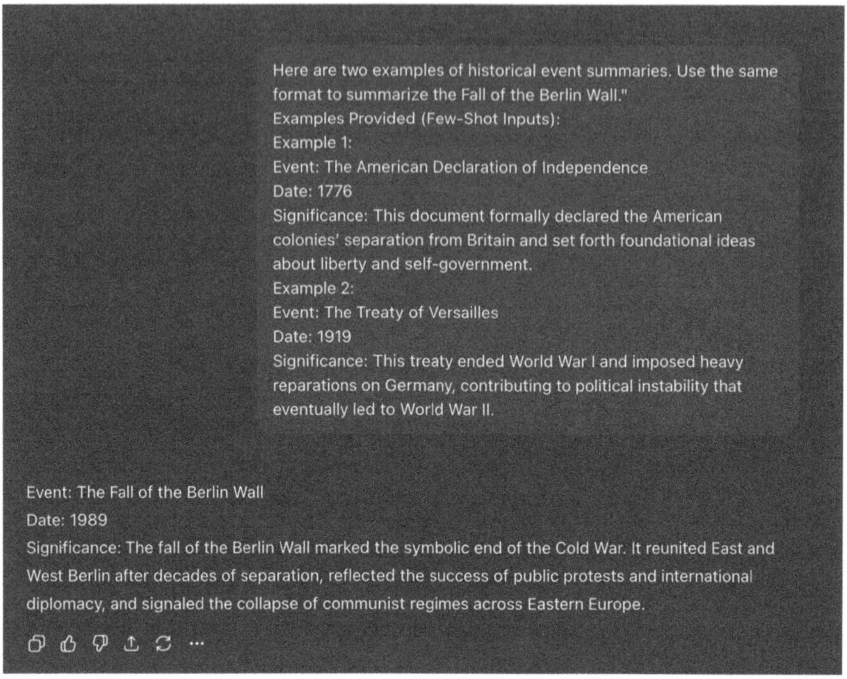

FIGURE 7.1 An example few-shot prompt given to ChatGPT. Notice how the response from the GenAI tool is the same as the examples given in the prompt.

Chain-of-thought prompting also proves valuable in medicine and anatomy. For example, when asked how to remember the branches of the brachial plexus, the AI can scaffold understanding by breaking the structure into a mnemonic (“*Randy Travis Drinks Cold Beer*”), then mapping the flow from roots to branches. Students are not simply memorising; they are guided through a systematic path that builds connections between components of knowledge. One such example is shown in Figure 7.2.

In practice, these structures can be combined. A teacher might use a few-shot structure to model analytical writing, followed by a chain-of-thought structure that asks the AI (and the student) to work through the reasoning process behind the analysis.

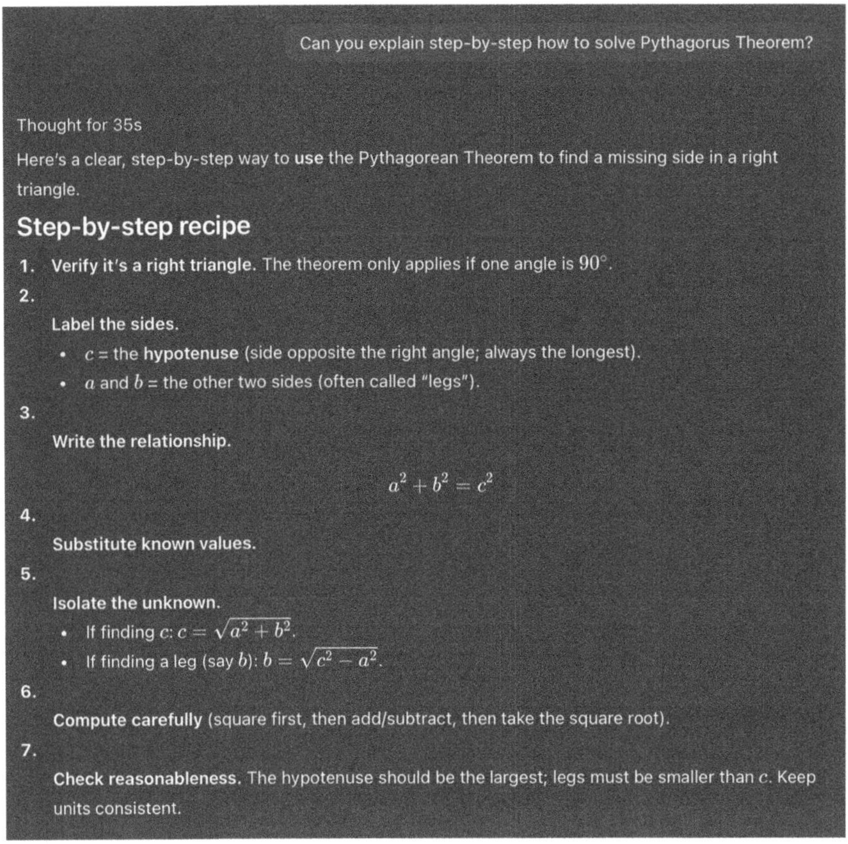

FIGURE 7.2 ChatGPT explains Pythagoras' Theorem by working through each step.

PROMPT ENGINEERING FOR EDUCATORS

As educators adapt to the integration of GenAI into classrooms, prompt engineering emerges as both a professional skill and a pedagogical strategy. Far from being a technical gimmick, prompt writing can streamline routine tasks, enhance creativity and support differentiated instruction. This section explores how educators can use prompt engineering across three core domains: content delivery, inclusive practice and curriculum design.

Prompt Engineering as Generative Dialogue

Incorporating GenAI into lesson planning aligns well with the principles of Generativism, introduced in Chapter 6: AI and the Top 5, which foregrounds knowledge as something actively co-constructed rather than passively received. In this view, prompt engineering becomes less about issuing commands and more about initiating a productive dialogue between educator and AI. When situated within Laurillard's Conversational Framework (Laurillard, 2013), the act of designing teaching activities becomes a recursive process in which the teacher articulates learning intentions, the AI generates possible interpretations or implementations, and the teacher then evaluates, refines or redirects the response.

This dialogic process unfolds across four iterative stages:

1. **Teacher Expression** (Articulating the learning goal):
    - Prompt: "Generate a 60-minute lesson plan on the water cycle for Year 6, including an inquiry-based activity and formative assessment."
2. **AI Feedback** (Initial output grounded in its language model training):
    - AI returns a structured lesson plan with suggested activities.
3. **Teacher Adaptation** (Evaluating for fit, tone, curriculum alignment):
    - Teacher revises or prompts further: "Make the group activity more interactive and integrate peer assessment."
4. **AI Refinement** (Revises content based on updated parameters):
    - AI returns an amended lesson with peer feedback rubrics and more dynamic group structures.

This recursive loop parallels Laurillard's conception of the discursive and adaptive elements of teaching, where both parties contribute to shaping pedagogical outcomes. The teacher's role remains epistemically dominant, but the AI functions as a generative interlocutor, responding, refining and adapting to successive prompts that are grounded in pedagogical intention.

Consider the following interaction that demonstrates this dialogic co-design:

Educator: "Design a short activity to help Year 9 students grasp the ethical implications of using facial recognition technology."

AI: "Propose a debate format: one group argues for increased surveillance in public spaces, another against. Include pre-reading on data privacy."

Educator: "Refocus on personal data use in schools, not public surveillance. Add a creative reflection task for after the debate."

AI: "Updated activity: Debate recontextualised to facial recognition for school attendance. Follow-up: students write a journal entry imagining their data footprint 10 years from now."

Here, the AI is not simply executing commands but participating in a structured conversation. Each cycle of refinement not only improves the activity but also models the teaching-as-design paradigm: iterative, reflective and co-creative.

Using Prompts to Differentiate Instruction

One of the long-standing challenges in education is addressing the diverse abilities, backgrounds and learning styles present in a single classroom. Prompt engineering enables rapid tailoring of content for:

Language Level:

> *Rewrite this explanation in simpler English for an ESL student.*

Learning Modality:

> *Convert this science explanation into a visual description suitable for a student who learns best through diagrams.*

Student Interest:

> *Explain Pythagoras' Theorem using an example from skateboarding.*

This responsiveness enables a level of differentiation that would otherwise be time-consuming or impractical for educators to deliver consistently. The process also supports a conversational model, where prompts are refined in response to how the AI interprets student needs.

Prompting for Curriculum Design and Assessment

Beyond day-to-day teaching, prompt engineering supports broader curriculum planning tasks. Teachers can initiate high-level design processes using generative prompts that are then iteratively refined:

Unit and Sequence Design:

> *Design a 6-week unit on climate change for Year 9, aligned with the Australian Curriculum.*

Rubric Creation:

> *Create a rubric for a Year 10 persuasive writing assignment with three levels of achievement.*

Formative Assessment Design:

> *Generate five quiz questions on Newton's Laws of Motion, with answers and explanations.*

Each of these tasks can begin with a single prompt, but the pedagogical value emerges through the refinement dialogue, in which the teacher probes the AI's response, adjusts scope or tone, and aligns the output with specific curricular objectives.

Prompt engineering, understood as an ongoing conversation, exemplifies how teachers can shape learning environments through co-design with GenAI. Rather than delegating intellectual labour, educators engage in a reflective practice of prompting, evaluating and redirecting, mirroring the very structure of effective pedagogy itself.

PROMPT ENGINEERING FOR STUDENTS AS DIALOGIC PRACTICE

While much of the discourse around GenAI in education has focused on how teachers can leverage it for instructional design, an equally critical frontier lies in helping students become active participants in prompt-driven dialogue. Teaching students how to craft and refine prompts positions them not as passive recipients of AI-generated information, but as co-authors of inquiry, engaged in an iterative learning conversation.

This approach aligns with Laurillard's Conversational Framework, in which learning emerges from meaningful interaction between a learner and a feedback-generating system. In this case, the AI functions as an interactive, semi-autonomous interlocutor, one that responds to student intent and evolves with student input. When students engage the AI through carefully constructed prompts, they participate in a discursive cycle of hypothesis, response, critique and refinement, which mirrors effective pedagogical dialogue.

Prompts to Support Inquiry-Based Learning

In inquiry-based models, learning begins with a question. Prompt engineering allows students to externalise their curiosity, generate speculative hypotheses and structure their investigative thinking. This transforms AI from a repository of answers into a platform for epistemic exploration.

Consider the following examples:

- "*What would happen if gravity were suddenly half as strong? Write a speculative explanation.*"
- "*Create three hypotheses to explain this scientific observation.*"
- "*What questions should I ask to better understand the causes of the Great Depression?*"

These prompts initiate a learning dialogue. The student offers a conceptual starting point; the AI responds; the student then evaluates, revises or deepens the prompt. This recursive loop fosters deeper subject-matter engagement, helping students refine both their questions and their understanding in tandem.

Reflective and Metacognitive Prompting

Reflection is central to metacognitive development, and prompt engineering can help students structure internal dialogue about their own learning. Within Laurillard's framework, this corresponds to reflective feedback, where learners receive insights about their understanding and strategies.

Examples of metacognitive prompting include:

- *"Explain this idea in your own words, then ask the AI if your explanation is accurate."*
- *"Generate three follow-up questions I should ask based on my last essay draft."*
- *"What are the weaknesses in my argument?"*

Here, the AI acts as a mirror, reflecting back possible interpretations of the student's ideas and offering directions for improvement. Students begin to internalise this feedback process, gradually developing a personal repertoire of prompts that serve as thinking tools.

Ethical and Critical Thinking Prompts

A key dimension of digital literacy is the ability to interrogate the limitations and implications of AI output. Students must be taught to see GenAI not as an oracle, but as a provisional voice and one that reflects training biases, lacks epistemic grounding and should always be critically examined.

Prompts that cultivate this sensibility include:

- *"Are there any biases in this summary?"*
- *"Provide both sides of the argument about universal basic income."*
- *"Cite sources for this claim. Are they credible?"*

These interactions require the student to assume an evaluative role in the dialogue. Within Laurillard's model, this reflects the adaptive phase of learning where the learner tests, challenges and redirects the information offered. Students thereby develop a stance of critical engagement, essential for ethical AI use and informed digital citizenship.

By embedding prompt engineering within a conversational framework, educators can help students move beyond instrumental use of AI. They become not just users of generative tools, but authors of learning conversations, capable of directing, evaluating and refining the dialogic process in service of intellectual growth.

META-AI LITERACY AND PROMPT FLUENCY

As GenAI becomes embedded in everyday learning, students and educators must move beyond simply using tools like ChatGPT; they must understand *how* and *why* these tools behave the way they do. This higher-order understanding is known as meta-AI literacy: the ability to reason about the capabilities, limitations and implications of GenAI. Central to this literacy is the development of prompt fluency, or the practised skill of crafting, evaluating and iterating prompts to achieve specific learning goals.

As discussed in Chapter 6: AI and the Top 5, Meta-AI literacy involves understanding not only how to interact with AI, but also how it works and why it generates particular kinds of responses. For example, knowing that AI does not "know" facts but predicts text based on probabilities can help students interpret answers with appropriate scepticism. Meta-AI literacy includes:

- Recognising the probabilistic nature of AI outputs
- Understanding model limitations (e.g., hallucinations, lack of lived experience)
- Identifying when to verify, revise or disregard a response
- Appreciating the ethical and social implications of using AI tools in academic work

Students who possess meta-AI literacy are not just consumers of AI-generated content; they are informed, reflective participants in a technological dialogue.

Developing Prompt Fluency as a Core Skill

Prompt fluency is the applied dimension of meta-AI literacy. Like any language skill, it improves with practice and feedback. In an educational context, developing prompt fluency means helping students:

- Write prompts aligned to learning objectives
- Refine prompts based on the quality of the AI's response
- Use prompts iteratively (e.g., revising, redirecting, scaffolding)
- Recognise when a prompt is ineffective and troubleshoot why

For example, a vague prompt like "*Tell me about climate change*" might lead to an overly broad or superficial answer. A more fluent prompt, such as "*Summarise three key impacts of climate change on agriculture, citing recent research*," is far more likely to generate a useful, accurate and relevant response.

Prompt Iteration and Evaluation

Prompting is not a one-time action but a cyclical process. Learners should be taught to:

1. Generate a prompt
2. Evaluate the output
3. Refine the prompt for clarity or depth
4. Compare results from multiple prompt attempts
5. Reflect on what was learned about both the content and the tool

This iterative approach strengthens both subject knowledge and digital literacy. It can be taught explicitly through scaffolded classroom activities, self-assessment checklists and peer comparison tasks that focus not just on content, but on the *prompting process* itself. An example of this process in a classroom environment follows.

EXAMPLE SCAFFOLDED CLASSROOM ACTIVITY: *PROMPT ITERATION FOR DEEPER INQUIRY*

Objective: Students will learn to craft, refine and evaluate AI prompts to deepen understanding of a curriculum-aligned topic and reflect on the process of AI-mediated learning.

Target Year Level: Year 10 (adaptable to other levels)

Subject Focus: Humanities (e.g., History – World War I causes)

Step 1: Introduction and Modelling (10 minutes)

To begin, the teacher demonstrates the prompting process explicitly, modelling how a single question can be reshaped through iteration to yield progressively more focused results. This helps students see prompting as a skill that involves testing, evaluating and refining, rather than as a one-off request.

Teacher models the process on screen:

- Initial prompt: *"What caused World War I?"*
- AI Output: Displays general summary
- The Teacher evaluates the output and poses a question to students: "This is broad. What if I want more detail on political alliances?"
- The prompt is refined based on consultation with students: *"Explain how political alliances contributed to the outbreak of World War I."*
- AI Output: Displays more targeted explanation
- Class discusses difference in depth and relevance

Step 2: Guided Practice (15 minutes)

With the modelling complete, students now take ownership of the process. They select a specific subtopic and begin experimenting with prompts of their own. The emphasis at this stage is not on getting the "perfect" output but on practicing the cycle of drafting, evaluating and refining.

- Students select a subtopic (e.g., militarism, imperialism, nationalism).
- Individually, students write an initial prompt related to their subtopic.
- Students input their prompt and read the AI response.
- Prompt refinement cycle:
    - Evaluate clarity, depth, tone
    - Rewrite and resubmit (up to 2 more times)

Teacher provides a checklist for evaluation, e.g.:
Is the response too general?
Did the AI misinterpret your question?
What terms could you add for precision?

Step 3: Comparison and Peer Review (10 minutes)
Learning is deepened when students compare their approaches with others. In this phase, they share their refined outputs with a partner and discuss the prompting strategies that led to stronger or weaker results. This introduces peer feedback as part of the learning dialogue, reinforcing that prompting is both a personal and collaborative process.

- Students exchange final AI outputs with a partner.
- Each partner answers:
  - What was strong about this prompt?
  - How might it be refined further?
  - What did you learn about prompting from this example?

Step 4: *Reflection and Meta-Prompting (10 minutes)*
Finally, students are guided to reflect on their own prompting journey. By articulating what they learned about both the topic and the prompting process, they begin to internalise strategies for future use. In some cases, they can even use the AI to refine their reflections, further reinforcing the iterative cycle.

- Students respond to a metacognitive prompt:
  - *"What did I learn about how prompt clarity affects AI response quality?"*
  - *"How did my understanding of the topic change as I refined my prompt?"*
- Option: Use AI to help refine their reflection into a paragraph summary.

EXTENSIONS

This activity can be expanded by having students compare AI responses to textbooks or teacher-provided readings, allowing them to critique not only the quality of their prompts but also the reliability of AI as a knowledge source. Another option is to conclude with a generative task where students ask the AI to produce a quiz on their subtopic, then attempt to answer it themselves, reinforcing both content mastery and critical digital literacy.

By structuring prompting as a cyclical and reflective process, educators help students see GenAI not as a shortcut to answers but as a medium for intellectual dialogue. Each stage of iteration, which includes generation, evaluation, refinement and reflection, mirrors the dynamics of Laurillard's Conversational Framework, where learning emerges through ongoing adaptation between intention and response. When students are taught to engage in this process deliberately, they not only strengthen their subject knowledge but also acquire a transferable digital literacy: the ability to interact critically and creatively with AI systems. In this way, prompt engineering becomes less about efficiency and more about cultivating habits of inquiry, reflection and responsible digital citizenship.

CHALLENGES AND LIMITATIONS

While prompt engineering offers significant pedagogical advantages, it is not without its limitations. As educators increasingly rely on AI to support teaching and learning, they must also confront the risks, uncertainties and ethical considerations associated with these technologies. This section outlines four major areas of concern: accuracy, pedagogy, bias and overreliance.

Hallucinations and Misleading Responses

GenAI tools can produce fluent and persuasive answers that are factually incorrect or entirely fabricated. These mistakes are commonly referred to as *hallucinations*. Even well-crafted prompts cannot fully eliminate this risk. For instance, an AI may confidently cite nonexistent academic articles or generate misleading explanations of scientific concepts. When students are unaware of this possibility, they may unknowingly internalise misinformation, particularly in domains where verification is complex or time-consuming.

For this reason, prompt engineering must be taught alongside strategies for critical verification. The emphasis should not be on trusting AI output, but on engaging in a dialogue that actively questions and tests it. This stance reflects Laurillard's Conversational Framework, where learners adapt their understanding by challenging and refining the responses of a conversational partner. Here, the AI acts as a partner that must always be interrogated.

Educators can model and scaffold this process by introducing students to practical strategies such as:

- **Verification Prompts**: Asking the AI to cite its sources and then checking whether those references exist and are credible.
    - Example: "*Provide three peer-reviewed sources to support this claim, including full citations I can check.*"
- **Cross-Checking Across Iterations**: Posing the same or similar question in multiple ways and comparing the outputs for consistency.
    - Example: "*List three causes of the Great Depression*" followed by "*Explain the role of banking failures in the Great Depression.*" Differences in responses reveal areas requiring further investigation.
- **External Validation**: Encouraging students to compare AI outputs with authoritative sources such as textbooks, scholarly databases or government reports.
    - Example: Using the AI's explanation of photosynthesis alongside a biology textbook to spot omissions or inaccuracies.
- **Bias and Perspective Checks**: Prompting the AI to present alternative viewpoints or highlight potential bias in its own output.
    - Example: "*What perspectives might be missing from this explanation of colonial history?*"

When framed as part of the prompting cycle, these strategies help students internalise a sceptical but constructive stance towards AI-generated responses. Rather than seeing hallucinations as failures, students can approach them as opportunities to practice critical literacy. By asking, evaluating and refining their prompts in relation to trustworthy sources, learners build resilience against misinformation while deepening their engagement with subject knowledge.

Prompt Dependency and Surface Learning

There is a risk that students may begin to rely on AI as a shortcut for thinking. Overuse of prompting for quick answer-generation, without proper scaffolding, may encourage surface learning such as memorising or regurgitating content rather than engaging deeply with it. If a student consistently relies on AI to generate explanations, paraphrases or writing templates, they may neglect to develop their own cognitive processes.

This challenge can be mitigated by reframing prompt engineering not as an end-product skill but as a thinking tool embedded in inquiry, reflection and revision. To ensure students remain cognitively engaged, educators can integrate the following strategies into classroom practice:

Require Student Input Before Prompting: Students first articulate their own explanation, hypothesis or draft before consulting AI. The prompt then becomes a tool for comparison and refinement rather than replacement. For example, students write a short paragraph explaining the causes of climate change, then prompt the AI with:

> *"Critique this explanation for accuracy and clarity. Suggest improvements."*

Design Prompts for Process, Not Just Product: Frame prompts that encourage analysis, questioning or reflection rather than simply requesting answers. For example, instead of asking "*What are the key themes in Macbeth?*" a student might prompt:

> *"Suggest three questions I should explore to identify key themes in Macbeth, and explain why they matter."*

Use Iteration as Evidence of Learning: Teachers can assess the quality of a student's prompts and refinements, rather than only the AI's final response. This shifts the focus from output to process. For example, students submit their original prompt, revised prompt and reflection on how the changes shaped the AI's response.

Integrate Self-Explanation Prompts: Students are asked to justify why they chose a particular prompt or how they judged the AI's response. This fosters metacognitive awareness. For example, "*Why did you choose to ask the AI this way? How did the wording influence the response?*"

Balance AI with Non-AI Tasks: Ensure students engage in activities where AI cannot substitute for effort, such as group debates, personal reflections or creative projects, so that prompting remains one tool among many.

By embedding these practices, prompt engineering shifts from a mechanism for outsourcing thinking to a scaffold for deeper inquiry. Students learn to approach AI as a partner in their cognitive process rather than as a replacement for it, thereby strengthening both disciplinary knowledge and transferable digital literacy skills.

Bias, Misinformation and Critical Use

GenAI models are trained on vast datasets that inevitably contain cultural, racial, gendered and ideological biases. Prompt engineering alone does not remove these underlying issues; in fact, poorly designed prompts can unintentionally reinforce them. For example, a request to "*describe the qualities of a good leader*" may return responses that privilege Western, male-centric or hierarchical views of leadership, overlooking collectivist or community-oriented traditions. Similarly, prompts related to historical events may reflect dominant narratives while omitting marginalised perspectives.

Recognising these risks is essential for both educators and students. Without critical awareness, learners may absorb misinformation or biased framings as objective truth. This makes AI not only a technical tool but also an ethical site of engagement, where questioning, contextualising and cross-referencing become indispensable practices.

To address these challenges, educators can model and scaffold bias-aware prompting strategies, such as:

- **Prompting for Multiple Perspectives**
  Encourage students to explicitly ask for alternative viewpoints or culturally diverse framings.
  - Example: "*Explain the causes of World War II from both European and Asian perspectives.*"
  - Example: "*What are different cultural understandings of leadership across Indigenous, collectivist and Western traditions?*"
- **Source Transparency and Verification**
  Train students to demand evidence and then evaluate it.
  - Example: "*Provide three peer-reviewed sources for your claim, and include the full references so I can verify them.*"

  - Students then cross-check whether the sources exist and assess their credibility.

- **Bias Awareness Prompts**
  Teach learners to directly interrogate the neutrality of AI outputs.
  - Example: "*What perspectives might be missing from your explanation of climate change responsibility?*"
  - Example: "*How might this answer differ if written from the perspective of a Global South researcher?*"

- **Comparative Validation**
  Encourage students to set AI responses against peer-reviewed literature, textbooks or authoritative datasets. This builds the habit of treating AI as a starting point rather than a final authority.

- **Classroom Discussions on Ethical AI Use**
  Incorporate activities where students critique the AI's biases together, surfacing how digital tools mirror social inequalities. For example, after generating outputs on gender roles, the class can debate what assumptions are embedded in the AI's framing.

By embedding these practices in teaching, AI becomes a lens for developing critical digital literacy. Students learn not only to identify bias and misinformation but also to use prompt engineering as a strategy to broaden perspectives and practice ethical inquiry. In this way, working with AI shifts from being a technical skill to becoming an exercise in responsible knowledge-making.

The Risk of Overreliance on AI in Learning

An overarching concern in integrating GenAI into education is the possibility of displacing the human elements that make learning transformative, dialogue, empathy, improvisation and collaborative meaning-making. While AI can streamline tasks and provide responsive support, it cannot replicate the relational dynamics between teacher and student that underpin deep understanding and personal growth. The danger is that students, and in some cases educators, may begin to substitute AI's efficiency for the slower, but more meaningful, processes of discussion, reflection and co-construction of knowledge.

This risk is not theoretical. Overreliance on AI can subtly reshape classroom habits: students might consult AI for quick answers instead of wrestling with complex ideas, or teachers might default to AI-generated lesson plans without critically adapting them to the needs of their learners. Such practices risk narrowing the scope of education to efficient content delivery, rather than cultivating intellectual resilience, curiosity and interpersonal skills.

To guard against these pitfalls, AI use should be framed as augmentation, not substitution. Prompt engineering can enhance pedagogy when it supports, rather than supplants, human-centred practices. Educators can model this balance through strategies such as:

- **Explicitly Valuing Human Dialogue**
  Pair AI-supported activities with teacher-led discussion or peer collaboration, ensuring that students engage in both machine-generated and human-generated dialogue. For example, after prompting AI for different interpretations of a poem, students discuss in groups which interpretations resonate most and why.

- **Positioning AI as a Catalyst, Not a Conclusion**
  Use AI to generate starting points for inquiry or drafts for debate, but require students to refine, critique and expand these ideas through personal reasoning and group dialogue. For example, AI generates a list of possible solutions to an environmental problem; students then debate the feasibility of each and propose their own alternatives.

- **Emphasising Reflection and Empathy**
  Create opportunities for students to reflect on how their thinking changes through interactions with AI and with peers, highlighting that empathy, creativity and ethical reasoning are uniquely human dimensions of learning.

- **Maintaining the Teacher as a Learning Designer**
  Reinforce the teacher's role as the architect of learning experiences, using AI to reduce administrative load but not to outsource pedagogical judgement or personal engagement with students.

By adopting this stance, educators help students see AI as one voice in a broader learning conversation, never the definitive authority. The irreplaceable value of education lies in its human dimension of the relational, dialogic and ethical interactions through which learners construct meaning together. Prompt engineering, when carefully integrated, can amplify these processes rather than erode them, ensuring that technology serves learning rather than the reverse.

PEDAGOGICAL FRAMEWORKS FOR PROMPT ENGINEERING

To embed prompt engineering meaningfully into educational practice, it must be guided by sound pedagogical principles. Just as teachers scaffold writing or problem-solving processes, they must also teach students how to design, test and reflect on prompts as part of their learning journey. This section introduces practical models for integrating prompt engineering into instructional design, classroom activities and assessment.

Integrating Prompt Engineering into Teaching Practice

Prompt engineering can be introduced across multiple points in the learning cycle, including during preparation, instruction and evaluation. Such practice aligns with the premise of *Generativism* discussed in Chapter 6: AI and the Top 5. Before a lesson, teachers might use generative tools to create case studies or develop provocative starter questions that frame the topic and spark curiosity. During instruction, students can interact with AI in small groups, working with structured prompts to probe the content, test their assumptions and generate alternative perspectives. After the lesson, learners can consolidate their understanding by prompting the AI to explain the concept in their own words and then critiquing the response for accuracy and depth. In this way, prompt engineering supports not only content delivery but also reflection and critical engagement across the full arc of learning.

By embedding prompt use into lesson flow, teachers can model critical thinking while demonstrating how to iteratively refine questions to deepen understanding.

Assessment of Prompting Skills

To legitimise prompt engineering as an educational practice, it must be assessed with the same rigour applied to other academic skills. If prompting is to be understood as a form of digital literacy, then students need opportunities not only to practise it but also to receive feedback on the effectiveness of their approach. The challenge for educators is to design assessments that foreground the *process* of prompting as much as the *product* of the AI's response.

Prompts can be evaluated according to several dimensions:

- **Clarity and Specificity**: Does the student articulate their request in precise, unambiguous terms? For example, "*Explain Newton's Laws*" may be too broad, whereas "*Explain Newton's First Law with a sports-related example for a Year 8 student*" demonstrates greater clarity.
- **Alignment with Task or Learning Goal**: Does the prompt directly support the intended learning outcome, or does it drift into tangential content? A well-aligned prompt shows evidence of purposeful design.
- **Capacity to Generate Relevant, High-Quality Output**: Does the AI's response provide material that is accurate, useful and appropriately detailed? While the AI cannot be held accountable, the student can be assessed on their ability to design prompts that elicit strong responses.
- **Evidence of Iterative Improvement**: Does the student refine and adapt their prompts based on earlier outputs? A series of revisions indicates an understanding of prompting as a cyclical process rather than a one-time query.

To operationalise these dimensions, educators can adopt several assessment strategies:

- **Rubric-Based Evaluation**
  Rubrics can include criteria such as clarity, alignment, effectiveness and reflection. For instance, a criterion might read: "*Student demonstrates the ability to refine an initial prompt to improve accuracy and relevance of output.*" Such rubrics help establish prompting as a formal skill worthy of structured evaluation.
- **Prompt Portfolios**
  Students can maintain a portfolio documenting their sequence of prompts, the outputs generated and reflections on what they learned from each iteration. This makes visible the evolution of their thinking and provides evidence of growth over time.

- **Justification of Prompt Design**
  Students may be asked to explain *why* they chose a particular prompt structure, what they hoped to achieve and how they evaluated the AI's response. This not only reinforces metacognitive skills but also allows educators to assess intentionality.

- **Peer Review of Prompts**
  Similar to peer feedback on writing drafts, students can exchange prompts and outputs, offering suggestions for improvement. This promotes collective reflection and models a community of practice around prompt engineering.

By treating prompt engineering as a skill that can be taught, practised and evaluated, educators reinforce its role as a legitimate and valuable component of 21st-century learning. Just as students are expected to demonstrate competence in essay writing, data analysis or oral presentation, so too can they be assessed on their ability to engage critically and creatively with GenAI. Framing prompting as an assessable literacy ensures that it is not dismissed as a superficial technical trick, but recognised as a core practice in navigating knowledge in the digital age.

BRINGING THE CONVERSATION FULL CIRCLE

As we come to the end of this chapter, it becomes clear that prompt engineering is not just about clever wording or getting the "right" answer out of an AI system. It is about learning to hold a conversation towards a dialogue that can open doors to new ideas, deepen understanding and spark curiosity. When teachers and students approach AI in this way, they are not replacing thinking, but extending it. A prompt becomes the beginning of a journey, not the end.

We have seen how prompts can support teachers in lesson design, help students explore difficult concepts and encourage reflection and critical questioning. We have also seen that the risks are real: hallucinations, surface learning, hidden biases and overreliance can all creep in if prompting is used carelessly. But rather than viewing these as reasons to shy away, they are reminders of why human judgement, empathy and collaboration remain at the centre of education. AI can generate possibilities; it is teachers and students who decide what to do with them.

What emerges, then, is a picture of prompt engineering as a new kind of literacy and one that belongs alongside reading, writing and critical thinking in the classrooms of today. It is a skill to be practised, assessed and refined, but more importantly, it is a habit of mind: asking better questions, revisiting answers and learning to see knowledge as something that grows through dialogue.

Chapter 8 steps back from the practicalities of prompting and turns instead to reflection. It is a chance to consider what all of this means for education more broadly and for the role of the teacher, the experience of the learner and the values we carry with us into a future shaped by GenAI. If this chapter has been about the *how*, the final one invites us to think about the *why*. Why we teach, why we learn and why the human heart of education must remain central, no matter how powerful the tools at our side become.

REFLECT AND REFRAME

1. Which frameworks (e.g., Bloom's Taxonomy, Laurillard's Conversational Model or Webb's DOK) most resonate with your approach to teaching? Why?
2. To what extent should students be expected to verify or critique AI outputs in your discipline?
3. How could prompt engineering streamline aspects of your teaching workload (e.g., lesson planning, feedback, content adaptation)?
4. How might you balance the efficiencies of AI-assisted teaching with the need for relational, human-centred pedagogy?

REFERENCES

Anderson, W. L., and Krathwohl, D. R., 2001. *A taxonomy for learning, teaching, and assessing: A revision of Bloom's taxonomy of educational objectives: complete edition*. Addison Wesley Longman, Inc..

Cole, M., Jolm-Steiner, V., Scribner, S., and Souberman, E., 1978. *VYGOTSKY, L. S. mind in society: Development of higher psychological processes*. Harvard University Press.

Jackson, J., 2025. Higher order prompting: Applying Bloom's revised taxonomy to the use of large language models in higher education. *Studies in Technology Enhanced Learning*, 4(1). https://doi.org/10.21428/8c225f6e.0915c17e

Laurillard, D., 2013. *Rethinking university teaching: A conversational framework for the effective use of learning technologies*. Routledge.

Niranon, P., and Triyason, T., 2024. *The efficiency of ChatGPT Vs google against self-learning of undergraduate students*. s.n.

Piaget, J., and Cook, M. 1952. *The origins of intelligence in children*. s.n.

Qiuzi, G., 2024. Prompting change: ChatGPT's impact on digital humanities pedagogy – a case study in art history. *International Journal of Humanities and Arts Computing*, 18(1),58–78.

Sasson, L. et al., 2025. The art of creative inquiry—from question asking to prompt engineering. *The Journal of Creative Behavior*, 59(1), e671.

Spessard, S. L., 2025. The prompt as pedagogy: Activating bloom's and advancing depth of knowledge through AI prompting.

Sweller, J., 1988. Cognitive load during problem solving: Effects on learning. *Cognitive Science*, 12, 257–285.

Webb, N. L., 1997. *Criteria for alignment of expectations and assessments in mathematics and science education. research monograph no. 6*. National Science Foundation.

Wei, Y. A., Liu, J., Qi, C., and Jia, R., 2024. *The advancement of personalized learning potentially accelerated by generative AI*. s.n.

Zhang, B., 2024. ChatGPT on student learning outcomes in higher education: A meta-analysis of early studies. *Using Artificial Intelligence in Teaching and Learning*, 189.

CHAPTER 8

Looking Back, Looking Forward

Reflections on AI in Education

AI is neither a miracle solution nor a looming threat, but a tool whose value depends on how thoughtfully it is woven into the fabric of education.

CHAPTER AIMS

The aim of this chapter is to:

1. *Reflect on the major themes explored across the book, drawing together historical, pedagogical, ethical and practical insights.*
2. *Re-examine the role of teachers and students in an AI-enhanced educational landscape.*
3. *Consider the values and principles that should guide education in the age of generative AI, and the futures we wish to design.*

IT'S NOT THE DESTINATION, IT'S THE PROCESS

As we arrive at the final chapter of this book, it is time to pause and take stock of the journey so far. We have explored the practicalities of prompt engineering, examined its risks and possibilities, and considered how

DOI: 10.1201/9781003624981-8

GenAI might reshape teaching, learning and curriculum design. Along the way, a consistent theme has emerged: AI is neither a miracle solution nor a looming threat, but a tool whose value depends on how thoughtfully it is woven into the fabric of education.

This chapter offers a space for reflection. Rather than focusing on the mechanics of prompting or the structure of classroom activities, it turns to the bigger questions: What kind of educators do we wish to be in an age of GenAI? What role should learners play when machines can generate content on demand? And what values must guide us as we design the future of teaching with these technologies at our side? By looking back across the key themes of the book and looking forward to the choices that lie ahead, this closing reflection seeks to connect practice with purpose, and to remind us that, at its heart, education remains a profoundly human endeavour.

Throughout this book, we have travelled across history, practice and philosophy to make sense of education's encounter with GenAI. We began by tracing the long tradition of anxiety surrounding new technologies in the classroom. From the printing press to calculators to the internet, each innovation unsettled familiar practices, raising questions about integrity, comprehension and equity. These patterns prepared us to see AI not as a sudden rupture, but as the latest chapter in a story of recurring tension between disruption and adaptation.

From there, we examined what AI actually is, its foundations, its capabilities and its limits. We explored how teachers and students alike are already navigating classrooms where AI-generated content competes with, and sometimes complements, human knowledge-making. Ethical questions, assessment redesign, the rise of generativism and the practice of prompt engineering all built towards a picture of education that is both unsettled and full of possibility.

The path through these chapters has not been about choosing sides, such as embracing or rejecting AI, but about finding the middle ground: thoughtful, critical and human-centred engagement.

If one theme has echoed consistently, it is that teachers remain central. AI may generate lessons, automate assessments or simulate dialogue, but it cannot replace the human work of interpretation, empathy and relational care. Teachers guide students not only through content but through the process of becoming learners who are curious, critical and resilient.

As we saw earlier, strategies such as "Step In, Step Up, Step Aside, Step Narrowly and Step Forward" highlight ways educators can reposition themselves in the AI era. These strategies remind us that survival is not about resisting change but about adapting intelligently. A teacher might step in by collaborating closely with AI tools for feedback, or step aside to emphasise uniquely human capacities like mentoring and empathy.

What emerges is a picture of the teacher as a designer of learning experiences, not merely a transmitter of knowledge. AI may lighten administrative load or provide new avenues for differentiation, but the teacher remains the one who ensures learning stays grounded in values of trust, inclusivity and growth.

Just as teachers must reimagine their roles, students must also see themselves differently in this new landscape. Prompt engineering showed us how learners can shift from passive consumers to active co-creators. By crafting, refining and questioning prompts, students learn not just about content, but about the very process of inquiry.

This emphasis on agency is crucial. If students rely on AI as a shortcut, they risk surface learning and intellectual dependency. But if they use AI as a thinking partner for posing questions, critiquing answers and comparing perspectives, they develop deeper literacy and autonomy. In this way, the learner's role expands beyond mastery of subject matter to mastery of dialogue itself: a capacity to engage critically with both human and machine-generated voices.

The challenge ahead is to support students in cultivating resilience, curiosity and responsibility. These are qualities that no algorithm can provide. AI can supply information, but it is the learner who must decide what matters, why it matters and how to act on it.

Throughout the book, we have returned to the question of values. What does it mean to learn in a world where machines can generate persuasive answers in seconds? The temptation is to focus on efficiency, but education has always been about more than speed. It is about meaning-making, empathy, creativity and ethical judgement.

The risks of bias, misinformation and overreliance are reminders that AI reflects the data it is trained on. It cannot offer neutrality. Educators and learners must therefore approach it critically, asking: Whose voices are represented here? Whose are missing? How should we respond when outputs reinforce stereotypes or erase perspectives?

In addressing these challenges, we reaffirm that education is not simply about transmitting knowledge but about cultivating wisdom. Tools come and go, but values such as fairness, trust and care remain constant. AI may reshape how we teach and learn, but it cannot determine what we hold dear. That responsibility rests with us.

HUMAN-CENTRED ANCHORING

At the heart of education lies something that no algorithm can replicate: the human connection between teacher and learner. While GenAI can produce content, structure lessons or simulate dialogue, it cannot recognise the subtlety of a student's hesitation, the spark of curiosity in a question, or the encouragement needed after a moment of failure. These moments remind us that education has always been more than the transfer of information. It is a relational practice, grounded in empathy, dialogue and care. As we navigate the possibilities of AI, anchoring ourselves in these human dimensions ensures that technology remains a tool in service of learning, never its substitute.

The Irreplaceable Role of Relationships

Education is not merely an intellectual exercise. It is fundamentally a human encounter. At its core are relationships of trust, empathy and mutual respect. These relationships allow teachers to perceive the emotional subtext of a student's silence, to offer encouragement precisely when it is needed and to foster a sense of safety that makes risk-taking in learning possible. While AI systems may be programmed to respond to input, they lack the emotional attunement that defines authentic relational exchange. The educator's ability to discern nuance, build rapport and cultivate an atmosphere of care cannot be outsourced to a machine. This relational dimension is not ancillary to education; it is constitutive of it.

To ensure that relational dimensions of teaching are not lost amid increasing reliance on AI, educators must adopt strategies that intentionally centre human connection. Prioritising consistent, meaningful interactions, whether through personalised feedback, check-in conversations or collaborative activities, helps sustain the interpersonal fabric of learning. Designing classroom routines that invite vulnerability and dialogue, such as peer review sessions or reflective journaling, reinforces a culture of trust and empathy. Importantly, educators can frame AI tools as conversation starters rather than content endpoints, using them to provoke discussion or deepen inquiry rather than to replace teacher-led engagement. Institutional support is also crucial: manageable workloads, smaller class sizes and professional development focused on relational pedagogy enable teachers to remain present and responsive to their students. By embedding these practices into everyday teaching, the human encounter at the heart of education can be protected, even in technologically mediated contexts.

FOR REFLECTION

1. How do I build and sustain trust, empathy and mutual respect in my learning environment?
2. In what ways has the integration of AI affected my relationships with students, positively or negatively?
3. What practices can I implement to ensure relational teaching remains central, even when using digital tools?
4. How can institutional structures better support the relational dimensions of my teaching?

The Value of Dialogue and Co-Presence

Much of what makes learning transformative occurs in real time and through unpredictable moments. A classroom debate that veers into uncharted territory, a spontaneous question that reframes an entire topic, or a shared moment of insight. All of these arise from live, dialogic interaction. These exchanges are not scripted or pre-programmed; they are responsive, embodied and situated in the unique chemistry of a particular group of learners and a teacher. AI can simulate conversation, but it cannot engage in true dialogue, which requires active listening, emotional reciprocity and a shared context. The presence of another thinking, feeling human being, co-present in the learning moment, is irreplaceable.

To preserve the vitality of dialogue and co-presence in AI-supported learning environments, educators must actively design for spontaneity and shared inquiry. This involves creating spaces, both physical and digital, where real-time interaction is prioritised over pre-scripted content delivery. Practices such as Socratic seminars, inquiry-based discussions and open-ended problem-solving tasks invite students to think aloud, challenge each other and co-construct understanding. Even in online or hybrid settings, synchronous sessions can be used strategically to cultivate immediacy and responsiveness, supported by norms that encourage listening and thoughtful turn-taking. Educators should also resist over-structuring classroom discourse around AI outputs, instead using these tools to provoke rather than conclude conversation. In doing so, they keep dialogue dynamic and relational, ensuring that the co-presence of human minds remains central to the learning process.

FOR REFLECTION

1. What forms of dialogue do I prioritise in my teaching, and how might these be enhanced or undermined by AI?
2. How do I currently design for spontaneity, co-presence and intellectual risk-taking?
3. In what ways can I use AI to provoke rather than replace meaningful human conversation?
4. What changes could I make to ensure live, embodied interaction remains central in hybrid or digital contexts?

The Importance of Values and Ethics

Teachers are not only conveyors of knowledge but also models of ethical conduct. In every decision, from grading fairly to navigating classroom conflict, they enact values such as integrity, compassion and justice. These are not abstract principles but lived practices that shape the moral climate of a learning environment. AI, by contrast, operates according to algorithms and optimisation metrics; it lacks a moral compass. Anchoring education in human values ensures that decisions about the use of AI are guided by ethical considerations, not just efficiency or convenience. It reaffirms that education is a fundamentally moral endeavour, concerned with the formation of persons as well as the transmission of knowledge.

To uphold values and ethics in AI-enhanced classrooms, educators must foreground moral reasoning as an explicit part of both curriculum and pedagogy. This can include engaging students in critical discussions about the ethical implications of AI use, fostering digital literacy that extends beyond functionality to include questions of bias, accountability and justice. Institutional policies should be transparent about where and how AI is used, ensuring that ethical safeguards, such as informed consent, data privacy and equitable access, are in place. Teachers can model ethical deliberation by articulating the rationale behind their choices, particularly when integrating AI tools into assessment or instruction. Professional development focused on ethics in technology use equips educators to respond to emerging dilemmas with integrity. By embedding ethical reflection into daily practice, teachers help students develop not only technical competence but also the moral discernment required to navigate a rapidly changing digital world.

FOR REFLECTION

1. What core values do I hope to model in my teaching, and how do these shape my decisions about AI use?
2. How do I create space for ethical reasoning in the curriculum?
3. In what ways do current AI tools align with or challenge my ethical commitments as an educator?
4. What institutional policies or professional development structures support ethical engagement with AI?

The Uniqueness of Human Creativity and Meaning-Making

While AI can generate content that mimics creative expression, it does so without understanding, intention or cultural context. Human creativity, by contrast, is deeply situated. It draws upon memory, emotion, experience and cultural knowledge to produce meaning. When learners engage with a topic creatively, whether it be through storytelling, design, experimentation or reflection, they are not just absorbing information. They are interpreting it, questioning it and weaving it into the fabric of their own lives. This process of meaning-making is inherently human. It is what allows knowledge to become wisdom, and information to become insight.

To preserve the centrality of human creativity and meaning-making, educators must design learning experiences that foreground interpretation, cultural context and personal voice. Assignments that invite multiple forms of expression, such as multimodal projects, narrative inquiry or community-engaged research, encourage students to draw upon their lived experiences and values. Instead of treating AI as a generative endpoint, teachers can position it as a tool for inspiration or critique, asking students to refine, contextualise or challenge AI-produced outputs. Educators should also explicitly teach the difference between reproduction and creation, helping learners recognise the value of process, struggle and revision. Cultivating environments where students are encouraged to take intellectual risks and make meaning on their own terms reinforces creativity as a relational, situated practice, one that no algorithm can replicate.

FOR REFLECTION

1. How do I currently foster creativity and personal meaning-making in my students' learning?
2. What types of assignments encourage interpretation, context and voice-over replication?
3. How can I help students distinguish between AI-generated output and authentic creative work?
4. What are the risks of outsourcing meaning-making to machines, and how do I address them in my practice?

Education as Formation, Not Just Information

The purpose of education extends far beyond the acquisition of facts and skills. At its best, it is a formative process. One that shapes identity, fosters character and prepares individuals to participate responsibly in society. Teachers play a central role in this formation. Through their guidance, learners develop resilience in the face of challenge, confidence in their abilities, curiosity about the world and empathy for others. These are not incidental outcomes; they are foundational to what it means to be educated. AI can assist in content delivery, but it cannot mentor a student through moments of self-doubt or help them imagine a different future for themselves.

To ensure that education continues to shape the whole person, educators must intentionally cultivate environments where identity, character and citizenship are central to learning. This means designing curricula that include reflective practices, ethical dilemmas and real-world problem-solving tasks that require learners to wrestle with uncertainty, values and the implications of their choices. Mentorship must be preserved as a core function of teaching, with structured opportunities for one-on-one dialogue, goal setting and personal growth. Educators can also scaffold metacognitive practices, encouraging students to examine how they learn, what motivates them and who they are becoming through the learning process. While AI can personalise content, only teachers can guide students in forming a coherent sense of self and purpose. By centring formation in both pedagogy and institutional priorities, education retains its deeper mission: the development of capable, compassionate human beings.

FOR REFLECTION

1. How do I integrate the formation of character, identity and civic responsibility into my teaching?
2. In what ways can AI support, but not supplant, mentorship and personal growth?
3. How do I help students reflect on who they are becoming through their educational journey?
4. What supports are needed to preserve the formative mission of education in an AI-integrated institution?

AI as Support, Not Substitute

The growing presence of AI in education invites both innovation and discernment. Rather than viewing AI as a replacement for human teaching, we must position it as a tool that supports and extends learning. Its strengths, which are speed, scalability and data processing, can complement human insight, but they must not displace the relational and ethical work that educators do. Framing AI as a partner rather than a proxy allows us to preserve what is most vital in education: the co-authorship of learning between teacher and student. In this vision, technology enhances education without eclipsing its human heart.

To uphold the role of AI as a support rather than a substitute, educators must implement it with clear pedagogical intent and firm ethical boundaries. This involves using AI tools to automate administrative tasks, provide formative feedback or differentiate instruction, always in ways that free educators to focus on deeper relational and instructional work. Teachers should maintain visibility over how AI-generated insights are applied, interpreting data in light of their professional judgement and contextual knowledge. In the classroom, AI can be introduced as a collaborative aid, helping students explore ideas or test solutions, but never replacing the teacher's role in guiding dialogue, nurturing critical thinking or providing moral clarity. Schools and institutions must also develop policies that reinforce the primacy of human oversight and the centrality of the teacher-learner relationship. By integrating AI into clearly defined pedagogical frameworks, educators can harness its strengths without compromising the human elements that make learning meaningful.

FOR REFLECTION

1. What boundaries do I set to ensure AI remains a support tool rather than a substitute for teaching?
2. How do I evaluate whether AI tools are complementing or displacing relational and ethical work?
3. In what ways do I retain pedagogical agency when interpreting AI-generated outputs or insights?
4. How can institutional frameworks reinforce the teacher-student relationship amid increasing automation?

While the human-centred foundations of education offer an anchoring vision, the integration of AI into learning environments is far from straightforward. Alongside its potential benefits, AI introduces a complex set of tensions and uncertainties that educators must navigate with care. These challenges are not simply technical but pedagogical, ethical and epistemological. They prompt difficult questions about authorship, agency, equity and the evolving nature of expertise. Acknowledging and critically engaging with these tensions is essential if we are to shape AI-enhanced education in ways that remain responsive to human needs and values.

TENSIONS AND UNCERTAINTIES

The promise of AI in education is often framed in terms of efficiency, personalisation and expanded access. Yet, alongside these possibilities come unresolved tensions that expose the limits of technological optimism. These are not peripheral concerns but central challenges that demand critical attention. The integration of AI into educational practice surfaces deep uncertainties about authorship, agency, trust, equity and the purpose of learning itself. For educators, these tensions are not merely theoretical as they manifest in everyday decisions about curriculum design, assessment and classroom interaction. Grappling with them requires a willingness to confront ambiguity, resist reductive solutions and engage in sustained ethical reflection.

Authorship and Originality

As AI becomes more capable of generating fluent, contextually appropriate text, longstanding notions of authorship are placed under pressure. When students use AI to draft essays or brainstorm ideas, the boundaries between original thought and machine-assisted output blur. This raises not only academic integrity concerns but also deeper questions about what it means to produce knowledge. Educators must reconsider how to teach and assess originality, ensuring that students are not merely consumers of generative tools but reflective agents capable of situating and transforming ideas. The challenge is to preserve the value of intellectual labour in an age where content creation is increasingly automated.

To safeguard authorship and originality, educators must foster a learning culture that emphasises critical thinking, reflective practice and intellectual ownership. Assignments should be designed to require personal insight, contextual analysis and iterative development, elements that resist full automation. Transparent discussions about the role of AI in the writing process can help students distinguish between support and substitution, encouraging them to document their use of generative tools and reflect on how these influenced their thinking. Educators can also implement process-based assessments that emphasise drafting, peer feedback and revision, thereby making the student's cognitive journey visible. By treating originality not as a static attribute but as a process of engagement, transformation and situated meaning-making, we reaffirm the centrality of the learner as a producer of knowledge, even in a context saturated with algorithmic output.

FOR REFLECTION

1. How do I define originality in my teaching context, and how might AI challenge that definition?
2. What practices can I adopt to help students reflect critically on their use of generative tools?
3. In what ways can I make students' thinking and authorship processes more visible?
4. How might assessments be redesigned to value interpretation, transformation and intellectual ownership over surface-level production?

Transparency and Trust

AI systems often operate as black boxes, with limited visibility into how decisions are made or outputs are generated. In educational contexts, this opacity can undermine trust. When a student receives feedback from an AI-powered system, or when algorithms influence grading or course recommendations, transparency becomes essential. Learners have a right to understand the logic behind these interventions, and educators must be equipped to explain or critique them. Without transparency, the use of AI risks reinforcing a culture of passive acceptance rather than critical engagement, eroding the trust that underpins effective pedagogy.

To promote transparency and sustain trust, educators must demystify how AI systems operate and make their integration into teaching and assessment as visible and accountable as possible. This involves clearly communicating to students when and how AI is used, what data it draws upon and what limitations or biases may affect its outputs. Where AI provides feedback or recommendations, educators should offer interpretive commentary that helps learners contextualise and question the results. Embedding critical AI literacy into curricula empowers students to interrogate the systems shaping their educational experiences, rather than accepting them uncritically. Institutions, likewise, must commit to ethical procurement and implementation of AI tools, prioritising explainability, auditability and alignment with pedagogical values. Through these measures, transparency becomes not merely a compliance issue but a foundation for cultivating informed, empowered and trusting learners.

FOR REFLECTION

1. How transparent am I with students about when and how AI is used in my teaching or assessment?
2. Do I understand how the AI tools I use function, and am I equipped to explain their outputs and limitations?
3. What strategies can I use to encourage students to question and critically engage with algorithmic feedback?
4. How might increased transparency support stronger trust and dialogue between educators and learners?

Bias and Inequity

AI systems are trained on data that reflect the biases of the societies from which they emerge. As a result, they can perpetuate or even amplify existing inequities, whether in language use, representation or access to resources. In education, these biases may manifest subtly in content recommendations, feedback patterns or linguistic norms. Marginalised students may find their ways of speaking, knowing or learning devalued by systems that privilege dominant cultural norms. Addressing this requires more than technical fixes; it demands a critical pedagogy that foregrounds equity and challenges the assumptions embedded in AI systems.

To confront bias and promote equity, educators must adopt a critical stance towards AI integration, ensuring that technology is deployed in ways that affirm, rather than marginalise, diverse learners and epistemologies. This begins with selecting or designing AI tools that have undergone rigorous evaluation for fairness and inclusivity, and demanding transparency from vendors about training data and algorithmic design. Educators should routinely audit AI-driven outputs for patterns of exclusion or misrepresentation and be prepared to challenge their validity when necessary. In the classroom, this means actively validating multiple forms of expression, cultural references and learning strategies, and using AI as a point of departure for critical conversations about power, identity and representation. Institutional policies must also prioritise equitable access to AI resources, ensuring that technological advantages do not exacerbate existing disparities. Through deliberate, justice-oriented pedagogy, educators can transform AI from a potential amplifier of inequity into a catalyst for more inclusive educational practice.

FOR REFLECTION

1. What biases might be embedded in the AI tools I use, and how can I surface and challenge them?
2. Who benefits from the AI systems in my educational setting, and who may be disadvantaged or excluded?
3. How do I incorporate culturally responsive and justice-oriented pedagogies in AI-supported environments?
4. What role can students play in identifying and interrogating issues of bias and representation in educational technologies?

OVERRELIANCE AND SKILL ATROPHY

The convenience of AI tools may inadvertently lead to the erosion of foundational academic skills. When students rely heavily on AI for drafting, editing or solving problems, they may bypass the slow, iterative processes through which deep learning occurs. Similarly, educators who outsource planning or feedback to AI risk losing touch with the pedagogical intuition that comes from sustained engagement with learners. The risk is not just of dependence, but of atrophy, of diminishing the very capacities that education seeks to cultivate. Safeguarding against this requires deliberate design choices that foreground human judgement and scaffold the development of core competencies.

To counteract overreliance and preserve essential academic capacities, educators must intentionally design learning experiences that prioritise depth, deliberation and manual cognitive effort. This includes structuring tasks that require sustained reasoning, original synthesis and iterative revision, processes that resist automation and reward persistence. Educators can scaffold these experiences by making stages of thinking visible through learning journals, annotated drafts or reflective commentaries. Where AI is used, it should be integrated as a supplementary tool rather than a shortcut, with clear boundaries that encourage learners to engage independently before consulting automated assistance. Professional development for teachers should emphasise maintaining pedagogical reflexivity, ensuring that reliance on AI does not displace the human insight and intuition essential to effective instruction. By preserving spaces for slow thinking and principled judgement, education can continue to cultivate the intellectual resilience and adaptive expertise that define deep learning.

FOR REFLECTION

1. Have I observed signs of overreliance on AI tools in my students' work, or in my own practice?
2. How can I better scaffold deep engagement and cognitive effort before students turn to automation?
3. What activities or assessments can I design to cultivate persistence, reasoning and intellectual risk-taking?
4. How do I balance technological support with the development of core academic competencies?

Shifting Definitions of Expertise

The rise of AI challenges traditional hierarchies of expertise. When machines can produce high-quality summaries, visualisations or even critical commentary, the role of the expert must be redefined. Educators are no longer the sole arbiters of knowledge but must position themselves as guides who help learners navigate, question and contextualise AI-generated content. This requires humility as well as critical literacy, a willingness to acknowledge the utility of AI, while also interrogating its limits. Reimagining expertise in this way opens space for more collaborative, inquiry-driven models of learning, but also requires a recalibration of authority within the classroom.

To respond constructively to shifting definitions of expertise, educators must adopt roles that emphasise facilitation, inquiry and critical mentorship. This begins with modelling how to engage AI outputs with discernment, by questioning their assumptions, identifying gaps and situating them within broader disciplinary contexts. Educators should invite students into this evaluative process, treating AI-generated content as a provisional starting point rather than an authoritative endpoint. Collaborative learning structures such as co-inquiry projects, peer teaching and dialogic assessment can reinforce the idea that knowledge is collectively constructed and constantly subject to reinterpretation. At the same time, teachers must retain and communicate the unique value of their human expertise, not as infallibility, but as interpretive depth, ethical judgement and the capacity to respond to learners' needs. By modelling humility alongside intellectual authority, educators can help students develop a more nuanced and participatory understanding of expertise in a world increasingly shaped by intelligent systems.

FOR REFLECTION

1. How is my role as an expert evolving in response to AI, and what aspects of expertise remain distinctly human?
2. What strategies do I use to model critical engagement with AI outputs in front of students?
3. How do I invite students to question, contextualise and extend AI-generated knowledge?
4. What new forms of authority and collaboration might emerge in AI-integrated learning spaces, and how do I prepare for them?

Moral Ambiguity and Decision Fatigue

Educators are increasingly confronted with ambiguous decisions about when, how and whether to incorporate AI into their practice. Should students be permitted to use AI for brainstorming? How do we differentiate between legitimate support and academic dishonesty? These decisions are rarely clear-cut and often context-dependent. Over time, the accumulation of such choices can lead to decision fatigue, especially in the absence of clear institutional guidance. To navigate this uncertainty, educators need shared frameworks for ethical reflection, spaces for collective deliberation and support for making principled yet adaptable choices.

To navigate the moral ambiguity surrounding AI use and mitigate decision fatigue, educators require structured support systems and ethical frameworks that guide consistent, principled choices. Institutions should establish clear, adaptable policies that outline acceptable uses of AI, provide examples of boundary cases and offer protocols for responding to violations. Equally important are collegial spaces for shared deliberation, such as ethics roundtables, professional learning communities or cross-disciplinary panels, where educators can discuss dilemmas, share practices and collectively interpret evolving norms. Embedding reflective decision-making models into professional development can also help teachers balance flexibility with integrity, enabling them to respond to context without losing coherence. By institutionalising ethical reflection and peer support, educators are better equipped to make sound, sustainable decisions in a pedagogical landscape increasingly marked by complexity and change.

FOR REFLECTION

1. What recent decisions about AI use have felt ethically ambiguous or emotionally taxing for me?
2. Are there shared guidelines or frameworks I can draw upon, or contribute to, within my institution?
3. How do I manage the tension between flexibility and consistency when students use AI in varied ways?
4. What kinds of professional learning or collegial dialogue would help me navigate AI-related dilemmas with greater confidence?

Engaging with these tensions is not about resolving them once and for all, but about developing the capacity to think with them, ethically, creatively and reflexively. As educators confront questions of authorship, trust, equity, expertise and moral responsibility, it becomes clear that AI is not simply a tool to be managed but a force that reshapes the epistemological and ethical terrain of education. These challenges demand more than reactive adjustments; they call for sustained inquiry into what we want education to become in the age of intelligent systems. This leads us to a set of future-oriented questions. Questions that resist easy answers but are essential for charting a path forward that keeps human flourishing at the centre.

FUTURE-ORIENTED QUESTIONS

The rapid integration of AI into education invites not only technical adjustments but deep, future-facing inquiry. Rather than asking solely how to implement AI, educators must ask what kind of educational future they wish to shape in its presence. These are not questions of optimisation but of orientation, meaning questions that reach beyond the immediate utility of tools to the broader purposes of teaching, learning and human development. The answers are necessarily provisional, shaped by evolving contexts and collective deliberation. Yet, posing the right questions now is essential if AI is to serve education without compromising its ethical and relational core. What follows are some of the most pressing questions we must carry forward. Questions designed not to close debate, but to keep it open, critical and grounded in human values.

What Kind of Education Do We Want AI to Serve?

Before asking what AI can do for education, we must first clarify what education is for. This is not a technical question but a moral and philosophical one. If education is reduced to efficient content delivery, standardised assessment or workforce preparation, then AI will be developed and deployed accordingly. But if education is understood as a formative, relational and democratic endeavour, one that cultivates critical thinking, empathy and civic responsibility, then the role of AI must be circumscribed by those ends. Articulating a clear educational vision is therefore not ancillary to technological implementation; it is foundational. Educators, institutions and communities must collectively define the human purposes AI is to serve, ensuring that technological tools remain subordinate to pedagogical values. In this light, AI should not shape the aims of education, but be shaped by them.

FOR REFLECTION

1. What do I believe is the core purpose of education in my context?
2. In what ways might AI support, or distort, this purpose?
3. Are our institutional goals clearly articulated in ways that can guide ethical AI use?
4. How do we ensure that educational aims are not quietly rewritten by the affordances of emerging technologies?

How Do We Redefine the Role of Educators in AI-Mediated Learning?

As AI systems take on functions once thought to be uniquely human, such as generating feedback, curating resources or even facilitating discussions, the role of the educator is undergoing a profound shift. Yet, rather than rendering teachers obsolete, this moment demands a reimagining of their professional identity. Educators are not merely transmitters of information but mentors, ethical guides and designers of learning environments. In AI-mediated classrooms, their responsibilities expand to include interpreting algorithmic outputs, modelling critical engagement with technology and safeguarding the relational core of education. This requires not only technical fluency but also pedagogical confidence and moral clarity. Redefining the role of educators means investing in their professional development, reaffirming their authority in matters of curriculum and care, and recognising their labour as central, not peripheral, to educational futures shaped by AI.

FOR REFLECTION

1. How is my role as an educator shifting in response to AI, and what aspects must remain non-negotiable?
2. In what ways can I model critical and ethical engagement with AI for my students?
3. What support or development do educators need to confidently and responsibly work with AI in their practice?
4. How do we protect time and space for the human work of teaching, which includes care, dialogue and judgement, in increasingly automated systems?

How Do We Design Equitable AI-Integrated Learning Environments?

AI has the potential to widen access to educational resources and personalise learning pathways, but without deliberate design for equity, it can also reinforce or exacerbate existing inequalities. Algorithms often reflect the biases of their training data, and unequal access to digital infrastructure can leave already-marginalised learners further behind. Designing for equity means asking who benefits from AI in education and who is left out. It requires inclusive design processes that involve diverse stakeholders, especially those historically excluded from educational innovation. Equity also demands transparency in how AI systems make decisions, robust mechanisms for accountability and culturally responsive pedagogy that values multiple ways of knowing. Ultimately, designing equitable AI-integrated learning environments is not about neutralising bias alone but about reimagining systems in ways that affirm justice, dignity and inclusion as non-negotiable educational commitments.

FOR REFLECTION

1. Who is most likely to be disadvantaged or excluded by the current use of AI in my educational setting?
2. How can I ensure that AI tools used in my context are accessible, culturally responsive and inclusive?
3. Are students aware of how bias and inequity can be embedded in algorithms – and how might we teach them to spot and challenge it?
4. What institutional structures are needed to hold AI systems accountable to principles of fairness and justice?

What Kinds of Pedagogies Are Most Resilient in the Face of Technological Change?

Not all pedagogies adapt equally well to rapid technological change. Approaches that prioritise memorisation, standardisation or passive content delivery are most vulnerable to automation. By contrast, pedagogies grounded in inquiry, dialogue, collaboration and reflection are inherently more resilient. These methods foreground human interaction, interpretation and meaning-making. These are capacities that cannot be outsourced to machines. Resilient pedagogies also embrace uncertainty and iteration, preparing learners to navigate complexity rather than seek definitive answers. In the context of AI, this means designing learning experiences that cannot be easily replicated by algorithms: slow thinking, ethical reasoning, open-ended exploration and deep disciplinary inquiry. The goal is not to reject technology, but to strengthen educational practices that endure and evolve and are anchored in human capacities for creativity, care and critical thought.

FOR REFLECTION

1. What aspects of my teaching practice are most resistant to automation, and how can I strengthen them?
2. How might I design learning experiences that emphasise slow thinking, interpretation or ethical reflection?
3. What role do uncertainty, dialogue and exploration play in my classroom, and how can these be enhanced?
4. How do I evaluate whether the pedagogies I use are preparing students for a world shaped by ongoing technological change?

What Ethical Frameworks Should Guide the Use of AI in Education?

As AI becomes increasingly embedded in educational infrastructure, ethical considerations must move from the margins to the centre of institutional decision-making. Questions of consent, privacy, bias, autonomy and accountability cannot be deferred to vendors or reduced to compliance checklists. Instead, educational institutions need robust ethical frameworks that are both principled and practical, grounded in commitments to justice, transparency, human dignity and the common good. These frameworks should be co-developed with input from educators, students, ethicists and technologists, and regularly revisited in light of new developments. Crucially, they must inform not only the selection and deployment of AI tools but also the pedagogical, relational and structural practices that surround their use. Ethical frameworks are not barriers to innovation; they are the conditions under which innovation can be truly responsible, inclusive and educative.

FOR REFLECTION

1. What values should guide my use of AI in teaching and learning, and how do I translate these into everyday decisions?
2. Does my institution have a clear, actionable ethical framework for AI use, and how is it communicated to staff and students?
3. How can I involve learners in ethical discussions about the tools they use and the systems that affect them?
4. What safeguards are in place to ensure that AI systems are used in ways that respect autonomy, fairness and accountability?

Who Gets to Decide?

At the heart of every conversation about AI in education lies a fundamental question of governance: who decides what technologies are adopted, how they are used and whose interests they serve? Too often, these decisions are made by external vendors, senior administrators or policymakers without meaningful input from educators and students, the very people most affected by the outcomes. Democratic participation in the governance of educational technology is essential if AI is to support, rather than subvert, pedagogical and ethical aims. This means creating structures for consultation, accountability and shared decision-making, especially when technologies have long-term implications for learning, privacy and equity. It also means interrogating whose voices are heard, whose knowledge counts and whose values are encoded into the systems we adopt. The future of education with AI must be co-created, not dictated.

FOR REFLECTION

1. Who currently makes decisions about AI use in my educational context, and who is left out of those conversations?
2. What mechanisms exist for students and educators to influence decisions about educational technology?
3. How might I advocate for more participatory and transparent governance of AI systems?
4. In what ways can decision-making processes be restructured to reflect shared responsibility and ethical accountability?

These future-oriented questions do not yield simple answers, but that is precisely their value. They serve as guideposts for an ongoing, collective inquiry into what education should become in the age of artificial intelligence. Rather than seeking finality, educators must remain engaged in a process of ethical reflection, pedagogical experimentation and institutional reimagining. The goal is not to resist change, nor to uncritically embrace it, but to shape it with intention and integrity. By holding fast to core human values, relationship, meaning, justice and care, we can ensure that AI serves not as a blueprint for education, but as one of many tools in a broader human project: the cultivation of thoughtful, capable and compassionate learners.

LOOKING FORWARD: DESIGNING EDUCATIONAL FUTURES

As we look ahead, the question is not whether AI will shape education because it already has. The question is how we, as educators and learners, will shape AI's role. Will classrooms become places of passive automation, where efficiency eclipses depth? Or will they remain spaces of dialogue, reflection and shared meaning-making, with AI serving as one more voice at the table?

The choice lies in how we design our practices. AI should be a catalyst, not a conclusion. It is a tool that sparks discussion, supports reflection and broadens inquiry. Teachers and students alike must remain authors of the learning conversation, using AI to generate possibilities but never surrendering their agency.

In the end, this book has been less about technology itself and more about us, including our practices, our values and our vision for what education can be. If we can hold fast to what is uniquely human while embracing what technology offers, we may find that GenAI does not diminish education, but deepens it.

As we close, the invitation is simple: to step into this future with clarity and courage. To look back at the lessons of history, to look forward with imagination and to remember always that education is, at its core, a profoundly human endeavour.

Index

Pages in *italics* refer to figures, pages in ***bold**-italics* refer to boxes and pages in **bold** refer to tables.

B

C

D

E

F

G

V

For Product Safety Concerns and Information please contact our EU representative GPSR@taylorandfrancis.com Taylor & Francis Verlag GmbH, Kaufingerstraße 24, 80331 München, Germany